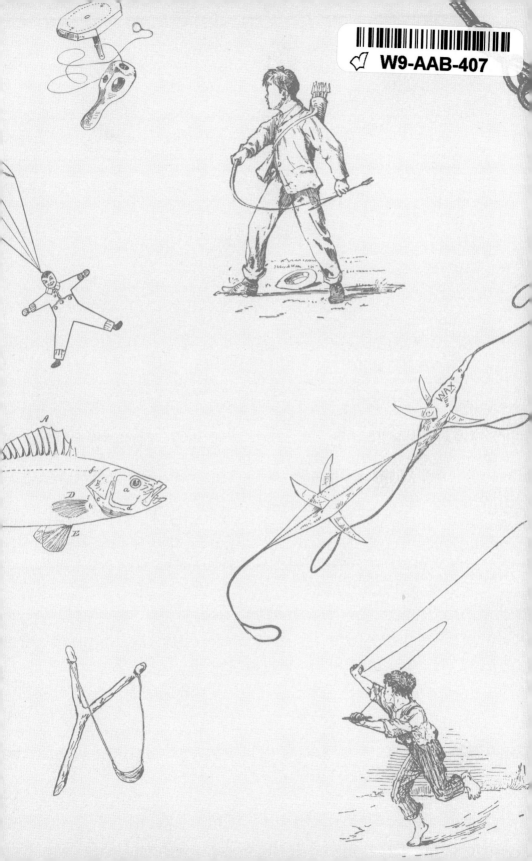

THE ORIGINAL
BOY'S
Handy Book

by **Daniel Carter Beard**
Co-founder of **THE BOY SCOUTS** *of* **AMERICA**

Published by Tess Press, an imprint of
Black Dog & Leventhal Publishers, Inc.
151 West 19th Street, New York NY 10011

This book was originally published in 1880
under the title *The American Boy's Handy Book*.

Cover design by Red Herring Design

ISBN: 978-1-60376-033-1

h g f e d c b a

Manufactured in the United States of America

PREFACE.

UNLESS boys have materially changed their habits in the last few years, it matters little what the preface of this book may contain, for it will be "skipped" without a passing glance. Still, in the established order of things, a preface, even if unnoticed by younger readers, is necessary to enable the author to state his purposes in undertaking the work, and to modestly put forward his claims on public attention.

It is the memory of the longing, that used to possess myself and my boy friends of a few years ago, for a real practical *American* boy's book, that has induced me to offer this volume.

The sports, amusements, and games embraced in this book are intended to reach the average American boy of any age, not too young to fly a kite or too old to enjoy a day's good fishing.

The book is based upon personal experiments and experiences, and is free, as far as lay within my power to make it, of foreign or technical terms or phrases.

Well do I remember the impracticable chemical experiments, necessitating professional skill and the use of compli-

cated and expensive apparatus, the impossible feats of leger-
demain and the time-worn conundrums, riddles, and games
that help to make up the contents of the boy's books of my
youth.

Unfamiliar and foreign terms, references to London shops
as places to procure the articles mentioned, glittering generali-
ties, and a general disregard for details are the marked characteristics of the books to which I refer.

Never shall I forget the disappointment experienced, when
after consulting the index, I sought the article on paper balloons and found only the bare statement of the fact that balloons made of paper and filled with heated air *would ascend.*
If I remember aright, the whole description occupies less than
four lines.

Although the greater portion of the contents of the present
volume has never been published before, some of it appeared
as short articles in the *St. Nicholas Magazine;* and the directions and descriptions then given have been tested by thousands of boys throughout the United States, and, judging from
the letters I have received, with uniform success.

Of course, such a book cannot, in the nature of things, be
exhaustive, nor is it, indeed, desirable that it should be. Its
use and principal purpose are to stimulate the inventive facul-
ties in boys, to bring them face to face with practical emergencies when no book can supply the place of their own common
sense and the exercise of personal intelligence and ingenuity.

Many new ideas will suggest themselves to the practical,
ready-witted American boy, many simplifications and improve-

ments on the apparatus here described; but it is hoped and expected by the author that the directions here given, as far as they go, will be found intelligible and practicable.

Nor is the volume, as is too often the case with this class of books, only to be made use of by lads with an almost unlimited supply of money at their disposal.

All apparatus described are either to be constructed of material easily obtained by almost any boy without cost, or by a very small outlay.

The author would also suggest to parents and guardians that money spent on fancy sporting apparatus, toys, etc., would be better spent upon tools and appliances.

Let boys *make their own kites and bows and arrows ;* they will find a double pleasure in them, and value them accordingly, to say nothing of the education involved in the successful construction of their home-made playthings.

The development of a love of harmless fun is itself no valueless consideration. The baneful and destroying pleasures that offer themselves with an almost irresistible fascination to idle and unoccupied minds find no place with healthy activity and hearty interest in boyhood sports.

CONTENTS.

SPRING.

CHAPTER I.

CHAPTER II.

CHAPTER III.

CHAPTER IV.

Contents.

Contents.

Contents.

CHAPTER XIX.

CHAPTER XX.

CHAPTER XXI.

CHAPTER XXII.

AUTUMN.

CHAPTER XXIII.

Contents.

WINTER.

Contents.

Contents.

Spring.

The American Boy's Handy Book.

CHAPTER I.

KITE TIME.

IT is a pleasant sensation to sit in the first spring sunshine and feel the steady pull of a good kite upon the string, and watch its graceful movements as it sways from side to side, ever mounting higher and higher, as if impatient to free itself and soar away amid the clouds. The pleasure is, however, greatly enhanced by the knowledge that the object skimming so bird-like and beautifully through the air is a kite of your own manufacture.

I remember, when quite a small boy, building an immense man kite, seven feet high. It was a gorgeous affair, with its brilliant red nose and cheeks, blue coat, and striped trousers.

As you may imagine, I was nervous with anxiety and excitement to see it fly. After several experimental trials to get the tail rightly balanced, and the breast-band properly adjusted, and having procured the strongest hempen twine with which to fly it, I went to the river-bank for the grand event.

My man flew splendidly; he required no running, no hoisting, no jerking of the string to assist him. I had only to stand on the high bank and let out the string, and so fast did the twine pass through my hands that my fingers were almost blistered.

People began to stop and gaze at the queer sight, as my man rose higher and higher, when, suddenly, my intense pride and enjoyment was changed into something very like fright.

The twine was nearly all paid out, when I found that my man was stronger than his master, and I could not hold him!

Japanese Square Kite.

Imagine, if you can, my dismay. I fancied myself being pulled from the bank into the river, and skimming through the water at lightning speed, for, even in my fright, the idea of letting go of the string did not once occur to me. However, to my great relief, a man standing near came to my assistance, just as the stick upon which the twine had been wound came dancing up from the ground toward my hands. So hard did my giant pull that even the friend who had kindly come to the rescue had considerable trouble to hold him in. The great kite, as it swung majestically about, high in the blue sky, attracted quite a crowd of spectators, and I felt very grand at the success of my newly invented flying-man; but my triumph was short-lived. The tail made of rags was too heavy to bear its own weight, and, breaking off near the kite, it fell to the ground, while my kite, freed from this' load, shot up like a rocket, then turned and came headlong down with such force, that dashing through the branches of a thorny locust-tree, it crashed to the ground, a mass of broken sticks and tattered paper. Although the sad fate of my first man-kite taught me to avoid building unmanageable giants, the experiment was, on the whole, satisfactory, for it proved beyond a doubt that it is unnecessary to follow the conventional form for a kite to make one that will fly.

Man Kite.

To make this kite you will require four sticks, some rattan and some paper. In regard to his size, I would suggest that the larger the man is, the better he will fly. Now let us suppose you are going to make this fellow four feet high. First, cut two straight sticks three feet nine inches long; these are to serve for the legs and body; cut another straight stick two and one-half feet in length for the spine, and a fourth stick, three feet five inches long, for the arms. For the head select a light piece of split rattan—any light, tough wood that will bend readily will do—bend this in a circle eight inches in diameter, fasten it securely to one end of the spine by binding it with strong thread, being careful that the spine runs exactly through the centre of the circle (Fig. 1). Next find the exact centre of the arm-stick, and with a pin or small tack fasten it at this point to the spine, a few inches below the chin (Fig. 2). After wrapping the joint tightly with strong thread, lay the part of the skeleton which

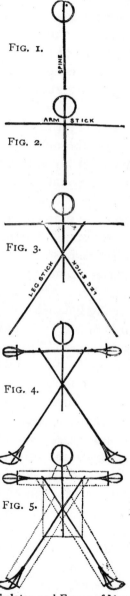

Fig. 1.

Fig. 2.

Fig. 3.

Fig. 4.

Fig. 5.

Skeleton and Frame of Man Kite.

is finished flat upon the floor, mark two points upon the arm-sticks for the shoulder-joints, each seven inches from the intersection of the spine and arm-stick, which will place them fourteen inches apart. At these points fasten with a pin the two long sticks that are to serve for the body and legs (Fig. 3). Now cross these sticks as shown in diagram, being careful that the terminations of the lower limbs are at least three feet apart; the waist-joint ought then to be about ten inches below the arm-stick. After taking the greatest pains to see that the arm-stick is perfectly at right angles with the spine, fasten all the joints securely. Upon the arms bind oblong loops of rattan, or of the same material as the head-frame. These hand-loops ought to be about three inches broad at their widest parts, and exact counterparts of each other. The loops for the feet must approach as nearly as possible the shape of feet, and these, too, must be exactly alike, or the kite will be "lopsided," or unequally balanced. Now cut two sticks three inches long for the ends of sleeves, and two others four inches long for bottoms of trousers (Fig. 4); fasten the two former near the ends of the arm-stick, and the two latter near the ends of the leg-sticks, as in the illustration. The strings of the frame must next be put on, as shown by the dotted lines (Fig. 5). Commence with the neck, at equal distances from the spine, and about seven inches apart; tie two strings to the arm-sticks; extend these strings slantingly to the head, and fasten them to the hoop, one on each side of the spine, and about five inches apart. Take another thread and fasten to the top of cross-stick of right arm, pass it over and take a wrap around the spine, continue it to top of cross-stick upon left arm, and there tie it. Fasten another string to bottom of cross-stick on right arm, draw it tight and wrap it on spine four inches below intersection of arm-stick, pass it on to the bottom of cross-stick on left arm, draw taut and fasten it. Tie the body-string at the right shoulder-joint, drop the thread down to a point exactly opposite the termination of spine upon the right leg, take a wrap, and draw the line across to point upon left leg exactly opposite, bind it there, then bring it up to left shoulder-joint and tie it. For the trousers fasten a string at a point on right arm-stick, eleven inches from the intersection of spine, extend it down in a straight line to inside end of cross-stick of left limb and fasten it there. Tie another string at a point one inch and a half to the left of spine upon right arm-stick, extend it down in a straight line to outside end of cross-stick of left limb. Go through the same process for right leg of trousers, and the frame-work will be complete.

For the covering of a kite of this size I have always used tissue paper; it is pretty in color and very light in weight. Paste some sheets of tissue paper together, red for the trousers, hands and face, blue for the coat, and black, or some dark color, for the feet. Use paste made of flour and water boiled to the consistency of starch. Put the paste on with a small bristle brush, make the seams or over-laps hardly more than one-fourth of an inch wide, and press them together with a soft rag or towel; measure the paper so that the coat will join the trousers at the proper place. When you are satisfied that this is all right, lay the paper smoothly on the floor and place the frame of the kite upon it, using heavy books or paper-weights to hold it in place. Then with a pair of scissors cut the paper around the frame, leaving a clear edge of one-half inch, and making a slit in this margin or edge every six or seven inches and at each angle; around the head these slits must be made about two or three inches apart to prevent the paper from wrinkling when you commence to paste. With your brush cover the margin with paste one section at a time, turn them over, and with the towel or rag press them down. After the kite is all pasted and dry, take a large paint-brush, and with black marking-paint, india ink, or common writing fluid, put in the buttons and binding on coat with a good broad touch. The face and hair must be painted with broad lines, so that they may be seen clearly at a great height. Follow this rule wherever you have to use paint upon any kind of kite.

The breast-band, or "belly-band," of the man kite should be arranged in the same manner as it is upon the common hexagonal or coffin-shaped kite with which all American boys are familiar; but for fear some of my readers may not quite understand I will try and tell them exactly how to do it. First, punch small holes through the paper, one upon each side of the leg-sticks just above the bottom of the pants, and one upon each side of the arm-stick at the shoulders. Run one end of the breast-band through the holes at the bottom of the left limb and tie it fast to the leg-stick; tie the other end at the right shoulder. Take another string of the same

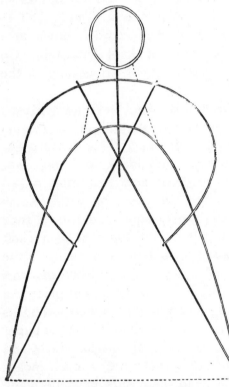

FIG. 6.—Frame of Woman Kite.

length as the first and fasten one end in the same manner at the bottom of the right leg, pass the string up, crossing the first band, and tie the end at the left shoulder. Attach your kite-string to the breast-band where the two strings intersect in such a manner that you can slide the kite-string up or down until it is properly adjusted. For the tail-band, tie a string (to the leg-sticks) at the bottom of the breast-band and let it hang slack from one leg to the other. Attach the tail to the centre of this string.

FIG. 7.—Foot of the Girl.

The Woman Kite, though differing in form, is made after the same method as the man kite, and with the aid of the diagram any boy can build one if he is careful to keep the proper proportions. Remember that the dotted lines in each of these diagrams represent the strings or thread of the framework (Fig. 6). Use small, smooth twine on large kites, and good strong thread on the smaller ones.

FIG. 8.—Comic Girl Kite.

A very comical effect can be had by making the feet of the woman kite of stiff paste-board, and fastening them on to the line which forms the bottom of the skirt with a string after the manner here illustrated (Fig. 7), allowing them to dangle loosely from below, to be moved and swayed by each motion of the

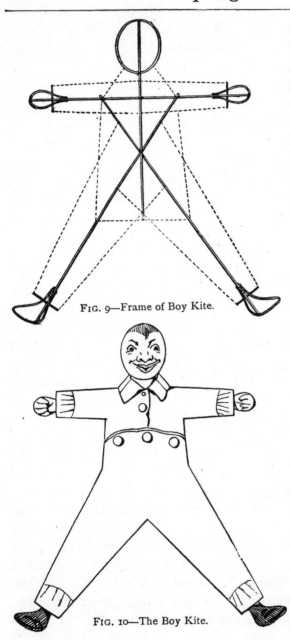

FIG. 9—Frame of Boy Kite.

FIG. 10—The Boy Kite.

kite, looking as if it was indeed a live woman or girl of the Kate Greenaway style, dancing and kicking in the clouds. Fig. 8 shows a girl kite with feet attached.

The costume given in the illustration may be varied according to fancy, with the same framework. A Dolly Varden or a Martha Washington costume can be made. A blue overskirt and waist covered with stars, and a red and white striped skirt, give us Columbia or a Goddess of Liberty. Attach the breast-band in the same manner as upon the man kite. Let the tail-band hang loosely below the skirt. By a slight modification of the frame of the man kite you can produce

A Boy Kite

that will create an unlimited amount of fun whenever he makes his appearance in his æsthetic Kate Greenaway suit. By carefully following the construction according to the diagram (Fig. 9) the average boy will find little difficulty in building a twin brother to the kite in the illustration (Fig. 10).

Still another strange looking kite can be made by using a piece of pliable wood bent in a circular form for the body, and allowing the leg-sticks to protrude above the shoulders to form short arms, the spine extending below the trunk some distance to form the tail to a

Frog Kite.

It is not worth while to build one less than two feet high. Let us suppose that the particular batrachian we are now about to make is to be just that height; in this case the leg-sticks must be each two feet long, and as you will want to bend them at the knees, these points should be made considerably thinner than the other parts of the sticks. The spine must be about one foot seven inches long, or a little over three-quarters of the length of the leg-sticks. Place the two latter one above the other, lay the spine on top of them, and see that the tops of all three are flush, or perfectly even. Then at a point eight inches from the top, drive a pin through all three sticks, carefully clamping it upon the other side where the point protrudes. For the body, take a piece of thin rattan two feet five or six inches in length, bend it into the form of a circle, allowing the ends to overlap an inch or two that they may be firmly bound together with thread by winding it around the joint. The circle will be about eight inches in diameter. Take the three sticks you pinned together and lay them on the floor, spreading them apart in the form of an irregular star, in such a manner that the top of the spine will be just half-way between the tops of the leg-sticks and about five inches from each ; when you have proceeded thus far place the rattan circle over the other sticks ; the intersection of the sticks should be the centre

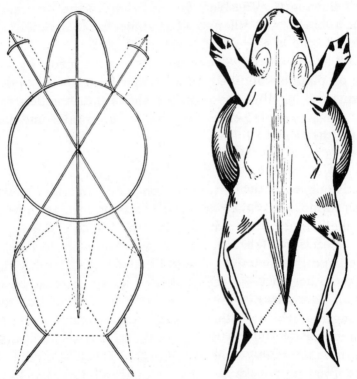

FIG. 11.—Frame of Frog Kite.   FIG. 12.—Frog Kite.

of the circle ; with pins and thread fasten the frame together in this position. The lower limbs will be spread wide apart ; they must be carefully drawn closer together and held in position by a string tied near the termination of each leg-stick. Cross-sticks for hands and feet may now be added, and the strings put on as shown in Fig. 11. This kite should be covered with green tissue paper. A few marks of the paint-brush will give it the appearance of Fig. 12. The breast and tail-band can be put on as described in the man kite.

The Butterfly Kite.

Make a thin straight stick of a piece of elastic wood, or split rattan; to the top end of this attach a piece of thread or string; bend the stick as you would a bow until it forms an arc or part of a circle; then holding the stick in this position tie the other end of the string to a point a few inches above the bottom end of the stick. At a point on the stick, about one-quarter the distance from the top, tie another string, draw it taut, and fasten it to the bottom end of the bow. Take another stick of exactly the same length and thickness as the first, and go through the same process, making a frame that must be a duplicate of the other. Then fasten the two frames together, as shown by Fig. 13, allowing the arcs to over-

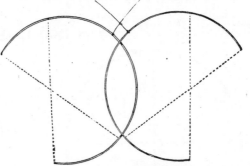

FIG. 13.—Frame of Butterfly Kite.

FIG. 14.—The Butterfly Kite.

lap several inches, and bind the joints securely with thread.

The head of the insect is made by attaching two broom-straws to the top part of the wings where they join, the straws must be crossed, the projecting ends serving for the antennæ or,

as the boys call them, the "smellers" of the butterfly. Now
select a piece of yellow or blue tissue paper, place your frame
over it, cut and paste as directed in the description of the man
kite. When the kite is dry, with black paint make some marking upon the wings similar to those shown in the illustration,
Fig. 14; or, better still, cut out some pieces of dark colored
paper in the form of these markings and paste them on, of
course taking care to have one wing like the other (Fig. 14), as
in nature.

The King Crab Kite.

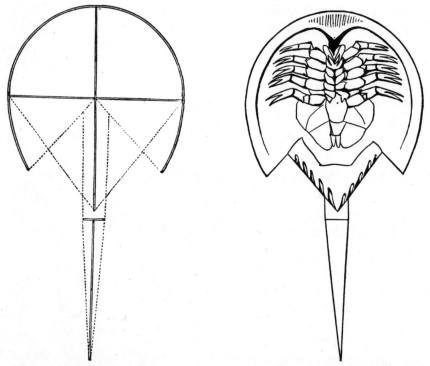

FIG. 15.—Frame of King Crab.   FIG. 16.—King Crab Kite.

The king, or "horse shoe crab," is familiar to all boys who
live upon the coast or spend their summer vacation at the sea-

side. It is a comparatively simple matter to imitate this crustacean in the form of a kite; in fact, all that is necessary is a slight modification of the old-fashioned bow kite to which a pointed tail must be attached. This tail can be made as shown in the illustration (Fig. 15), or may be cut out of a piece of paste-board and joined to the kite by a paper hinge ; this will allow the tail to bend backward when the wind blows against it, giving it a natural appearance ; the kite and pointed tail, which is part of the kite, should be covered with yellow paper. If you think that you do not possess sufficient skill with the brush to represent the under side of the crab, as shown in the illustration (Fig. 16), you can, at least, paint two large eye-spots some distance apart near the upper end, and then your kite will represent a back view. Attach the breast and tail bands as on an ordinary bow kite.

Fish Kite.

Cut two straight pine sticks; shave them down until they are thin enough to bend readily; see that they are exactly the same length and of about the same weight. Fasten the top ends together by driving a pin through them. Bend each stick in the form of a bow, and hold them in this position until you have secured a third stick across them at right angles about one-third the way down from the top, or ends where they are joined together. The fish should be about half as broad as it is long. Let the lower ends of the side or bow sticks cross each other far enough up to form a tail to the fish, and fasten the sticks together at their intersection. Before stringing the frame see that the cross-stick protrudes an equal distance from each side of the fish. To make the tail, tie a string across the bottom from the end of one cross-stick to the end of the other, and to this string midway between the two side-sticks tie another string, pass it up to the root of the tail, draw it taut and fasten it there at the intersection of the side-sticks ; this will make a natural hooking-fork to the caudal fin (Fig. 17).

The remainder of the strings can be put on by referring to the diagram, care being taken that the dorsal or back-fin is made exactly the same size as the fin on the belly of the fish. Yellow, red, and green are all appropriate colors for the paper

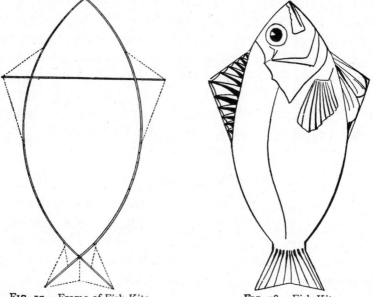

FIG. 17.—Frame of Fish Kite.   FIG. 18.—Fish Kite.

covering of this kite. After the paper is pasted and dry you **may** amuse yourself by painting the outlines of the gills and fins (Fig. 18). The kite will look all the better for not having the scales painted upon it. Tie the strings of the breast-band to the side-sticks near the head and tail, and let them cross each other as in a common kite. Attach the tail-band to the tail of the fish.

The Turtle Kite

is so simple in its construction that a lengthy description of how to make it would be out of place. All that is necessary

is to place the diagram before you (Fig. 19) and go to work.
Suppose you want your kite to measure two feet from tip of
nose to end of tail, the spine or centre-stick must then, of
course, be two feet long; make the leg-sticks each one and a
half foot long, place the stick for the fore-legs at a point on the
spine seven inches below the top, put the stick for the hind-

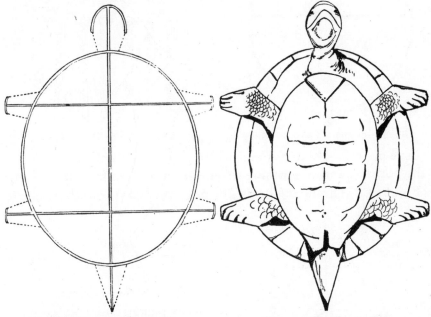

FIG. 19.—Frame of Turtle Kite.   FIG. 20.—The Turtle Kite.

legs eight inches below the fore-legs.   Adjust the hoop so that
it will extend four inches above the fore-leg stick and the same
distance below the hind-leg stick.   Let the diameter across the
centre from side to side be about fifteen inches.   Put the cross-
pieces on for the head and feet, run a thread over the bottom
end of the spine for a tail, cover the whole with green tissue
paper and your kite is done (Fig. 20).

2

The Shield Kite.

Make the frame of four sticks, two straight cross-sticks and two bent side-sticks (Fig. 21); cover it with red, white, and blue

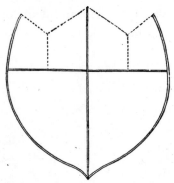

FIG. 21.—Frame of Shield Kite.

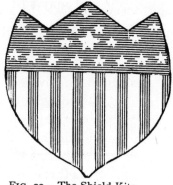

FIG. 22.—The Shield Kite.

tissue paper. Paste red and white paper together in stripes for the bottom, and use a blue ground with white stars for the top (Fig. 22). The next kite is not original with the author, but is

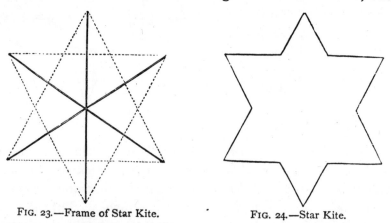

FIG. 23.—Frame of Star Kite.

FIG. 24.—Star Kite.

well known in some sections of the country. I have made a diagram of it at the request of a number of boys who did not know how to make

A Star Kite.

Build it according to the diagrams (Figs. 23 and 24), making the sticks all of equal length, and cover the kite with any colored paper that may suit your fancy.

The Chinese Dragon Kite.

This kite is a most resplendent affair, and glitters in the sunlight as if it were covered with jewels. It is rather complicated to look at, but not very difficult to make. The one I have before me was made in China.

The top or horizontal stick (Fig. 25, 1–2) is three feet long, half an inch wide, and one-eighth inch thick. The face can be simplified by using a loop, as in the man kite. Two more loops, as shown in the diagram, will serve as frames for the wings. Paper is pasted

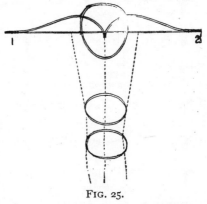

FIG. 25.

upon this, and hangs loose like an apron in front below the cross-stick (1–2). Cut the paper long enough to cover the first

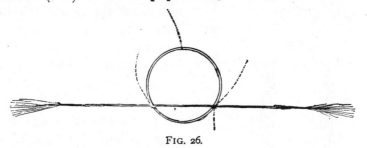

FIG. 26.

disk of the tail-piece, as shown in the finished kite, Fig. 27. The head-piece is ornamented with brilliant colors, bits of

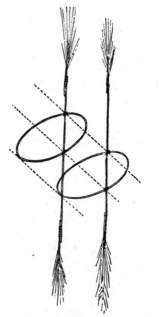

FIG. 27.—Portion of Framework of Tail.

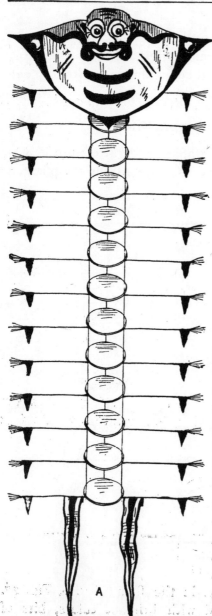

A

FIG. 27.—The Chinese Dragon Kite.

looking-glass pasted on or attached with strings, so that they dangle loosely, etc. ; this makes the top rather heavy, as, in fact, it ought to be, for then it serves to balance the tail, which, in this instance, is a succession of circular kites, ten inches in diameter, and thirteen in number, connected with one another by strings. Attached to each of these paper disks is a slender piece of reed or grass with a tufted head ; a similar tuft is fastened by a string to the opposite end to balance it. The breast-band is made like that upon an ordinary kite; the cross-strings, being attached to the face at the top and bottom, intersect each other about opposite a point between the eyes.

Fig. 26 represents the top view of a single disk, showing where the reeds and string are attached. Fig. 27 shows a side view of two disks, and the way in which they are connected by strings, six and a half inches space being left between each two disks. A (Fig. 27) is a front view of finished kite.

The Japanese Square Kite

is not, as its name might imply, perfectly square. It is rectangular in form, and made with a framework of very thin bamboo or cane sticks, bound together as shown in Fig. 28. This frame is covered with Japanese paper, to which all the sticks are tightly glued. The kite is bent backward, making the front slightly convex, and held in this position by strings tied from end to end of the cross-sticks at the back; the breast-band may be attached as on an ordinary six-sided kite. Instead of a tail-band, with a single tail attached, this foreigner carries two tails, one tied at each side to the protruding ends of the diagonal sticks at the bottom of the kite.

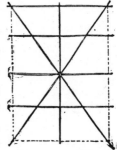

FIG. 28.—Japanese Square Kite Frame.

The illustration on page 4, of two boys making ready to fly one of these kites, is a copy from a picture made by a Japanese artist.

The Moving Star

is a paper lantern attached to the tail of any large kite.

A Chinese lantern will answer this purpose, although it is generally so long and narrow that the motion of the kite is apt to set fire to it.

To make a more suitable lantern, take a circular piece of light board five inches in diameter, drive three nails in the centre just far enough apart to allow a candle to fit between them firmly. Make of rattan or wire a light hoop of the same diameter as the bottom-piece; fasten these to a strap or handle

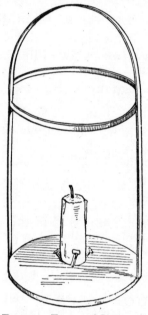

FIG. 29.—Frame of Lantern.

of wood, or wire, as shown in the diagram (Fig. 29), and cover the body of the lantern with red tissue paper.

This lantern fastened to the tail of a large kite that is sent up on a dark night will go bobbing around in a most eccentric and apparently unaccountable manner, striking with wonder all observers not in the secret.

CHAPTER II.

WAR KITES.

LIKE all soldiers, war kites should be trim and martial in appearance. Their uniform may be as brilliant and fanciful as the ingenuity and taste of the builder suggests, always remembering that lightness and strength are essential qualities. An appropriate name or emblem, marked, painted, or pasted on, would serve not only to distinguish the combatants from their more peaceful brother aërostats, but would give to each kite an individuality, and thus allow successful veterans to become famous throughout kitedom. There are but two " arms " to this novel " service," or rather two modes of warfare. The first, *unarmed*, might be compared to the friendly jousts of the knights of old when they met for trials of skill. The second, *armed*, is more like the mortal combat where but one survives.

Unarmed War Kite.

The usual form of the unarmed fighting kite is that of the ordinary bow kite. It should be made about two and one-half feet high. Base of bow, fourteen inches below top of spine or centre-stick, and twenty-seven inches broad. Cover the frame with paper cambric. Make the tail of string, with stripes of colored paper inserted in loops an inch or so apart. A paper tassel at the end will give it a finished look. Ten feet is about the proper length of tail for a kite of this size.

In fighting with this unarmed soldier the object is to capture your opponent's kite by entangling its tail in your own string. To do this you must make your kite dart under the twine of your enemy. As soon as it darts let out string rapidly enough to keep your fighter under control, and at the same time allow it to fall to the rear of the other kite. Having accomplished this, drop your ball of string and pull in hand over hand, as fast as possible. If your enemy is not very spry and well up in these tactics, this manœuvre will hopelessly entangle his kite-tail on your string. Then, although the battle is half won, a great deal depends upon your superior quickness, skill, and also upon the strength of your twine, which may break, or your victim may escape with the loss of part of its tail. If, however, you are successful in capturing your prisoner you can write on your kite the date of the victory, and the name of the vanquished warrior. The captive must, in all cases, be returned to its proper owner after the latter has signed his name to the record of his defeat written upon your kite. Thus is the successful hero soon covered with the records of his victories, while the unsuccessful fighter carries a bare blank face.

Armed Kites

are of a more relentless and bloodthirsty order than the strategic unarmed warrior. The peculiar mission of these rampant champions of the air is to cut the enemy off from his base of supplies; then with a satisfied wriggle, and a fiendish wag of the tail, this ferocious flyer sails serenely on, while his ruined victim falls helplessly to the earth, or ignominiously hangs himself on some uncongenial tree, where his skeleton will struggle and swing until beaten to pieces by the very element that sustained him in his elevation before his thread of life was cut. In this sport, new to most Northern boys, they will find an exciting and healthy pastime, one that will teach them to think and act quickly, a quality that when acquired may be of infinite service to them in after years.

Armed Kite Fighting.

These aëro-nautical cutters might be appropriately named the Scorpion, "Stingerree," Wasp, or Hornet, because they fight with their tails, the sting of the insect being represented on the kite-tail by the razor-like cutters.

The tactics used in these battles of the clouds are just the opposite from those employed in fighting with unarmed kites.

To win the battle you so manœuvre your warrior that its tail sweeps across and cuts the string of your antagonist.

Armed kites are usually made after the pattern of the American six-sided or hexagonal kite. They are two and one-half feet high, covered with paper cambric, or, when economy is no object, with silk.

As a successful warrior looks well after his arms, so should the tail of a war kite receive the most careful attention.

One very popular style of tail is made of strips of bright-colored cloth about one inch wide tied securely in the middle to a strong twine, the tail ending in a fancy tassel.

Another style is made of long narrow strips of white cloth securely sewed together. This tail is not so apt to become knotted or tangled as the first.

How to Make the Knives.

The "cutters" to be attached to the tail are made of sharp pieces of broken glass called knives.

From a thick glass bottle, broken off below the neck, chip off pieces. This can be done with the back of a heavy knife blade or a light hammer. The workman cannot be too careful or cautious in breaking or handling the glass, as the least carelessness is sure to result in bad cuts and bloody fingers.

From the slivers or chips of glass select pieces thick on the outside curve, but with a keen sharp inside edge. It may take time, experience, and several bottles to get knives to exactly suit you.

How to Make Cutters.

Fasten three knives together with wax (Fig. 30) so that each shall point in a different direction, bind on this three slips of thin wood lengthwise to hold the wax and glass firmly, and cover it neatly with cloth or kid.

A piece of twine looped at each end should pass through the apparatus lengthwise. This, of course, to be put in before the slips are bound together. Excellent cutters can be made of blades from an old penknife.

A much simpler weapon is made with a piece of stout twine one foot long, dipped in glue and rolled in pounded glass until thickly coated with a glistening armor of sharp points. Two of these incorporated in the lower half of the kite's tail will be found to be effective cutters.

Boys participating in this war of kites should always bear in mind the fact that it requires but little skill to cut an unarmed kite, and that there is no honor or glory to be gained in vanquishing a foe who is unable to defend himself.

There are many other attachments, improvements, and amusing appliances that suggest themselves to an enthusiastic kite-flyer.

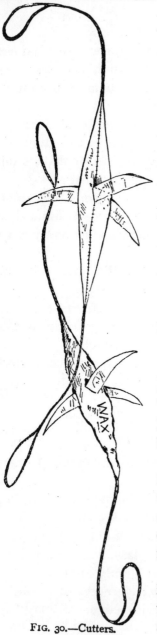

FIG. 30.—Cutters.

Kite Clubs.

The field is a large one, and the opportunities for originality and ingenuity almost unbounded. If some enthusiastic, energetic boy will take the initiatory steps, kite clubs might be formed throughout the country with appropriate names, rules, and regulations, which, during the kite season, would have their meets and tournaments, and award prizes to the steadiest stander, the highest flyer, and the most original and unique design besides the prizes awarded at the jousts of the war kites.

The organization of such clubs would give a new impetus to an amusement deserving of greater popularity than it has ever attained in this country.

Kite Time.

CHAPTER III.

NOVEL MODES OF FISHING.

The Bell Pole.

In the Gulf States, upon some of the plantations that border the sluggish streams or bayous peculiar to that part of the country, the field hands have a simple and ingenious contrivance by which they are enabled to fish without interfering with the discharge of their duties.

The apparatus used consists of an ordinary cane-pole to which a long line with any number of hooks is attached; an old bell is hung at the end of the cane where the line is fastened.

The sable sportsmen set a number of poles, rigged in this manner, thrusting the butt ends of the rods into the soft bank so that they stand almost upright along the edge of the water upon which the plantation borders.

After the hooks are baited the lines are cast out as far as they will reach into the stream and left to take care of themselves. As soon as a fish is hooked it struggles to free itself, but the first plunge the unwary creature makes rings the bell at the end of the rod and summons the laborer from the field, who leaves his ploughing or planting just long enough to land the fish and re-bait the hook. It is seldom that the setting sun sees the dusky workmen return to their cabins empty-handed.

By far the oddest and most original mode of fishing practised by the colored people of the Southern States is called by them

"Jugging for Cats."

Early one morning, while sauntering along the levee of a small town upon the Mississippi, the author met an old colored friend, Uncle Eanes.

"Whars I gwine?" queried the old man. "I was jus gwine to git de traps together to jug for cats,—Hi, Hi, neber hea tell of dat? De Lor! no sah, not presactly pussy cats — cullored folks eats 'bout de same as white folks (when dey can git it). Yes, sah! we's seed purty tight times since de war, Suah! but we hasent come to eating pussy cats just yet, Boss! Hi, Hi! Take a big jug suah enough to hold a tolerable sized mud cat! but we don't cotch dem in de jugs. You jest come along and I'll show you how 'tis." Uncle Eanes's invitation was accepted, and the author was initiated into the mysteries of

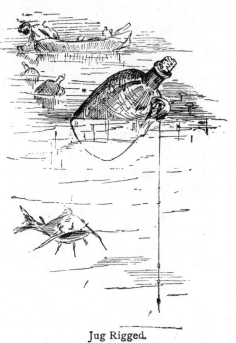

Jug Rigged.

"jugging for cats," which he found to combine exercise, excitement and fun in a much greater degree than the usual method of angling with rod and reel.

The tackle necessary in this sport is very simple; it consists of five or six empty jugs tightly corked with corn cobs, as many stout lines, each about five feet long with a sinker and large hook at the end. One of these lines is tied to the handle of each jug. Fresh liver, angle worms, and balls made of corn meal and cotton, are used for bait; but a bit of cheese, tied up in a piece of mosquito netting to prevent its washing away, appears to be considered the most tempting morsel.

When all the hooks are baited, and the fisherman has inspected his lines and found everything ready, he puts the jugs into a boat and rows out upon the river, dropping the earthenware floats about ten feet apart in a line across the middle of the stream. The jugs will, of course, be carried down with the current, and will have to be followed and watched. When one of them begins to behave in a strange manner, turning upside down, bobbing about, darting up stream and down, the fisherman knows that a large fish is hooked, and an exciting chase ensues. It sometimes requires hard rowing to catch the jug, for often when the fisherman feels sure of his prize and stretches forth his hand to grasp the runaway, it darts off anew, frequently disappearing from view beneath the water, and coming to the surface again, yards and yards away from where it had left the disappointed sportsman.

One would think that the pursuit of just one jug, which a fish is piloting around, might prove exciting enough. But imagine the sport of seeing four or five of them start off on their antics at about the same moment. It is at such a time that the skill of a fisherman is tested, for a novice, in his hurry, is apt to lose his head, thereby losing his fish also. Instead of hauling in his line carefully and steadily, he generally pulls it up in such a hasty manner that the fish is able, by a vigorous flop, to tear himself away from the hook. To be a successful "jugger," one must be as careful and deliberate in taking out his fish as though he had only that one jug to attend to, no matter how many others may be claiming his attention by their frantic signals. The illustration shows how the line is rigged.

The Dancing Fisherman

is another method of catching fish, in principle similar to jugging, by means of a jumping-jack, or small, jointed man, whose limbs are moved by jerking a string attached to them. This little figure is fastened to a stick, which is secured in an upright position on a float made of a piece of board. Through a hole in the float is passed the string attached to the figure, and tied securely to this are the hook and line. After the hook is baited, the float is placed on the surface of the water, and the little man, standing upright, is left to wait in patience.

Presently a fish,

FIG. 31.

attracted by the bait, comes nearer the surface, seizes the hook quickly, and darts downward, pulling the string, and making the little figure throw up its arms and legs as though dancing for joy at having performed its task so well. The capering of

Jack is the signal to his master that a fish has been caught and is struggling to free itself from the hook. This manner of fishing is necessarily confined to quiet bodies of water, such as small lakes or ponds ; for in rough water poor little Jack would be upset. Fig. 31 shows how to rig the " dancing fisherman."

Toy Boats for Fishing.

Trolling, by means of rudely made toy boats, is a sport the novelty of which will certainly recommend itself.

The boat can be made out of a piece of plank any where from a foot to two and one-half feet long, according to the size

FIG. 32.

of the fish to be caught. Sharpen the plank at one end and rig it with one or two masts and sails of paper or cloth. The rudder must be very long in proportion to the size of the boat, to prevent its making lee way and to keep it on a straight course. To nails in the stern of the boat tie fish lines rigged with spoon or live bait (Fig. 32). This diminutive fishing-smack will not alarm the finny inhabitants of the water as a larger boat might, but when sailing before the wind will troll the bait in a manner that appears to be irresistible to bass or pickerel, and sometimes even the mud-loving cat-fish will rise and swallow the hook. A whole fleet of these little vessels may be attended by one boy if he has a boat in which to row immediately to the assistance of any of his toy boats, whose suspicious movements betray the presence of a fish in tow.

The Wooden Otter

consists of a board two feet long, three inches wide, and one-half-inch thick, made to float on edge in the water by weighting the lower part of the plank with lead, iron, or even stones, tied on with strings. By means of a breast-band rigged like that on a kite, a strong tow-line is fastened to the " otter." At intervals along the tow-line, shorter lines are attached baited with artificial flies, spoon hooks, dead or live bait, as the case may be, the bait of course depending altogether upon the fish you are after. As you walk or row, the " otter " sheers off and the baits comb the water in a tantalizing way that is fatal to trout, bass, or pickerel. So " killing " is this instrument that it should only be used to replenish the larder when provisions are running short in camp.

Fishing for Fresh-Water Clams.

Mussels, or fresh-water clams, are prized by many boys on account of the pearly opalescent substance of which the shell is composed, it being an excellent material of which to make finger-rings and charms. Not unfrequently pearls of great beauty are found concealed within the shells of these bivalves.

The empty shells found upon the beach are never very highly prized, and are called by collectors dead shells. Shells of any kind which contain the living animal when collected, are ever after called live shells, for they still retain all their freshness and lustre after the inmate has been removed. To

3

collect live mussel shells, you must wade, dive, or, if the water
is clear enough for you to distinguish objects upon the bottom,
fish for them, not with a hook and line, but with a long twig,
from which all branches and leaves have been removed excepting a single bud on the end (Fig. 33). As soon as you detect
a bivalve, you will discover its shells to be partially open.

Carefully insert the bud, that you have left upon the end
of your stick, between the gaping lips of the shell, the instant

FIG. 33.

FIG. 34.

that the animal within feels the touch it will close its doors
firmly, of course holding the switch between the shells. The
bud at the end prevents the stick from slipping out, and the
animal is caught by taking advantage of the very means it uses
for protection.

A simple contrivance for catching small frogs, eels, and liz-
ards, for the aquarium consists of an elder stick, with one end
cut like a quill pen with the points spread apart, as shown in
sketch (Fig. 34).

To use this you must approach a pond or brook very cautiously so as not to frighten your game. Through the clear
water the little creatures can be seen resting quietly on the
bottom. If you are careful not to make any disturbance or
sudden movement you may get your elder lance poised over
your lizard, newt, or frog, within an inch or so of its body, without disturbing him; then with a quick movement push the stick
and animal both into the mud. On drawing out the stick you
will find your captive squirming between the split ends of the

elder—from which he can be removed without serious injury. With practice you can perfect yourself in this aquarian sport so as seldom to lose or injure your specimens.

The snare made of fine wire in the form of a slip noose is so well known to the boys in general, that it is no novelty and unnecessary to describe.

CHAPTER IV.

HOME-MADE FISHING TACKLE.

The Rod.

IT not unfrequently happens that an amateur is unable to take advantage of most excellent fishing, for the want of proper or necessary tackle.

It may be that he is accidentally in the neighborhood of a pickerel pond or trout stream, or that his fishing tackle is lost or delayed in transit. Under such circumstances a little practical ingenuity is invaluable. If within reach of any human habitation you can, in all probability, succeed in finding sufficient material with which to manufacture not only a rod which will answer your purpose, but a very serviceable reel. To rig up a home-made trout rod, you need a straight, slender, elastic pole, such as can be found in any wood or thicket, some pins, and a small piece of wire. File off the head of several pins, sharpen the blunt ends, and bend them into the form of the letter U. At a point about two feet from the butt end of the rod drive the first pin, leaving enough of the loop above the wood to allow the fish line to pass freely through; drive the other pins upon the same side of the rod and at regular intervals. Make the tip of a piece of wire by bending a neat circular loop in the centre, and then knitting or binding the wire on the end of the pole (Fig. 35). Should you have enough wire, it will answer much better for the other loops than the pins. If at a farm-house look in the attic for an old bonnet frame, or some similar object likely to be at hand, and it will furnish you with plenty of material. Cut the wire in pieces about two and

a half inches long, make a simple loop in the centre of each
piece, and with a "waxed end" or strong thread bind the
ends of the wire lengthwise on the rod, then give each loop a

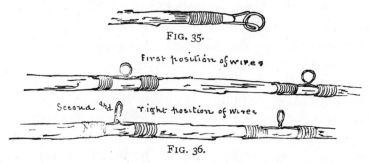

FIG. 35.

turn, twisting it in proper position (Fig. 36). With a large
wooden spool, an old tin can, and a piece of thick wire, a first-
rate reel may be manufactured.

Tin and Spool Reel.

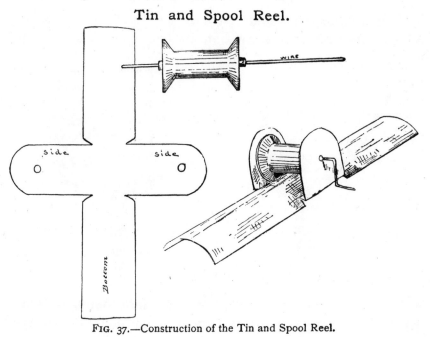

FIG. 37.—Construction of the Tin and Spool Reel.

Put the wire through the spool, allowing about one inch to protrude at one end and about three inches at the opposite end. Wedge the wire in firmly by driving soft pine sticks around it, and trim off the protruding ends of the sticks. Cut a piece of tin in the shape shown by the diagram (Fig. 37), punch a hole in each side piece for the wire to pass through, leaving plenty of room for the spool to revolve freely. Turn the side-pieces up upon each side of the spool, and bend the long end of the wire in the form of a crank. Hammer the bottom piece of tin over the rod until it takes the curved form, and fits tightly, then with strong wax string bind it firmly to the rod. If it should happen that a piece of tin could not be procured, a reel can be made of a forked stick and a spool.

The Forked-Stick Reel.

Cut a forked stick and shave off the inside flat, as in Fig. 38, cut two notches near the bottom, one upon each side ; this

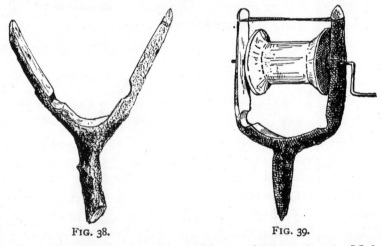

FIG. 38.   FIG. 39.

will allow the fork to bend readily at these points. Make a small groove for a string at the top of each prong. Put the spool between the prongs, allowing the wire to protrude through holes bored for that purpose. Bend the long end of the wire in the form of a crank. Tie a string across from end to end of the prongs to hold them in proper position, and you have a rustic but serviceable reel (Fig. 39). It may be attached to the pole in either manner shown by Figs. 40 and 41. Boys who find

FIG. 40.   FIG. 41.

pleasure in outdoor sports should always be ready with expedients for any emergency. A fish hook is rather a difficult thing to manufacture, though I have seen them made of a bird's claw bound to a piece of shell by vegetable fibre. I would not advise my readers to attempt to make one. A better plan is to always carry a supply about your person, inside the lining of your hat being a good place to deposit small hooks. For black bass, pickerel, and many other fish, live minnows are the best bait. To catch them you need a net.

Home-Made Nets.

A simple way to make a minnow net is to stretch a piece of mosquito netting between two stout sticks. If deemed necessary, floats may be fastened at the top and sinkers at the bottom edge of the net (Fig. 42). Coarse bagging may be used if mosquito netting is not obtainable. But with a forked stick and a ball of string for material, a jack-knife, and your fingers for tools, a splendid scoop-net can be made that will not only last, but be as good, if not better, than any you could purchase. Cut a good stout sapling that has two branches (Fig. 43). Trim off all other appendages, and bend the two branches until the ends over-lap each other for some distance, bind the ends firmly and neatly together with waxed twine, if it can be had—if not, with what string you have (Fig. 44).

Fasten the pole in a convenient position so that the hoop

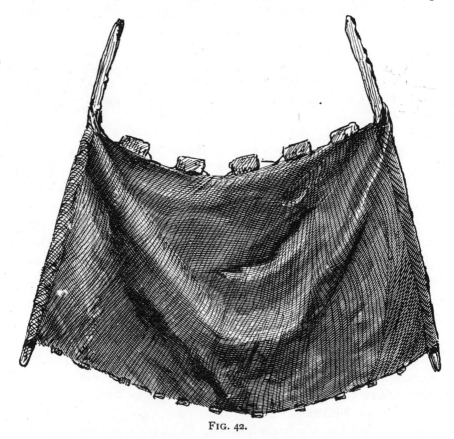

FIG. 42.

is about level with your face. If you want the net two feet deep, cut a number of pieces of twine seven or eight feet long, double them, and slip them on the hoop in the manner shown by the first string (Fig. 45).

Beginning at the most convenient point, take a string from each adjoining pair and make a simple knot of them, as shown

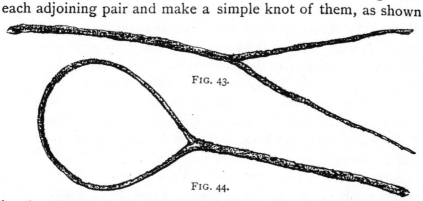

FIG. 43.

FIG. 44.

by the diagram. Continue all the way around the hoop knotting the strings together in this manner. Then commence on the next lower row and so on until you reach a point where, in your judgment the net ought to commence to narrow or taper down. This can be accomplished by knotting the strings a little closer together, and cutting off one string of a pair at four equidistant points in the same row. Knot as before until you come to a clipped line; here you must take a string from each side of the single one and knot them, being careful to make it come even with others in the same row. Before tightening the double knot pass the single string through, and

FIG. 45.

after tying a knot close to the double one cut the string off close. (See Fig. 45 A.)

Continue as before until the row is finished, only deviating from the original plan when a single string is reached. Proceed in a like manner with the next and the next rows, increasing the number of strings eliminated until the remaining ones meet at the bottom, being careful not to let one drop mesh come directly under another of the same kind.

A scoop-net can be made of a piece of mosquito netting by sewing it in the form of a bag, and fastening it to a pole and hoop made of a forked stick like the one just described.

Minnows must be kept alive, and tin buckets, with the top half perforated with holes, are made for that purpose. These buckets, when in use, are secured by a string and hung in the water, the holes in the sides allowing a constant supply of fresh breathing material to the little fish within.

A Home-Made Minnow Bucket.

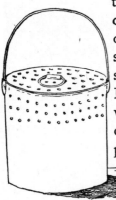

Take any tin bucket that has a lid to it and punch holes in the top and upper part with a nail and hammer, or some similar instruments. If a tin bucket cannot be had, a large-sized tin can will answer the purpose. The illustration (Fig. 46) shows a minnow bucket made in this manner. Fig. 47 shows the proper manner of baiting with a live minnow. The cartilaginous mouth of a fish has little or no feeling in it. A hook passed from beneath the under jaw through it and the upper lip will neither kill nor injure the minnow. As it allows the little creature to swim freely, there is a much greater chance of getting a bite than with a dead or mangled bait. The latter is a sign of either cruelty or ignorance on the part of the fisherman.

Fig. 46.

Inhabitants of the Water.

How natural it is to speak of a love for the sea, or an intimate acquaintance and knowledge of the ocean, when, in reality, it is only the top or surface of the water that is meant, while the hidden mysteries that underlie the billows, the sea-world proper—its scenery, inhabitants, and history—are but

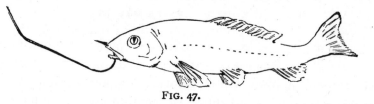

FIG. 47.

partially known, except to our most learned naturalists. The occasional glimpses we have of queer and odd specimens kidnapped from this unknown realm make it natural for us to feel a curiosity to know and a desire to see the life and forms that are concealed beneath the waves.

What boy can sit all day in a boat, or upon the green shady bank of an inland stream, watching the floating cork of his fish line without experiencing a longing for some new patent transparent diving bell, in which, comfortably ensconced at the bottom of the water, he might see all that goes on in that unfamiliar country.

In the next chapter I propose to show how this natural curiosity or desire for knowledge may be gratified, not exactly by placing you at the bottom of the water, but by transporting a portion of this curious world, with its liquid atmosphere and living inhabitants into your own house, where you may inspect and study it at your leisure.

CHAPTER V.

HOW TO STOCK, MAKE, AND KEEP A FRESH-WATER AQUARIUM.

ALTHOUGH marine animals may surpass the inhabitants of fresh water in strangeness of form and tint, there are some fresh-water fish upon whom Mother Nature appears to have lavished her colors ; and there are enough aquatic objects to be found, in any stream or pond, to keep all my readers busy and happy for years in studying their habits and natural history. One must have a certain amount of knowledge of the habits of an animal before he can expect to keep it in a thriving condition in captivity. This knowledge is gained by observation, and success depends upon the common sense displayed in discreetly using the information thus obtained.

Do not make the common mistake of supposing that an aquarium is only a globe or ornamental tank, made to hold a few lazy gold-fish. Do not have china swans floating about upon the top of the water, nor ruined castles submerged beneath the surface. Such things are in bad taste. Generally speaking, ruined castles are not found at the bottoms of lakes and rivers, and china swans do not swim on streams and ponds. If you determine to have an aquarium, have one whose contents will afford a constant source of amusement and instruction—one that will attract the attention and interest of visitors as soon as they enter the room where it is. Sea-shells, corals, etc., should not be used in a fresh-water aquarium; they not only look out of place, but the lime and salts they contain will injure both fish and plant. Try to make your aquarium a miniature lake in all its details, and you will find the effect more pleasing to the eye. By making the artificial home of the aquatic creatures conform as nearly as possible to their natural ones you can keep them all in a healthy and lively condition.

At the bird-stores and other places where objects in natural history are sold, you may buy an aquarium of almost any size you wish, from the square tank with heavy iron castings to the small glass globe ; the globes come in ten sizes.

Some time ago, when the author, then quite a small boy, was spending the summer upon the shores of Lake Erie, the older members of the household frequently went out on the lake after black bass, taking with them for bait a pail of the beautiful " painted minnows " found in the little brooks of Northern Ohio. Upon the return of a fishing party the minnows left in the pail were claimed by the children as their share of the spoils, but the little fish would scarcely live a day ; in spite of all that could be done they would, one by one, turn upon their backs and expire. This was the source of much disappointment and remorseful feelings on the part of the children. One day half the minnows from the pail were poured into a large flat dish, that they might be better seen as they swam about ; here they were forgotten for the time ; on the morrow all the fish in the pail were found to be dead, but those in the flat dish were perfectly lively and well. This discovery led to a series of experiments which the author has continued at times up to the present date, and he feels no hesitancy in saying that, if the manufacturers of aquariums in this country had made it their object to build vessels in which no respectable fish could live, they could hardly have succeeded better, for they all violate this first rule : the greater the surface of water exposed to the air, the greater the quantity of oxygen absorbed from the atmosphere. Amateurs must bear in mind that " the value of water depends not so much on its bulk as on the advantageous distribution of its bulk over large spaces." In other words, flat, shallow vessels are the best.

In the light of this fact the author set to work to build his first aquarium. The materials for its construction were bought of the town glazier's son. The amount paid was several marbles, a broken-bladed Barlow knife, and a picture of the school teacher sketched in lead pencil upon the fly-leaf of a spelling-book. In exchange for these treasures, several fragments of window-glass, some paint, an old brush, and a lump of putty, was received. Two or three days' work resulted in the production of an aquarium. It was only twelve inches long, eight inches wide, and four inches high ; but, although this tank was small, it was a real aquarium, and would hold water and living pets. A piece of glass 12 × 8 inches formed the bottom. The sides were fastened on by simply pasting paper along the outside edges ; if left in this condition of course the water would leak through the cracks, soften the paper, and produce disastrous results.

To prevent this the cracks upon the inside were carefully puttied up and the putty covered with thin strips of glass, which the glazier good-naturedly cut for the purpose ; this not only prevented the tank from leaking, but added greatly to its strength. The paper corners and all the outside, excepting the front was then covered with two or three coats of paint. The front glass was left clean for observation. A piece of pine board formed the base of the little aquarium. After it was carefully puttied around the bottom, where the glass set in the board, the latter was nicely painted to correspond with the rest of the structure, the whole was left to dry. Crude as this tank may appear from the description, it did not look so, and best of all it never leaked.

With a dip-net, made of an old piece of mosquito-netting, what fun it was to explore the spaces between the logs of the rafts in front of the old saw-mill! and what curious creatures were found lurking there! Little gars, whose tiny forms looked like bits of sticks; young spoon-bill fish (paddle-fish), with exaggerated upper lips one-third the length of their scaleless bodies; funny little black cat-fish, that looked for all the world like tadpoles, and scores of other creatures. Under the green vegetation in those spaces they found a safe retreat from the attacks of larger fish.

If a constant supply of fresh water can be kept flowing in an aquarium, or the water constantly aërified by agitation, the ordinary misshapen tank may be run successfully. The glass globe, the most unnatural of all forms for aquariums, can be utilized in this way. There used to be in the window of a jewelry store, in an Ohio town, an ordinary glass fish-globe, in which lived and thrived a saucy little brook trout. Brook-trout, as most of my readers know, are found only in cool running water, and will not live for any great length of time in an ordinary aquarium. In this case, an artificial circulation of water was produced by means of a

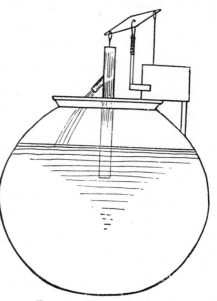

FIG. 48.—Globe and Pump.

little pump run by clock-work. Every morning the jeweller wound up the machine, and all day long the little pump worked, pumping up the water from the globe, only to send it back

again in a small but constant stream which poured from the
little spout, each drop carrying with it into the water of the
globe a small quantity of fresh air, including, of course, oxygen
gas. (See Fig. 48.) And the little speckled trout lived and
thrived, and, for aught I know to the contrary, is still swimming around in his crystal prison, waiting, with ever-ready
mouth, to swallow up the blue-bottle flies thrown to him by his
friend the jeweller. It is a great mistake to suppose that it is
necessary to change the water in an aquarium every few days.
The tank should be so arranged as to seldom if ever require a
change of water. This is not difficult to accomplish.

If possible, have your aquarium made under your own eyes.
Suppose you wish one, two feet long ; then it should be sixteen
inches wide and seven inches high ; or 24″ × 7″ × 16″. Figure
49 shows an aquarium of the proper form and proportions.

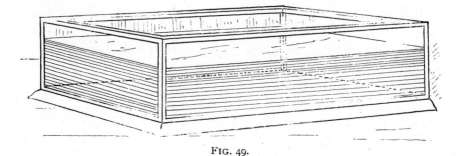

FIG. 49.

Figure 50 shows the popular, but unnatural and improper form.
With a properly made aquarium, after it is once stocked with
the right proportion of plant and animal life, there is no necessity of *ever* changing the water.

Both animals and plants breathe, and what is life to the
plant is poison to the animal. Animals absorb oxygen and
throw off carbonic acid gas ; this gas the plants inhale, separat-
ing it into carbon and oxygen, absorbing the carbon, which is

converted into their vegetable tissue, and throwing off the free oxygen for the animals to breathe. By having plants as well as animals in your tank, both classes are supplied with breathing material. When you start your aquarium, first cover the bottom with sand and gravel. Then build your rockery; it is better to cement it together and into place.

After this is all arranged, go to the nearest pond or brook, and dredge up some water plants. Any, that are not too large, will do—starwort, milfoil, bladder-wort, pondweed, etc. Fast-

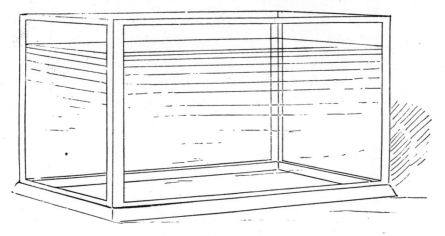

FIG. 50.

en the roots of your plants to small stones with a bit of string, and arrange them about the tank to suit your taste. Fill the tank with water, and let it stand in the window for a week or two, where it will receive plenty of light and but little sun. By that time all your plants will be growing, and numerous other little plants will have started into life of their own accord. Then you may add your animals, and, if you do not overstock the tank, you need *never change the water.* Be sure not to handle the fish; if, for any cause, you wish to remove them, lift them gently with a dip-net.

4

Should you wish to keep a little turtle, a crawfish, or any such animal, you must have your rockery so arranged that part

Fig. 51.

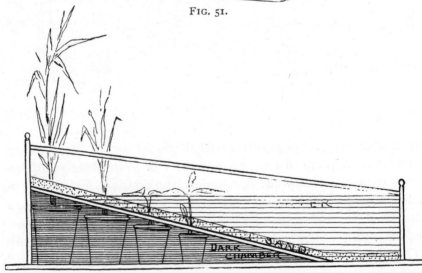

Fig. 52.

of it will protrude above the water; or, better still, have a vivarium or land-and-water aquarium, such as is shown in Figures 51 and 52. With a tank made upon this plan you can have aquatic plants as well as land plants and flowers, a sandy beach for the turtle to sleep upon, as he loves to do, and a rockery for the crawfish to hide in and keep out of mischief. Some species of snails like to crawl occasionally above the water-line. Such an aquarium makes an interesting object for the conservatory.

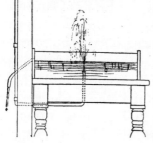

Figure No. 53 shows how a fountain can be made. The opening of the fountain should be so small as to allow only a fine jet of water to issue from it; the reservoir or supply-tank should be out of sight, and quite large, so that, by filling it at night, the fountain will keep playing all day. The waste-pipe should open at the level you intend to keep the water, and the opening should be covered with a piece of mosquito-netting or wire-gauze to prevent any creature from being drawn in.

In an aquarium with a slanting bottom, only the front need be of glass; the other three

FIG. 53.

sides can be made of slate, which is also a good material for the false bottom. In ponds, rivers, and lakes, the only light received comes from above; so we can understand that a vessel admitting light upon all sides, as well as from the top, forms an unnaturally luminous abode for fish. The glass front is sufficient for the spectator to see through.

The author has a tank twenty-five inches long, eleven inches wide, and twelve inches high—far too narrow and deep; but these defects have been, in a measure, overcome by filling it only two-thirds full of water, and allowing the green vegetation to grow undisturbed upon three sides of the aquarium ; the remaining side is kept clean by rubbing off all vegetable matter once a week with a long-handled bottle-washer. A rag or a piece of sponge, tied upon the end of a stick, will answer the same purpose. This tank has been in a flourishing condition for three years, and the water has been changed only once, and then all the water was removed so that some alteration could be made in the rockery.

But one of the inmates has died since last summer, and that was a bachelor stickleback, who probably received a nip from the pincers of one of the craw-fish. Two of these creatures have their den in the rockery that occupies the centre of the tank. A German carp, from the Washington breeding-ponds, browses all day long upon the mossy surface of the rocks, or roots around the bottom, taking great mouthfuls of sand and then puffing it out again like smoke. A striped dace spends most of his time lying flat upon his stomach on the bottom, or roosting like some subaqueous bird upon branches of the aquatic plants or on a submerged rock. A big and a little " killie " dart around after the boat-bugs, which they seldom catch ; and if they do, they drop them again in great trepidation. A diminutive pond-bass asserts his authority over the larger fish in a most tyrannous manner. An eel lives under the sand in the bottom, and deigns to make his appearance only once in several months, much to the amazement of the other inhabitants, all of whom seem to forget his presence until the smell of a bit of meat brings his long body from his retreat. Numerous little mussels creep along the bottom ; periwinkles and snails crawl up and down the sides ; caddice-worms cling to the plants, and everything appears perfectly at home and contented.

And why? Because their home is arranged as nearly as possible like their natural haunts, where they were captured. *Learn the habits of any creature, and give it a chance to follow them, and you will find little difficulty in keeping it healthy in captivity.*

Stocking.

Feed your fish on insects once or twice a week. Do not try to force them to eat ; if they are hungry, they need little persuasion. Boat-bugs, whirligig-beetles, and, in fact, almost all the aquatic bugs and beetles, will eat lean, raw meat, if given to them in small bits.

Water-bugs and insects will become almost as tame as the fish, and even dispute with the latter over a dainty piece of food. One of the most amusing sights is a tiny thread-like eel and a pugnacious whirligig-beetle fighting for the possession of a fly. The eel generally comes off victorious : if he succeeds in once getting a good hold of the fly, he will make a corkscrew or spiral of his body, then commence revolving so rapidly as to often throw the whirligig out of the water.

Remember that aquatic animals, like all other creatures, are very variable in their appetites ; some are gluttons, some eat sparingly, some prefer animal food, while others live entirely upon vegetable matter. Carp, dace, and such fish will eat bread ; bass, pickerel, and gars will not.

Never allow any food to remain in the bottom of the aquarium to spoil, for it will contaminate the water. The vegetarians in your tank will feed upon the plants growing therein, and they will all eat bread. Most fish will like the prepared food which you can obtain at any aquarium store.

In selecting fish for your aquarium, be careful to have the perch, sun-fish, and bass much smaller than the dace, carp, or gold-fish ; otherwise the last-named fish will soon find a resting-place inside the former.

Never put a large frog in an aquarium, for he will devour everything there. A bull-frog that I kept in my studio for more than a year swallowed fish, live mice, and brown bats; he also swallowed a frog of nearly his own size; but when he engulfed a young alligator, we were almost as amazed as if he had swallowed himself.

The Frog.

For the benefit of the curious, here is a partial record of Mr. Frog's meals from May until November:

May 14th.—Over a dozen brown beetles.

May 15th.—One full-grown live mouse.

May 19th.—One full-grown spotted frog.

May 24th.—A piece of beef one-third size of the frog himself.

June 2d, 9 A.M.—One live mouse.

June 2d, 1 P.M.—One live mouse.

June 5th.—A piece of steak one-half size of the frog.

July 18th.—One full-grown live mouse.

July 20th.—One young alligator 11 ¼ inches long.

This was a pet alligator, and I just came in in time to see the tip of his tail sticking out of the frog's mouth. Taking hold of the alligator's tail I helped Mr. Frog disgorge my pet, but the saurian was dead.

July 27th.—One full-grown live mouse.

July 29th.—One full-grown live mouse.

August 9th.—One full-grown live mouse.

September 17th.—One large brown bat.

September 20th.—One live craw-fish.

September 21st.—Two live craw-fish.

September 22d.—One live craw-fish.

September 25th, 27th, and October 8th.—Each one full-grown live mouse.

November 15th.—This gluttonous frog ate two-thirds of a white perch and

November 17th.—Died of a fit of indigestion.

But so celebrated had the frog become on account of his pluck and voracious appetite, that his obituary was published in several papers.

Craw-fish are very mischievous; they pull up the plants, up-set the rockery, nip the ends off the fishes' tails, crack the mus-sel-shells, pull out the inmates and devour them, squeeze the caddice-worm from his little log-house, and, in fact, are incorri-gible mischief-makers. But, from that very fact, I always keep one or two small ones. The other inhabitants of the aquarium soon learn to dread the pincer of these fresh-water lobsters, and keep out of the way. Tadpoles are always an interesting addi-tion to an aquarium.

Pickerel and gars should be kept in an aquarium by them-selves.

Pond-bass make very intelligent pets. I once had three hundred of these little fellows, perfectly tame. Down in one corner of the cornfield I found two patent washing-machines, the beds of which were shaped like scow-boats. These old ma-chines were fast going to ruin, and I readily gained permission to use them for whatever purpose I wished; so, with a hatchet, I knocked off the legs and top-gear; then removed a side from each box, and fastened the two together, making a tank about four feet square. The seam, or crack, where the two parts joined, was filled with oakum, and the whole outside was thickly daubed with coal-tar. The tank was then set in a hole dug for that purpose, and dirt filled in and packed around the sides. Back of it I piled rocks, and planted ferns in all the cracks and crannies, and also put rocks in the centre of the tank, first covering the bottom with sand and gravel. After filling this with water and plants, three hundred little bass were introduced, and they soon became so tame that they would follow my finger all around, or would jump out of the water for a bit of meat held between the fingers. Almost any wild creatures will yield to persistent kind treatment, and become tame. Generally, too, they learn to have a sort of trustful affection for their keepers, who, however, to earn the confidence of such friends, should be almost as wise, punctual, and unfailing as good Dame Nature herself.

Gold-Fish versus Bass.

One of the same bass, which I gave to a friend of mine, lived in an ordinary glass globe for three years. It was a very intelligent fish, but very spiteful and jealous. My friend's mother thought it was lonesome, and so, one day, she brought home a beautiful gold-fish—a little larger than the bass—to keep it company. She put the gold-fish in the globe, and watched the bass, expecting to see it wonderfully pleased; but the little wretch worked himself into a terrible passion, erected every spine upon his back, glared a moment at the intruder, and then made a dart forward, seized the gold-fish by the abdomen, and shook it as a terrier-dog shakes a rat, until the transparent water was glittering all over with a shower of golden scales. As soon as possible, the carp was rescued; but it was too late. He only gasped and died. The vicious little bass swam around and around his globe, biting in his rage at all the floating scales. Ever after, he was allowed to live a hermit's life, and he behaved himself well. At last the family went away for a couple of weeks, and, when they returned, the poor little bass lay dead at the bottom of his globe.

It might be well to state, before finishing this article, that common putty, after being exposed to the action of water, is very apt to soften and crumble away, or drop off in large flakes. Painting it will not prevent this. In New York, and I suppose other large cities, the aquarium-stores keep a substance which they call aquarium cement. It looks like red putty, but I have found that it withstands the action of water admirably. For fifty cents enough can be purchased to cement a large aquarium; but for the benefit of those among my readers who live out of the cities, the following receipt from the *Scientific American* is inserted.

"*Aquarium Cement.*—Linseed oil, 3 oz.; tar, 4 oz.; resin, 1 lb.; melt together over a gentle fire. If too much oil is used the cement will run down the angles of the aquarium; to obviate this it should be tested before using by allowing a small quantity to cool under water; if not found sufficiently firm, allow it to simmer longer or add more tar and resin. The cement should be poured in the corners of the aquarium while warm (not hot). This cement is pliable, and is not poisonous."

Whirligig and the Eel.

CHAPTER VI.

HOW TO KEEP AQUATIC PLANTS IN THE HOUSE OR FLOWER-GARDEN.

In gathering plants for your aquarium you will undoubtedly see many much too large for your purpose, and yet so beautiful that you naturally desire to keep them. Some water plants are extremely lovely and all of them odd when seen growing anywhere but in their accustomed places. Water-lilies growing in the midst of a lawn will be sure to excite surprise, and cat-tails flourishing in a conservatory will be a novelty. Yet it is a comparatively simple matter to rear these and other aquatic plants in your house and garden.

Water-Lily.

Select a spot in your flower-bed and make an excavation of sufficient depth to set a water-tight barrel in, so that the top of the barrel will be even with the surface of the ground. Set the barrel in and fill the earth around. In the bottom of the barrel put about eight or ten inches of black pond-mud; plant the water-lily roots firmly in centre of mud. Fill the barrel with water, being careful to pour it in gradually, so as not to disturb or displace the mud. Figure 54 shows a cross-section of ground and barrel. Everything being then as it is in the natural or wild state, the lily will flourish and bloom, adding a beautiful and curious feature to your plat. Supply fresh water only as the water in the barrel evaporates.

Fig. 54

Fig. 55.

Fig. 56.

DAN BEARD

Cat-Tails.

Cat-tails are of graceful form and make a pretty background. At the nearest marsh dig up a bunch of good healthy ones and plant them in some of their native mud in a water-tight box or pail. Set the box or pail in the earth. A cover of plank, with a round hole in the centre for the cat-tails to come through, should be put over the top and covered with the sod. Half an inch of water over the surface of the mud in box or pail is all that is necessary. (See illustration, Fig. 55.) Figure 56 shows how cat-tails may be disposed of in-doors, or where it is inconvenient to make room for them in the soil. A very unique and effective floral arrangement may be made by grouping pot-plants around them.

CHAPTER VII.

HOW TO STOCK AND KEEP A MARINE AQUARIUM.

THE first introduction of the aquarium revealed another world and its inhabitants : a world of enchantment, far surpassing any described in the " Arabian Nights " or fairy tales ; a world teeming with life so strange that some of it we can scarcely believe to be real.

The marine aquarium has laid bare secrets that have been locked in the breast of the ocean for ages. Through the crystal sides of the tanks are now shown living animals, of forms so lovely and delicate as to remind us of the tracery of frost-work. We can behold in the transparent waters fishes circling about, with distended fins that resemble the gorgeous wings of butterflies ; and we can see, glancing here and there, other fish, the glitter of whose glossy sides dazzles us and is as various in hue as the rainbow. The rocks at the bottom are carpeted with animals in the forms of lovely flowers !

The remarks in regard to the form and general construction of fresh-water aquariums will apply equally to marine tanks. The best form for the latter is the shallow vessel with a slanting false bottom, described in a preceding chapter and illustrated by Figures 51 and 52.

If you have a common rectangular tank, such as can be purchased at any aquarium-store (Fig. 50), it may be rendered inhabitable for marine animals by making a few improvements. Four tall glass panels admit too much light ; therefore give the outside of the glass a coat of green paint on all but one side, leave that clean and transparent to serve as a window, through which may be observed the interior and its occupants. The rockery or arch that is to occupy the centre of the aquarium should be cemented together with marine cement. Although this is not absolutely necessary, it is the best plan, and prevents many accidents. The following receipt I cull from the *Scientific American :*

Cement for Marine Aquaria.—Take 10 parts, by measure, litharge, 10 parts plaster-of-Paris, 10 parts dry white sand, 1 part finely powdered resin, and mix them when wanted for use into a pretty stiff putty with boiled linseed oil. This will stick to wood, stone, metal or glass, and hardens under water. It resists the action of salt water. It is better not to use the tank until three days after it has been cemented.

The arch may be built out of clean cinders or ragged and irregular stones ; an old oyster-shell with its rough side upper-most can be used as a top-piece. To make the arch steady and not liable to upset, the bottom should be composed of rather large flat stones.

Cover the bottom of the aquarium to a depth of an inch or more with sand from the beach. Procure the salt water from the ocean itself, and if possible obtain the supply some distance from shore. In no case must you dip the water for your aqua-rium up from the mouth of a fresh-water stream or muddy creek. If the tank is narrow and deep, fill only about one-third of it. Let the water stand in the aquarium for several days before introducing the plants. Select the bright algæ or sea-weeds that you find attached to small pebbles ; the stones will of course sink to the bottom of your aquarium and keep the plants in an upright and stationary position. After all is ar-ranged to your satisfaction, choose a place for the location of your tank where there will be light enough to plainly see its contents and cause little bubbles of oxygen to collect and rise from the vegetation. A window facing the north or northeast is the best situation. When you observe that the plants are in a thriving condition, and that a new vegetation has apparently sprung spontaneously into existence, carpeting the rockery and sides of the glass with green, then and not until then introduce the animals. Be very careful not to overstock the tank. Remember, no matter how bright and pleasant a room may be with one or two persons in it, the atmosphere of that same room will become foul and heavy in the presence of a large crowd, and if the ventilation be insufficient, headache, dizziness, and death will ensue, as was the case in the terrible Black Hole of Calcutta. Unless you want to make a miniature " black hole " of your aquarium, do not overcrowd it. Let the water have light, but no sunshine. Put a glass cover over the tank to keep out the dust, but let the cover fit loosely enough to allow a free circulation of air. The glass top-piece will in a measure prevent evaporation. If, however, any water is lost from this cause, recollect that the salts contained in sea water do not evaporate, and consequently the tank may be replenished with fresh water equalling the amount evaporated. Beware of the hot summer months. I have always found it more difficult to keep the water pure during July and August than any other part of the year. Do not allow smoking in the room where your aquarium is, as the foul atmosphere taints the water. I once lost almost all the inhabitants of a thriving marine tank, by allowing a party of gentlemen to smoke in the room where it was standing. If you have company in the evening, the room, as a rule, will become overheated, and you should take the precaution to wrap the sides of the tank with wet towels.

The prepared food mentioned in the preceding chapter will answer for some salt-water animals. Lean beef, cut in very small bits, may be dried and kept for feeding marine pets when oysters or clams cannot be had. The clams and oysters should be chopped up very fine when used.   Anemones and madrepores should be fed in quantities regulated by the size of the animals, and not more frequently than once a week.   The food should be placed gently within their reach by means of a pair of forceps or some similar instrument.   Crabs will soon learn to come out of their hiding-places at meal-times, and the fish will not be behind time in getting their share of chopped clam.   If you have a vivarium (Figs. 51 and 52), a handful of fiddler-crabs may be kept upon your artificial beach, where they will soon make themselves at home and afford a constant source of amusement by their antics.   I kept a lot of little " fiddlers " in a fish globe, and for more than a year they lived without salt water, happy and contented with a bit of damp sand to dig in and an occasional piece of chopped oyster to eat.   It would be difficult to find odder or more easily satisfied pets than the grotesque little fiddlers. Each male crab has one large claw which for exercise or amusement he keeps in constant motion, only folding it up when preparing to enter his hole or scamper sideways across the sand.   The pedunculated eyes of these little creatures stand up in a manner that gives them a very pert appearance.

Remove all dead animals or particles of food not devoured by the inmates, from the aquarium, to prevent the water from becoming tainted with poisonous gases emanating from the decaying animal matter.   Dead vegetation, though not as injurious as dead animals, should nevertheless be removed, for it is unsightly, and makes the water turbid and muddy.   No matter how foul sea-water may become, you must not waste it, for the injury is never permanent, and can soon be remedied by filtering or exposing it in earthenware vessels to the air and gently stirring it occasionally with a stick or piece of glass.

A filter may be made of a flower-pot, by stopping up the hole in the bottom with a perforated cork in which a small

quill has been inserted, and then filling the pot half full of powdered charcoal, sand, and gravel—the charcoal at the bottom,
the sand next, and the fine gravel or coarse sand on top. This
filter when in use should be hung over, but some distance
above, an earthen-ware dish, and the water allowed to fall drop
by drop, or in a small stream, from the pot to the dish, or the
filter may be hung over the aquarium, and each drop of water
as it falls will carry with it into the tank below particles of the
purifying, life-giving oxygen gathered up on its journey through
the air.

5

Fiddler Crabs.

CHAPTER VIII.

HOW TO COLLECT FOR MARINE AQUARIUM.

NEAR high-water mark, among the sea-weed and drift that have been washed up by a storm, is a veritable curiosity shop, and one well worth inspecting, but most of the animals to be found in this heterogeneous mass of drift, shells, plants, and pieces of wreck are either badly injured or dead, and, though many valuable specimens may here be obtained for the cabinet or museum, it is not a good place to find living, healthy animals for the aquarium.

If you are going on a collecting tour in search of living objects you must go prepared for a good rough-and-tumble time among slippery stones, muddy bottoms, or grimy old docks and piers.

You should wear no clothing that you care to preserve. Salt water will ruin shoes, so put on any old pair that will protect your feet from the shells or sharp stones; if the shoes have holes that let the water in, console yourself with the thought that the water can run out the same way. In fact, you must be prepared for a slip-up in the mud, or a good ducking in the shallow water, where the bottom is often so slippery that it is hard to wade far without involuntarily sitting down once or twice. After you have rigged yourself out in " old togs," next equip yourself with a basket to hold upright some glass preserve-jars or a lot of wide-mouthed bottles; then, armed with a small hammer, an old case-knife or trowel, a dip-net made of coarse bagging or fine mosquito-netting, you are ready for any game from a lobster to the minute little crustacean found among the algæ.

You should time your excursion so as to be on the hunting-ground at extreme low tide. As soon as you reach the beach wade right into your work ; look under the stones, scoop up the sand or mud with your net from the bottom of all the pools left by the tide, examine every promising-looking bunch of sea-weed, and before the tide comes in you will have material enough to stock forty aquariums. When you reach home sort out your specimens, discard all weak and sickly animals, and put the healthy ones in flat earthenware dishes of salt water, where they may be examined at leisure, and the proper ones taken out and put into your aquarium. In the mud and sand between the tides, or in the shallow water at extreme low tide, live many curious creatures.

If you should discover among the dirt in the bottom of your dip-net some queer-looking tubes, preserve them carefully, for they may contain some of those odd and often brilliantly colored marine worms. The inland boy, who is accustomed to see only the unsightly angle-worm, has no idea what really beautiful creatures some of the marine worms are. See, for instance, there is something in the mud that looks like a drop of blood. Put it in a plate of salt water and watch how one by one it begins to put forth its tentacles until its whole appearance is changed. This is a worm with a long scientific* name, which you may learn by and by if you become interested enough in your recreation to make a study of it.

Do not neglect to collect a few barnacles for your aquarium, and you will find yourself amply repaid for the trouble you found in detaching them from their native posts or rocks, when you see them each put forth an odd hand-shaped member, open-

* Polycirrus eximius.

ing and closing the numerous long, slender fingers as if the animals inside the shells were grasping for something in the water, as, indeed, they are, for it is by this means that the little hermits in their acorn-shaped houses obtain their food.

For collecting in deep water, dredges are used; these are described among the summer sports, page 86.

The Young Collectors.

Summer.

FIG. 57.

CHAPTER IX.
KNOTS, BENDS, AND HITCHES.

THE art of tying knots is an almost necessary adjunct to not a few recreations. Especially is this true of summer sports, many of which are nautical, or in some manner connected with the water.

Any boy who has been aboard a yacht or a sail-boat, must have realized that the safety of the vessel and all aboard may be imperilled by ignorance or negligence in the tying of a knot or fastening of a rope.

With some, the knack of tying a good, strong knot in a heavy rope, or light cord, seems to be a natural gift; it is certainly a very convenient accomplishment, and one that with practice and a little perseverance may be acquired even by those who at first make the most awkward and bungling attempts.

A bulky, cumbersome knot is not only ungainly, but is generally insecure.

As a rule, the strength of a knot is in direct proportion to its neat and handsome appearance.

To my mind, it is as necessary that the archer should know how to make the proper loops at the end of his bow-string, as it is that a hunter should understand how to load his gun.

Every fisherman should be able to join two lines neatly and securely, and should know the best and most expeditious method of attaching an extra hook or fly; and any boy who rigs up a hammock or swing with a " granny," or other insecure knot, deserves the ugly tumble and sore bones that are more than liable to result from his ignorance.

A knot, nautically speaking, is a " bend " that is more permanent than a " hitch." A knot properly tied never slips, nor does it jam so that it cannot be readily untied. A " hitch " might be termed a temporary bend, as it is seldom relied upon for permanent service. The " hitch " is so made that it can be cast off, or unfastened, more quickly than a knot.

It is impossible for the brightest boy to learn to make " knots, bends, and hitches " by simply reading over a description of the methods; for, although he may understand them at the time, five minutes after reading the article the process will have escaped his memory; but if he take a piece of cord or rope, and sit down with the diagrams in front of him, he will find little difficulty in managing the most complicated knots; and he will not only acquire an accomplishment from which he can derive infinite amusement for himself and a means of entertainment for others, but the knowledge gained may, in case of accident by fire or flood, be the means of saving both life and property.

The accompanying diagrams show a number of useful and important bends, splices, etc. To simplify matters, let us commence with Fig. 57, and go through the diagrams in the order in which they come:

The "English," or "common single fisherman's knot" (Fig. 57, I.), is neat and strong enough for any ordinary strain. The diagram shows the knots before being tightened and drawn together.

When exceptional strength is required it can be obtained by joining the lines in the ordinary single fisherman's knot (Fig. 57, I.), and pulling each of the half knots as tight as possible, then drawing them within an eighth of an inch of each other and wrapping between with fine gut that has been previously softened in water, or with light-colored silk.

An additional line, or a sinker may be attached by tying a knot in the end of the extra line, and inserting it between the parts of the single fisherman's knot before they are drawn together and tightened.

The "fisherman's double half knot," Fig. 57 (II. and III.). After the gut has been passed around the main line and through itself, it is passed around the line once more and through the same loop again, and drawn close.

Fig. 57 (IV., V. and IX.). Here are three methods of joining the ends of two lines together; the diagrams explain them much better than words can. Take a piece of string, try each one, and test their relative strength.

Fig. 57 (VI.). It often happens, while fishing, that a hook is caught in a snag, or by some other means lost. The diagram shows the most expeditious manner of attaching another hook by what is known as the "sinker hitch," described further on (Fig. 57, D, D, D, and Fig. 58, XIV., XV., and XVI.).

Fig. 57, VII. is another and more secure method of attaching a hook by knitting the line on with a succession of hitches.

How To Make a Horse-Hair Watch-Guard.

The same hitches are used in the manufacture of horse-hair watch-guards, much in vogue with the boys in some sections of the country. As regularly as "kite-time," "top-time," or "ball-time," comes "horse-hair watch-guard time."

About once a year the rage for making watch-guards used to seize the boys of our school, and by some means or other almost every boy would have a supply of horse-hair on hand. With the first tap of the bell for recess, some fifty hands would dive into the mysterious depths of about fifty pockets, and before the bell had stopped ringing about fifty watch-guards, in a more or less incomplete state, would be produced.

Whenever a teamster's unlucky stars caused him to stop near the school-house, a chorus of voices greeted him with " Mister, please let us have some hair from your horses' tails."

The request was at first seldom refused, possibly because its nature was not at the time properly understood; but lucky was the boy considered who succeeded in pulling a supply of hair from the horses' tails without being interrupted by the heels of the animals or by the teamster, who, when he saw the swarm of boys tugging at his horses' tails, generally repented his first good-natured assent, and with a gruff "Get out, you young rascals!" sent the lads scampering to the school-yard fence.

Select a lot of long hair of the color desired ; make it into a switch about the eighth of an inch thick by tying one end in a simple knot.   Pick out a good, long hair and tie it around the switch close to the knotted end ; then take the free end of the single hair in your right hand and pass it under the switch on one side, thus forming a loop through which the end of the hair must pass after it is brought up and over from the other side of the switch.   Draw the knot tight by pulling the free end of the hair as shown by Fig. 57, VII.   Every time this operation is repeated a wrap and a knot is produced.   The knots follow each other in a spiral around the switch, giving it a very pretty, ornamented appearance.   When one hair is used up select another, and commence knitting with it as you did with the first, being careful to cover and conceal the short end of the first hair, and to make the knots on the second commence where the former stop.   A guard made of white horse-hair looks as if it might be composed of spun glass, and produces a very odd and pretty effect.   A black one is very genteel in appearance.

Miscellaneous.

Fig. 57, VIII. shows a simple and expeditious manner of attaching a trolling hook to a fish-line.

Fig. 57, F is a hitch used on shipboard, or wherever lines and cables are used.   It is called the Blackwall hitch.

Fig. 57, E is a fire-escape made of a double bowline knot, useful as a sling for hoisting persons up or letting them down from any high place ; the window of a burning building, for instance.   Fig. 58, XVIII., XIX. and XX. show how this knot is made.   It is described on page 77.

Fig. 57, A is a "bale hitch," made of a loop of rope.   To make it, take a piece of rope that has its two ends joined ; lay the rope down and place the bale on it ; bring the loop opposite you up, on that side of the bale, and the loop in front up, on the side of the bale next to you; thrust the latter loop under and through the first and attach the hoisting rope. The heavier the object to be lifted, the tighter the hitch becomes. An excellent substitute for a shawl-strap can be made of a cord by using the bale hitch, the loop at the top being a first-rate handle.

Fig. 57, B is called a cask sling, and C (Fig. 57) is called a butt sling. The manner of making these last two and their uses may be seen by referring to the illustration. It will be noticed that a line is attached to the bale hitch in a peculiar manner (a, Fig. 57). This is called the "anchor bend." If while aboard a sail-boat you have occasion to throw a bucket over for water, you will find the anchor bend a very convenient and safe way to attach a line to the bucket handle.

Fig. 58, I. and II. are loops showing the elements of the simplest knots.

Fig. 58, III. is a simple knot commenced.

Fig. 58, IV. shows the simple knot tightened.

Fig. 58, V. and VI. show how the Flemish knot looks when commenced and finished.

Fig. 58, VII. and VIII. show a "rope knot" commenced and finished.

Fig. 58, IX. is a double knot commenced.

Fig. 58, X. is the same completed.

Fig. 58, XI. shows a back view of the double knot.

Fig. 58, XII. is the first loop of a "bowline knot." One end of the line is supposed to be made fast to some object. After the turn or loop (Fig. 58, XII.) is made, hold it in position with your left hand and pass the end of the line up through the loop or turn you have just made, behind and over the line above, then down through the loop again, as shown in the diagram (Fig. 58, XIII.); pull it tight and the knot is complete. The "sinker hitch" is a very handy one to know, and the

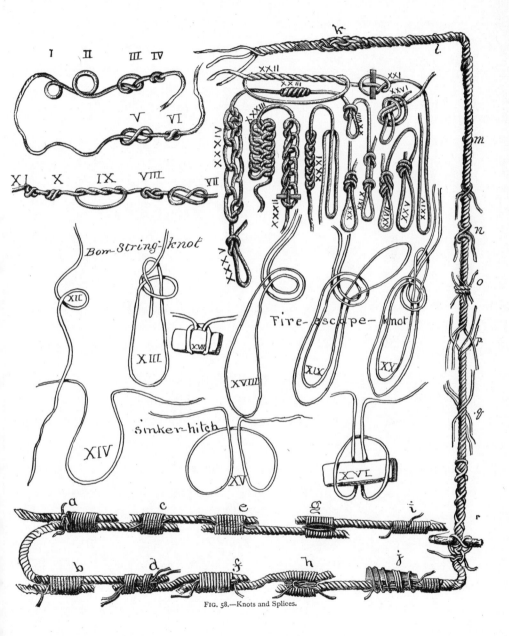

FIG. 58.—Knots and Splices.

variety of uses it may be put to will be at once suggested by the diagrams.

Lines that have both ends made fast may have weights attached to them by means of the sinker hitch (Fig. 57, D, D, D).

To accomplish this, first gather up some slack and make it in the form of the loop (Fig. 58, XIV.) ; bend the loop back on itself (Fig. 58, XV.) and slip the weight through the double loop thus formed (Fig. 58, XVI.) ; draw tight by pulling the two top lines, and the sinker hitch is finished (Fig. 58, XVII.).

The "fire-escape sling" previously mentioned, and illustrated by Fig. 57, E, is made with a double line.

Proceed at first as you would to make a simple bowline knot (Fig. 58, XVIII.).

After you have run the end loop up through the turn (Fig. 58, XIX.), bend it downward and over the bottom loop and turn, then up again until it is in the position shown in Fig. 58, XX. ; pull it downward until the knot is tightened, as in Fig. 57, E, and it makes a safe sling in which to lower a person from any height. The longer loop serves for a seat, and the shorter one, coming under the arms, makes a rest for the back.

Fig. 58, XXI. is called a "boat knot," and is made with the aid of a stick. It is an excellent knot for holding weights which may want instant detachment. To detach it, lift the weight slightly and push out the stick, and instantly the knot is untied.

Fig. 58, XXII. Commencement of a "six-fold knot."

Fig. 58, XXIII. Six-fold knot completed by drawing the two ends with equal force. A knot drawn in this manner is said to be "nipped."

Fig. 58, XXIV. A simple hitch or "double" used in making loop knots.

Fig. 58, XXV. "Loop knot."

Fig. 58, XXVI. shows how the loop knot is commenced.

Fig. 58, XXVII. is the "Dutch double knot," sometimes called the "Flemish loop."

Fig. 58, XXVIII. shows a common "running knot."

Fig. 58, XXIX. A running knot with a check knot to hold.

Fig. 58, XXX. A running knot checked.

Fig. 58, XXXI. The right hand part of the rope shows how to make the double loop for the "twist knot." The left hand part of the same rope shows a finished twist knot. It is made by taking a half turn on both the right hand and left hand lines of the double loop, and passing the end through the "bight" (loop) so made.

Whip-Lashes.

Fig. 58, XXXII. is called the "chain knot," which is often used in braiding leather whip-lashes. To make a "chain knot," fasten one end of the thong or line ; make a simple loop and pass it over the left hand ; retain hold of the free end with the right hand ; with the left hand seize the line above the right hand and draw a loop through the loop already formed ; finish the knot by drawing it tight with the left hand. Repeat the operation until the braid is of the required length, then secure it by passing the free end through the last loop.

Fig. 58, XXXIII. shows a double chain knot.

Fig. 58, XXXIV. is a double chain knot pulled out. It shows how the free end is thrust through the last loop.

Fig. 58, XXXV. Knotted loop for end of rope, used to prevent the end of the rope from slipping, and for various other purposes.

Splices, Timber-Hitches, etc.

Although splices may not be as useful to boys as knots and hitches, for the benefit of those among my readers who are interested in the subject, I have introduced a few bands and splices on the cables partly surrounding Fig. 58.

Fig. 58, *a* shows the knot and upper side of a " simple band."

Fig. 58, *b* shows under side of the same.

Fig. 58, *c* and *d* show a tie with cross ends. To hold the ends of the cords, a turn is taken under the strands.

Fig. 58, *e* and *f*. Bend with cross strands, one end looped over the other.

Fig. 58, *g* shows the upper side of the "necklace tie."

Fig. 58, *h* shows the under side of the same. The advantage of this tie is that the greater the strain on the cords, the tighter it draws the knot.

Fig. 58, *i* and *j* are slight modifications of *g* and *h*.

Fig. 58, *p* shows the first position of the end of the ropes for making the splice *k*. Untwist the strands and put the ends of two ropes together as close as possible, and place the strands of the one between the strands of the other alternately, so as to interlace, as in *k*. This splice should only be used when there is not time to make the "long splice," as the short one is not very strong.

From *l* to *m* is a long splice, made by underlaying the strands of each of the ropes joined about half the length of the splice, and putting each strand of the one between two of the other ; *q* shows the strands arranged for the long splice.

Fig. 58, *n* is a simple mode of making a hitch on a rope.

Fig. 58, *o* is a " shroud knot."

Fig. 58, *r* shows a very convenient way to make a handle on a rope, and is used upon large ropes when it is necessary for several persons to take hold to pull.

Fig. 59, A. Combination of half hitch and timber hitch.

Fig. 59, B. Ordinary half hitch.

Fig. 59, C. Ordinary timber hitch.

Fig. 59, D. Another timber hitch, called the " clove hitch."

Fig. 59, E. "Hammock hitch," used for binding bales of goods or cloth.

Fig. 59, F. "Lark-head knot," used by sailors and boatmen for mooring their crafts.

Fig. 59, P shows a lark-head fastening to a running knot.

Fig. 59, G is a double-looped lark-head.

Fig. 59, H shows a double-looped lark-head knot fastened to the ring of a boat.

Fig. 59, I is a "treble lark-head." To make it you must first tie a single lark-head, then divide the two heads and use each singly, as shown in the diagram.

Fig. 59, J shows a simple boat knot with one turn.

Fig. 59, K. "Crossed running knot." It is a strong and handy tie, not as difficult to make as appears to be.

Fig. 59, L is the bowline knot, described by the diagrams XII. and XIII. (Fig. 58). The free end of the knot is made fast by binding it to the "bight" or the loop. It makes a secure sling for a man to sit in at his work among the rigging.

Fig. 59, M, N, and O. "Slip clinches," or "sailors' knots."

Fig. 59, Q shows a rope fastened by the chain hitch. The knot at the left-hand end explains a simple way to prevent a rope from unravelling.

Fig. 59, R. A timber hitch; when tightened the line binds around the timber so that it will not slip.

Fig. 59, S. Commencement of simple lashing knot.

Fig. 59, T. Simple lashing knot finished.

Fig. 59, U. "Infallible loop;" not properly a timber hitch, but useful in a variety of ways, and well adapted for use in archery.

Fig. 59, V. Same as R, reversed. It looks like it might give way under a heavy strain, but it will not.

Fig. 59, W. Running knot with two ends.

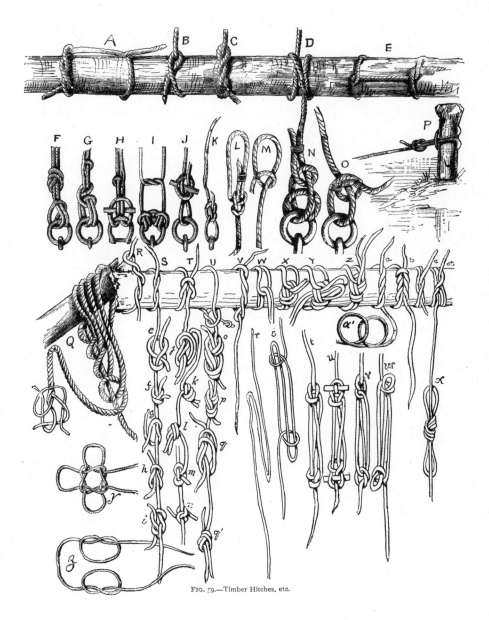

FIG. 59.—Timber Hitches, etc.

Fig. 59, X. Running knot with a check knot that can only be opened with a marline-spike.

Fig. 59, Y. A two-ended running knot with a check to the running loops. This knot can be untied by drawing both ends of the cord.

Fig. 59, Z. Running knot with two ends, fixed by a double Flemish knot. When you wish to encircle a timber with this tie, pass the ends, on which the check knot is to be, through the cords before they are drawn tight. This will require considerable practice.

Fig. 59, *a* shows an ordinary twist knot.

Fig. 59, *a'* shows the form of loop for builder's knot.

Fig. 59, *b*. Double twist knot.

Fig. 59, *c*. Builder's knot finished.

Fig. 59, *d* represents a double builder's knot.

Fig. 59, *e*. "Weaver's knot," same as described under the head of Becket hitch (Fig. 57, V).

Fig. 59, *f*. Weaver's knot drawn tight.

Fig. 59, *g* shows how to commence a reef knot. This is useful for small ropes; with ropes unequal in size the knot is likely to draw out of shape, as *m*.

Fig. 59, *h* shows a reef knot completed.

Of all knots, avoid the "granny;" it is next to useless under a strain, and marks the tier as a "landlubber."

Fig. 59, *i* shows a granny knot; *n* shows a granny under strain.

Fig. 59, *j* shows the commencement of a common "rough knot."

Fig. 59, *k*. The front view of finished knot.

Fig. 59, *l*. The back view of finished knot. Although this knot will not untie nor slip, the rope is likely to part at one side if the strain is great. Awkward as it looks, this tie is very useful at times on account of the rapidity with which it can be made.

6

Fig. 59, *o* and *p*. Knot commenced and finished, used for the same purposes as the Flemish knot.

Fig. 59, *q* and *q'*. An ordinary knot with the ends used separately.

Fig. 59, *s*. Sheep-shank, or dog-shank as it is sometimes called, is very useful in shortening a line. Suppose, for instance, a swing is much longer than necessary, and you wish to shorten it without climbing aloft to do so; it can be done with a sheep-shank.

Fig. 59, *r* shows the first position of the two loops. Take two half hitches, and you have a bend of the form shown by *s*. Pull tightly from above and below the shank, and you will find that the rope is shortened securely enough for ordinary strain.

Fig. 59, *t*. Shortening by loop and turns made where the end of the rope is free.

Fig. 59, *u*. A shortened knot that can be used when either end is free.

Fig. 59, *v*, *w*, and *x*. Shortening knots.

Fig. 59, *y* and *z*. A " true lover's knot," and the last one that you need to practise on, for one of these knots is as much as most persons can attend to, and ought to last a lifetime.

CHAPTER X.

THE WATER-TELESCOPE.

NEARLY three-fourths of the whole world is covered by water. Old Isaak Walton in his quaint book says that this vast expanse of territory is "Nature's storehouse, in which she locks up all her wonders." The previous chapters on fresh water and marine aquariums have already shown how a portion of the "wonders" may be kept in your own house, in what might be termed little glass side-shows to the great marine menagerie. This chapter will tell you how to make an instrument through which you can peep under the watery tent of the big show itself, and see the curiosities swimming about in their native haunts.

The water-telescope is not made of aqueous fluid, as its name might imply, but is a contrivance made of wood or metal, through which, when one end is partly submerged, objects beneath the water can be plainly seen that would otherwise be invisible.

It is astonishing how many fathoms of water become almost as transparent as air when viewed through one of these simple and amusing contrivances. In Norway, the fishermen make practical use of the water telescope when searching for herring shoals or cod, often by its means discovering new and unlooked-for fish.

How to Make a Wooden Water-Telescope.

All that is necessary is a long wooden box, a piece of glass for one end, and some paint and putty for making the seams water-tight. Fix the glass in one end of the box, and leave the other end open to admit the eyes of the observer, as shown in the illustration (Fig. 60).

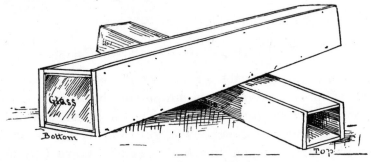

FIG. 60.—Wooden Water-Telescopes.

A Tin Water-Telescope,

is a funnel-shaped tin horn, about three or four feet long, eight to ten inches in diameter at the bottom, and broad enough at the top to admit both eyes of the observer (Fig. 61). Sinkers should be soldered on near the bottom, as shown in the illustration (Fig. 61). This in a measure counteracts the buoyancy of

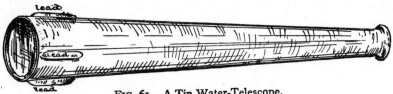

FIG. 61.—A Tin Water-Telescope.

the air contained in the water-tight funnel, and helps to submerge the big end.

The inside of the funnel should be painted black, to prevent the light from being reflected upon the bright surface of the tin.

If any difficulty is found in procuring a circular piece of glass, the bottom may be made square and square glass used, and fitted into a leaden frame made for the purpose.

Any tinner can, at a moderate cost, make an instrument like the one just described.

A water-telescope will add greatly to the entertainment of a boating party or picnic, furnishing a new and novel feature that will become popular wherever it is introduced.

Mr. Fred. Holder tells me that while collecting marine animals with his father, Dr. Holder, the naturalist, they had a boat built with a glass in the hull, arranged and worked upon the same principle as a water-telescope. It was of great service where the water was not too deep. While one person rowed the other watched the bottom, which Mr. Holder describes as having the appearance of a beautiful panorama passing beneath him. Fish of all colors and forms filled the intervening space, and sometimes a " devil fish " would cross the scene, flapping its great wing like fins as it flew rather than swam through the clear water.

CHAPTER XI.

DREDGE, TANGLE. AND TRAWL FISHING.

A New Sport.

THIS new pastime not only insures the fisherman something to show for his day's work, but, by furnishing an incentive, it lends an additional charm to rowing or sailing, and combines the pleasures of fishing and boating, perhaps, in a greater degree than any other sport upon the list of out-door exercises. There is no good reason why the "dredge" and "tangle" should be monopolized by a few learned scientists, nor why the sport should not be indulged in by all boys, as well as men, who love the open air, the salt sea breeze, Nature and her wonders.

To put this new pastime within the reach of the boys, this chapter illustrates and describes the "regular" dredge made upon the most improved pattern, and it also shows how service-able dredges and tangles may be made out of simple materials to be found about any house.

The dredge is an instrument made to drag along the bot-tom of the water and scoop up the objects, such as corals, sponges, etc., that are found there.

The common oyster dredge is a familiar object at all sea-side places, but it has two or three defects which make it objection-able to the amateur dredger. In the first place, it requires a skilled hand to keep it right side up when in use. Nothing is more discouraging to a beginner than to discover, after a long pull, that on account of the dredge being towed upside down the scraper has been unable to perform its duty. The meshes of an oyster dredge are made very large purposely, that all small objects may slip through. Among these small objects are some of the curiosities most prized by the collector.

To remedy the first defect, the collector's dredge is made with a scraper upon both sides (Fig. 65). The second defect is overcome by using a net with very fine meshes.

The net, if unprotected, would soon be cut and torn into shreds by the sharp-edged shells or rough bottom. To prevent this, it is enclosed in a leather or canvas bag open at both ends (Fig. 65). The dotted line shows the net inside.

The handles and scrapers are composed of iron.

If the machine become fast between the rocks of the bottom, the string that binds the joint marked in the diagram (Fig. 65) will part, thus allowing the machine to turn edgewise and free itself.

Many curious objects were frequently brought up clinging to the cable or the frayed edges of the canvas cover of the dredges first used, and it was noticed that the dredge itself seldom con-tained any of these objects. This fact gave birth to

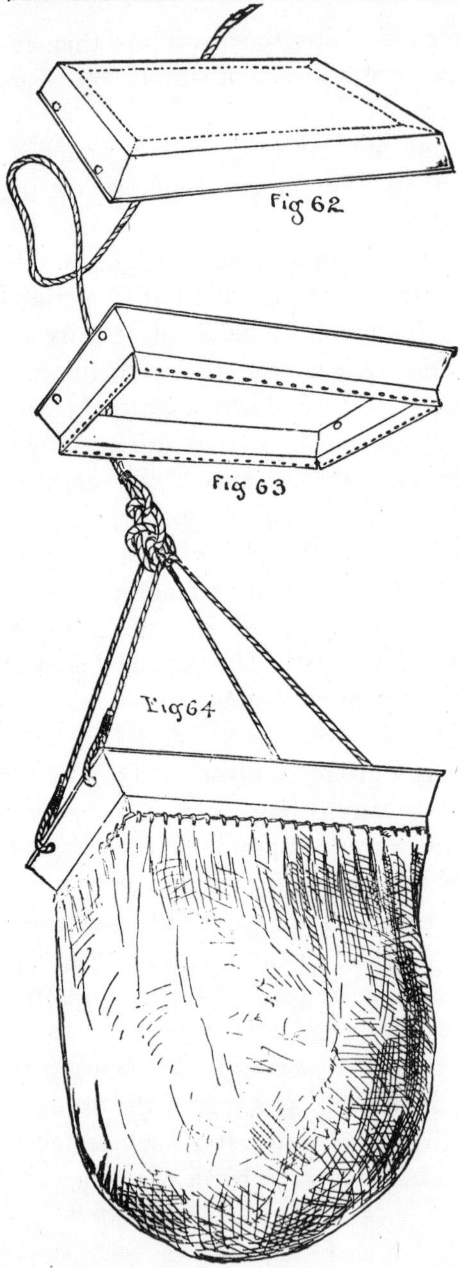

Fig 62

Fig 63

Fig 64

FIGS. 62, 63, and 64.—Construction of Bake-Pan Dredge.

The Tangle,

a name given to tassels of hemp that are often attached to the bottom of the dredge itself or used separately (Figs. 66 and 67).

The Trawl.

If the bottom to be explored be smooth a trawl can be used (Fig. 68). This consists of a net larger than the one connected with the dredge. The front of the net is attached to a rod at the top and hangs slack at the bottom, being weighted by small sinkers. The rod is fastened to runners which allow the trawl to slide smoothly over the bottom. Weights are sometimes fastened to the ends of the runners. It is a good idea to have pockets in the net, to prevent the fish from escaping. The end of the net should be gathered and tied with a string, so that by untying the string the contents can be dumped out in less time than it takes to tell of it.

How to Make a Bake-Pan Dredge.

There is a sort of flat sheet-iron pan used in the kitchen for holding bread or biscuit while baking. It is seldom that the cook cannot show you one of these pans (Fig. 62) that has served its time and been discarded. Such a one will make a first-rate frame for a dredge. The only difficulty will be found in cutting the bottom out neatly. If there be a tin shop in the neighborhood it is best to take the pan there and have the tinner cut it for you; or you may do it yourself with a can opener or some other convenient instrument. Cut as shown by the dotted lines in Fig. 62, which represents the pan bottom upwards. This will leave a margin of about an inch and a half still adhering to the pan; with a strong nail and a hammer punch holes all around the marginal piece of the bottom. Make two larger holes in each end to admit the ropes forming the handles.

Bend the bottom pieces out as illustrated by Fig. 63, and it will produce a compact and handy frame for a small dredge.

An old coffee sack can be readily adapted so as to serve as a net, but if the canvas cover be used as in Fig. 65, mosquito netting of double thickness will answer for the inner pouch.

Fig. 64 shows a " bake-pan dredge " with ropes attached ready for use. Although the framework of a " regular " dredge can be made by any blacksmith at trifling cost, it is more fun to make a dredge for one's self. When once the principles upon which a machine is made are thoroughly understood, it requires but little ingenuity to produce home-made substitutes that will perhaps answer as well, if not better, than the originals.

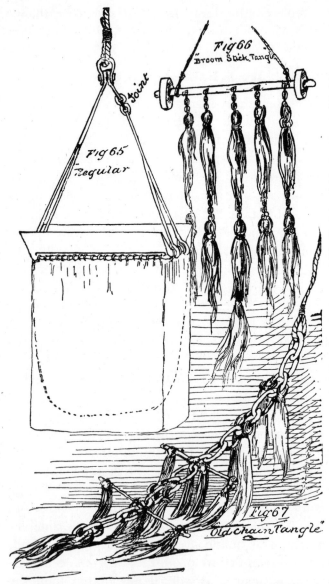

Fig 65
Regular

Fig 66
"Broom Stick Tangle"

Fig 67
"Old Chain Tangle"

Joint

FIGS. 65, 66, and 67.—Regular-made Dredge, Broomstick and Old Chain Tangle.

A Tin-Pail Dredge.

Take any old tin bucket, knock the bottom out, and attach a piece of coffee sack for a net. Tie bunches of hemp to the rim, first punching holes for the purpose, and you will have a make-shift dredge like the one in the tail-piece that only requires a few minutes to manufacture. Even with such a crude apparatus as this, many things may be captured for the cabinet or aquarium, the hempen tangles serving not only to entangle star-fish, sea-urchins, and the like, but in a measure preventing other crea tures that have been scooped up by the pail from making their escape.

How to Make a Broomstick Tangle.

Saw off from an old broom handle a piece of stick about two and one-half feet long ; hunt up three or four pieces of chain about the size used for large dog-chains ; with small iron staples fasten these chains at intervals along the broomstick. Tie bunches of hemp securely along the chains. If you have no hemp, unravel pieces of old rope ends and tie them to the chains as in the illustration (Fig. 66). The broomstick, being light, will possibly float in spite of the chains. This can only be prevented by attaching weights to the stick.

If a couple of iron wheels can be procured and put upon the ends of the broomstick they will not only counteract the buoy-ancy of the stick, but will also, in a measure, prevent the tangle from fouling stones or other objects on the bottom.

In the place of the iron wheels, simple weights of lead or other material may be used, and instead of the chains, weighted strings can be tied to the stick and the hempen knots fastened to them. Still another tangle can be made of a piece of old chain.

The Old Chain Tangle,

as may be seen by the illustration (Fig. 67), is simply a piece of iron chain decorated with hempen tassels and occasional cross-sticks. A rope is attached to one end, and by its means the tangle is hauled over the bottom to gather up its load of curiosities.

Hints and Suggestions to Amateurs.

If dredging from a sail-boat, divide the crew into two parties, one to manage and sail the boat, the other to attend to the casting and hauling of the dredge. It is as necessary that the boat be carefully managed as it is that at least one person's undivided attention be given to handling the dredge. The dredging rope should be about twice as long as the water is deep. A wooden reel or windlass attached to one side of the boat near the stern will be of very great assistance, especially when the net comes up filled with mud or heavy stones, as it frequently does ; in which case, if there be but one boy to attend to it he will find it no light task to pull in the line hand over hand.

A piece of old oilcloth or tarpaulin will answer to dump the contents of the dredge upon, although a large wooden tray, or "picking-over board," as it is called, is much better. A small board of the kind intended for a row-boat is shown in the illustration at the head of this chapter.

Common glass preserve jars, or wide-mouthed bottles, make excellent receptacles for living specimens. A convenient rack for carrying these easily and safely may be made from any wooden box, by nailing laths or slats across the top from end to end and side to side, making the squares thus formed just large enough to hold the jars or bottles in an upright position.

The sail-boat is best for long excursions, but for a short trip a row-boat is preferable, it being more readily handled and independent of the wind.

Although a dredge without tangles will bring up many curious and interesting objects, the specimens are apt to be confined to the mollusca or shell-fish, mixed, of course, with all manner of rubbish.

If properly managed, the pouch, when it reaches the surface, will be about half full. After it has been emptied upon the "picking-over" board, the mud and sand may be washed away by pouring water over the mass. Although not absolutely necessary, a large sieve is a desirable addition to the dredger's outfit, and furnishes valuable assistance when the mud or sand is to be searched for minute objects. Some dredgers use a " nest of sieves," so arranged that the strainers, four in number, fit freely within one another. The top sieve is of course smaller than the others, but the meshes are larger The second sieve is a little larger, with finer meshes. The third is still larger, with a much finer mesh, and the fourth, the largest sieve of the lot, has a mesh so close as only to allow the finest sand or mud to pass through. The contents of a dredge when filtered through a " nest of sieves " is divided up into a graduated series, the largest objects at the top and the smallest at the bottom. Mr. Emerton, in his " Life on the Seashore," describes a sieve for hanging over the side of a boat " in the shape of a half cylinder," the bottom being made of strong wire ; but, as before remarked, sieves are not absolutely necessary, and may be dispensed with when the object is only a day's fun with the curiosities of the sea.

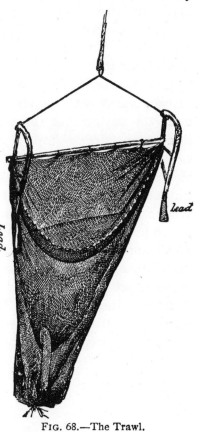

FIG. 68.—The Trawl.

The Use of the Tangle.

Partially buried in the mud of the bottom are to be found many pretty corals, queer and curious sponges, and those funny animals called sea-cucumbers. The dredge may skip these, but the hempen tangles, when they sweep the bottom, catch all such rough or irregular objects and bring them to the surface, along with a miscellaneous assortment of star-fish, sea-urchins, crabs, shrimps, and hundreds of other creatures.

Wyville Thomson, in his interesting account of the dredging cruise of the Porcupine and Lightning, mentions one haul when the tangles contained not fewer than 20,000 sea-urchins, which "were warped through and through the hempen fibres and actually filled the tangles; and," adds Mr. Thomson, "they hung for days round the bulwarks like nets of pickling onions in a green-grocer's shop." At times the tangle, when it comes to the surface, is completely covered with curious little shrimp-like creatures called Caprellas. Indeed, so many surprises await the dredger and tend to keep up the excitement, that this new sport cannot fail to interest and delight all who participate in it; and when the young dredgers return home they need not do so empty-handed, but may, if they choose, bring curiosities from the bottom of the sea that will not only astonish their parents, but most likely puzzle their teachers and professors.

Under the head of TAXIDERMY, among the autumn sports, will be found some hints which will aid the reader in preserving marine specimens for the cabinet or for future study.

Tin-Pail Dredge.

CHAPTER XII.

HOME-MADE BOATS.

Birth of the "Man-Friday" Catamaran.—The Crusoe Raft.

NOT so very many years ago I remember visiting, in company with my cousin Tom, a small lake at the head waters of the Miami. High and precipitous cliffs surround the little body of water. So steep were the great weather-beaten rocks that it was only where the stream came tumbling down past an old mill that an accessible path then existed. Down that path Tom and I scrambled, for we knew that large bass lurked in the deep, black holes among the rocks.

We had no jointed split bamboo rods nor fancy tackle, but the fish there in those days were not particular and seldom hesitated to bite at an angle-worm or grasshopper, though the hook upon which the bait squirmed was suspended by a coarse line from a freshly cut hickory sapling.

Even now I feel the thrill of excitement and expectancy as, in imagination, my pole is bent nearly double by the frantic struggles of those "gamy" black bass. After spending the morning fishing we built a fire upon a short stretch of sandy beach, and cleaning our fish and washing them in the spring close at hand, we put them among the embers to cook.

While the fire was getting our dinner ready for us we threw off our clothes and plunged into the cool waters of the lake. Inexpert swimmers as we were at that time, the opposite shore, though apparently only a stone's-throw distant, was too far off for us to reach by swimming. Many a longing and curious glance we cast toward it, however, and strong was the temptation that beset us to try the unknown depths intervening. A pair of brown ears appeared above the ferns near the water's edge, and a fox peeped at us; squirrels ran about the fallen trunks of trees or scampered up the rocks as saucily as though they understood that we could not swim well enough to reach their side of the lake; and high up the face of the cliff was a dark spot which we almost knew to be the entrance to some mysterious cavern.

How we longed for a boat! But not even a raft nor a dug-out could be seen anywhere upon the glassy surface of the water or along its reedy border. We nevertheless determined to explore the lake next day, even if we should have to paddle astride of a log.

The first rays of the morning sun had not reached the dark waters before my companion and I were hard at work, with axe and hatchet, chopping in twain a long log we had discovered near the mill. We had at first intended to build a raft; but gradually we evolved a sort of catamaran. The two pieces of log we sharpened at the ends for the bow; then we rolled the logs down upon the beach, and, while I went into the thicket to chop down some saplings, my companion borrowed an auger from the miller. We next placed the logs about three feet apart, and marking the points where we intended to put the cross-pieces, we cut notches there; then we placed the saplings across, fitting them into these notches. To hold them securely we bored holes down through the sapling cross-pieces into the logs; with the hatchet we hammered wooden pegs into these holes. For the seat we used the half of a section of log, the flat side fitting into places cut for that purpose. All that remained to be done now was to make a seat in the stern and a pair of rowlocks. At a proper distance from the oarsman's seat we bored two holes for a couple of forked sticks, which answered admirably for rowlocks; across the stern we fastened another piece of log, similar to that used for the oarsman's seat. With the help of a man from the mill our craft was launched; and

The Man-Friday.

with a pair of oars made of old pine boards we rowed off, leaving the miller waving his hat.

Our catamaran was not so light as a row-boat, but it floated, and we could propel it with the oars, and, best of all, it was our own invention and made with our own hands. We called it a "Man-Friday," and by its means we explored every nook in the length and breadth of the lake; and ever afterward when we wanted a boat we knew a simple and inexpensive way to make one—and a safe one, too.

The Crusoe Raft,

is another rustic craft, but it is of more ambitious dimensions than the "Man-Friday." Instead of being able to float only one or two passengers, the "Crusoe," if properly built, ought to accommodate a considerable party of raftsmen. Of course the purpose for which the raft is to be used, and the number of the crew that is expected to man it, must be taken into consideration when deciding upon the dimensions of the proposed craft.

All the tools that are necessary for the construction of a good stout raft are an axe, an auger, and a hatchet, with some strong boys to wield them.

The building material can be gathered upon any wooded bank of lake or stream.

For a moderate sized raft collect six or seven logs, the longest not being over sixteen feet in length, nor more than a foot in diameter ; the logs must be tolerably straight. Pick out the longest and biggest for the centre ; sharpen one end ; roll the log into the water and there secure it.

Select two logs as nearly alike as possible, to lie one at each side of the centre log. Measure the centre log, and make the point of each side log, not at its own centre, but at that side of it which will lie against the middle log, so that this side-point shall terminate where the pointing of the middle log begins. (See Fig. 69.)

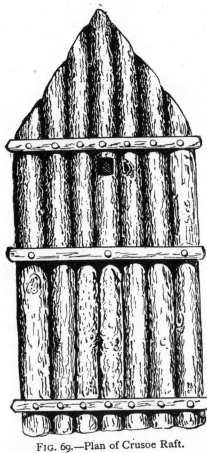

FIG. 69.—Plan of Crusoe Raft.

After all the logs needed have been trimmed and sharpened in the manner just described, roll them into the water and arrange them in order (Fig. 69). Fasten them together with

" cross-strips," boring holes through the strips to correspond with holes bored into the logs lying beneath, and through these holes drive wooden pegs. The water will cause the pegs to swell, and they will hold much more firmly than iron nails.

The skeleton of the cabin can be made of saplings ; such as are used for hoop-poles are the best.

These are each bent into an arch, and the ends are thrust into holes bored for that purpose. Over this hooping a piece of canvas is stretched, after the manner of old-fashioned country wagons (Figs. 70 and 71).

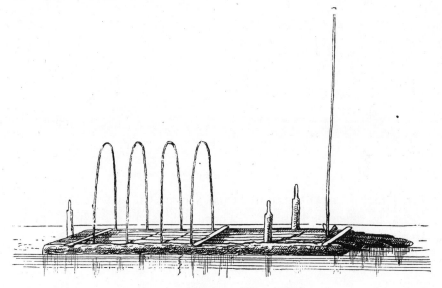

FIG. 70.—Skeleton of Crusoe Raft.

Erect a " jack-staff," to be used as a flag-pole or a mast to rig a square sail on.

A stout stick should be erected at the stern, and a similar one upon each side of the raft near the bow ; these sticks, when their ends are made smaller, as shown in the illustration (Fig. 70), serve as rowlocks.

For oars use "sweeps"—long poles, each with a piece of board for a blade fastened at one end (Fig. 72).

Holes must be bored through the poles of the sweeps about

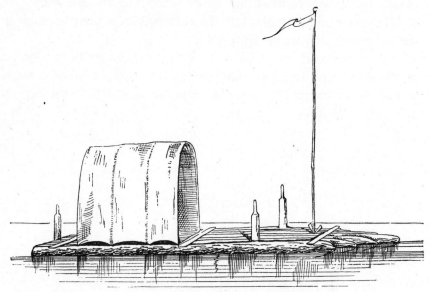

FIG. 71.—Crusoe with Cabin Covered.

three feet from the handle, to slip over the pegs used as row-locks, as described above. These pegs should be high enough to allow the oarsman to stand while using the sweeps.

A flat stone placed at the bow will serve as a fireplace.

FIG. 72.—Sweeps.

If the cracks between the logs under the cabin are filled up to prevent the water splashing through, and the cabin is floored with cross-sticks, a most comfortable bed at night can be made of hay by heaping it under the canvas cover in sufficient quantities.

The " Crusoe " raft has this great advantage over all boats : you may take a long trip down the river, allowing the current to bear you along, using the sweeps only to assist the man at the helm (rear sweep) ; then, after your excursion is finished, you can abandon the raft and return by steamboat or cars.

The Scow.

There can be but few boys who are not familiar with that large and useful tribe of flat-bottomed, perpendicular-sided boats called "scows." These crafts are used as coal barges, lighters, flat-boats, sail-boats, and row-boats ; but it is only to the construction of the last named class that this chapter will be devoted.

To build a scow-shaped row-boat is not a difficult feat, even for a boy ; and when it is finished he will find it to be a very convenient boat, roomy, and not hard to row.

The material necessary consists of eight or ten three-quarter-inch pine boards, one one-inch board, some fivepenny nails, and about a half pound of wrought-iron nails of the same size as the ones just mentioned.

A saw, a plane, and a sharp hatchet are requisite in the way of tools. Other tools, if not absolutely necessary, should not on that account be ignored, as they may come in very handy at times.

When selecting the lumber for the boat, pick out those pieces which are free from large knots and other blemishes. Reserve two of the best boards for the sides, and let them measure 11 feet in length and 12 inches in width when trimmed. Measuring toward the centre, mark a point 2½ feet from each end of one of the side boards upon the edge selected for the bottom. Measuring from the bottom edge toward the top, mark a point upon each end 8 inches from the bottom. Saw off the triangular pieces between these points (Fig. 73). Round off the angles with a plane, and make the other side board an exact duplicate of the one just described (Fig. 74).

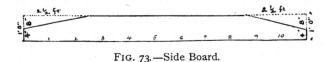

FIG. 73.—Side Board.

For the ends of the boat use the 1½-inch plank, making of it two small boards to fit between the ends of the side boards.

The side pieces now measure 4 inches upon each end (Fig. 73), hence the end boards ought to be 4 inches wide; but to make sure of neat joints, it is best to allow ½ inch extra. Make the end pieces 3 feet long, 4½ inches wide, and 1 inch thick. Set the side pieces parallel to each other upon their straight or top edges, and between their ends fit the end boards (Fig. 74). After seeing that all the corners are square, nail the end boards in place. Plane off the protruding edges at the bow and stern, so that the bottom pieces overlapping them will make close joints; then nail the bottom boards on crosswise, as

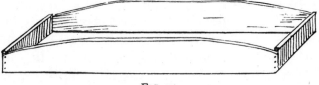

FIG. 74.

shown in the illustration (Fig. 75). All nails must be driven in so that their heads are below the surface of the board, or as carpenters call it, countersunk, and the indentations made should be puttied up.

Turn the scow over, and upon the inside, at the middle of the bottom, nail a ¾-inch long bottom board (Figs. 76 and 77). Next cut two small boards of ¾-inch plank; make them 7 inches wide and about 1 foot 5 inches long; cut out a place in one end of each, as shown by A, Fig. 76; these are to serve as row-

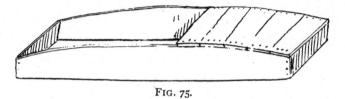

FIG. 75.

locks, and should be nailed with wrought-iron nails to the inside of the boat, so that the centres of the rowlocks are about 4 feet 10 inches from the end which will be the stern of the boat; this is the simplest style of rowlock, but a much neater one can be made by using thole-pins (Fig. 77, B).

Turn the boat upon its side and nail a strip 11 feet long, 2 inches wide, and 1 inch thick upon the upper edge of the side board; repeat the operation on the other side, using wrought nails and clinching them. If thole-pins are intended to be used,

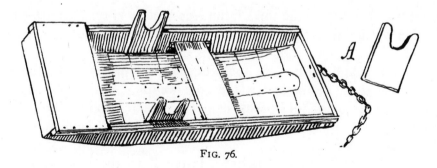

FIG. 76.

before nailing the strips upon the sides, 4 feet 9 inches from one end of each strip cut a notch in the side ½ inch deep and 1½ wide; 3 inches from this notch, or 5 feet from the same end, cut another similar notch. When these strips are nailed on

. the sides (Fig. 77) the notches cut in them form the rowlocks. Put in more nails near the rowlocks than elsewhere, to help to withstand the greater strain that that part has to bear. The end of the boat nearest the rowlocks is the stern. Of oak or some hard wood make four thole-pins to fit into the rowlocks (Fig. 77, B).

For a seat use a board about 1 foot wide ; it should be 3 feet long to fit inside the boat ; the seat rests upon two cleats

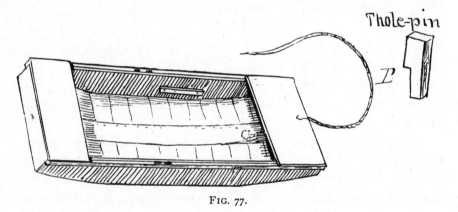

Thole-pin

B

FIG. 77.

set 6 inches below the top of the side boards (Fig. 77) ; the aft edge of the seat should be about 1 foot forward of the row-locks.

A bow and stern seat should be made for passengers ; these seats need not set so low as the one occupied by the oarsman, and may be made of boards nailed across the top of the boat at the bow and stern, and the space underneath them may be used for lockers.

If a chain " painter " is used, fasten it to the bow with an iron staple (Fig. 76) ; but if a rope is preferred, or is more easily obtained, run one end of it through a hole bored for the purpose in the bow seat, and knot the end so that it cannot slip out (Fig. 77). When such a boat is built with clean, close-fitting joints, and the cracks daubed with thick paint, it is often unnecessary to do any further caulking. A good method is to saturate pieces of woollen cloth with paint and place them between the different parts before they are joined. After the carpenter work is done, go to the paint shop and get a can of white paint, first telling the painter to weigh the can. After you have used what paint is necessary, return the can, have it weighed, and pay only for the amount used. If you are well known the painter will not hesitate to allow you to do this, and you will find it the most economical way. After the first coat of paint is dry put on a second coat ; as soon as that is hardened, which will be in two or three days, according to the weather, your boat is ready for launching ; it may leak at first, but after the seams have swelled it will be almost perfectly dry inside.

A Floating Camp, or the Boy's Own Flat-Boat.

Flat-boats are essentially inland craft, having their origin with the birth of trade in the West before the puffing and panting steam-boats plowed their way through the turbid waters of Western rivers. They are craft that can be used on any stream large enough to float a yawl, but the St. John's River, Florida, is perhaps the most tempting stream for the amateur flat-boatman. The numerous inlets and lakes connected with the river, the luxuriant semi-tropical foliage on the banks, the strange-looking fish and great, stupid alligators, the beautiful white herons and hundreds of water-fowl of many descriptions —all form features that add interest to its navigation and inducements to hunters, fishermen, naturalists, and pleasure-seekers scarcely equalled by any other accessible river of the United States.

To build the hull of the flat-boat, use pine lumber. For the sides select two good, straight 2-inch planks, 14 feet long and about 16 inches wide. Take one of the planks (Fig. 78), measure 6 inches from the top upon each end, and mark the points A, a (Fig. 78); then upon the bottom measure from each end toward the centre 2 feet, and mark the points B, b (Fig. 78). Saw off the corners A, B and a, b, and round the

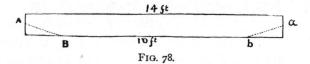

FIG. 78.

angles in the manner described on page 102 and illustrated by Fig. 74. Next take two 2-inch planks, 6½ inches wide and 6 feet long, for the stem and stern; set the side pieces on edge upside down, and nail on the two end pieces (see Fig. 79). Then, allowing 4 inches—the thickness of the two sides—there will be a space inside the boat of 5 feet 8 inches. Take three pieces of scantling about 3 inches thick and 5 feet 8 inches long; place one near the end flush with the bottom of the boat just where the sheer of bow and stern begins (see A and B, Fig. 79). After fitting them carefully, nail them firmly. Nail the other piece of scantling in place at the point C (Fig. 79), so

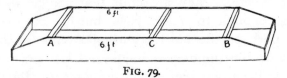

FIG. 79.

that it will measure 6 feet from the outside of the brace A to the outside of the brace C. Plane off the protruding edges of the bow and stern.

A bottom may now be put on as described on page 102 and illustrated by Fig. 75, or a regular flat-boat bottom can be made by selecting good, straight ½-inch lumber a little over 14 feet long, to allow for the curve.

Nail an end of one of the bottom boards to the stern board

(see Fig. 80); its side edge must be flush with the outer edge of the side piece. Bend the bottom board carefully along the curve to the first cross piece A (Fig. 80) and nail it firmly; nail it again at C and at the bow, being careful to make it conform to the curve of the sides. Follow the same plan with the next board, keeping it close up against the first board so as to

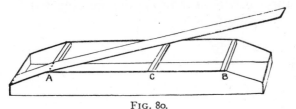

FIG. 80.

leave no crack when the bottom is finished. Caulk up any accidental cracks with oakum; give the whole hull a coating of coal tar, and allow it to harden. The remainder of the work is comparatively easy.

After the coal tar has hardened, turn the boat over and erect four posts, one at each end of the cross piece A and one at each end of the cross piece C (Fig. 79 or 80).

The tops of the posts for this size boat should be about 3½ feet above the bottom of the hull. Put a cross piece on the top of the post at A and another at C, and the framework of your cabin is done. It may now be covered with canvas, or, as in the illustrations, with thin planks, in which case make the roof of ¼-inch boards, bending them in an arch so that the middle will rise about one foot higher than the sides.

The eaves should overhang about six inches beyond the cabin upon each side.

Board up the sides with the same material used for the roofing, leaving openings for windows and doors. Pieces of shoe leather make very good hinges for the door, but iron hinges are of course the best. The cabin can then be floored, a bunk or two may be built, and as many other conveniences as your taste or necessities may indicate, can be provided ; a few clothes-hooks, etc.

Put in rowlocks ; those used in the Crusoe raft are best for large flat-boats, but for this one make rowlocks on the same plan as the ones illustrated by Fig. 76, A (page 103). There should be three rowlocks, one for the steering oar and two near the front for rowing (see Fig. 81).

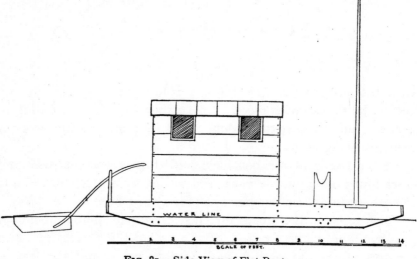

FIG. 81.—Side View of Flat-Boat.

Set a seat in front of the rowlock with a hole in it for the "jack-staff" to pass through. The jack-staff should be made so that it can be taken out and put in at pleasure. This can be done by making a simple socket underneath the seat for the end of the staff to fit in.

The flat-boat is now ready to be launched, which should be done with appropriate ceremonies. Fig. 81 shows the side view of a 14-foot flat-boat ; the cabin, to better show its construction, is increased in height in the drawing, and, according to the scale, it measures about five feet at the sides and six feet at the ridge-pole.   Fig. 82 shows a front view of the same.

Fig. 83 shows a top view of a flat-boat as it would appear looking down upon the roof of the cabin.

The large diagram (Fig. 84) drawn in perspective shows how a cabin for a little larger boat can be arranged.   The diagram is drawn on the scale of feet marked below it.   The floor is about six feet long by six feet wide, and the side walls are five feet high.   A cabin of these dimensions can be arranged with four folding berths, two upon

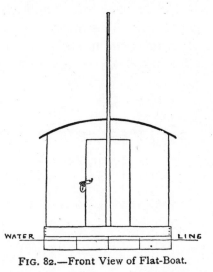

FIG. 82.—Front View of Flat-Boat.

each side, made of boards each two feet wide and fastened to the sides by hinges.   The top berths may be supported by their hinges and a cross beam upon the inside, and by two broad

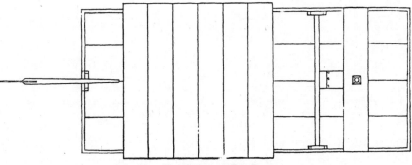

FIG. 83.—Top View of Flat-Boat.

straps upon the outside; the straps button on to knobs in the ends of the berths.   The lower berths can be provided with folding legs, as shown by the illustration (Fig. 84), which shows two berths down on the left-hand side and two folded up on the right-hand side. The lockers underneath the bottom berths can be used for storing away bed-clothes.

In the rear, under a looking-glass, can be seen a device for a folding desk, which is simply a square board attached to

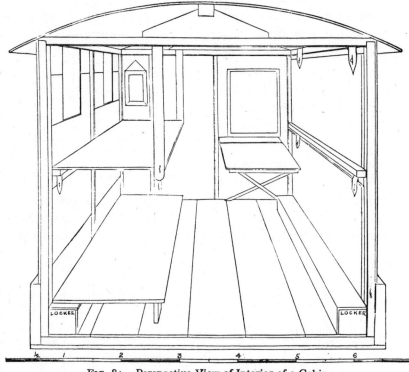

Fig. 84.—Perspective View of Interior of a Cabin.

the wall, like the berths, by hinges, and which may be let down so as to hang flat against the wall, out of the way when the berths are to be used. The legs to the desk are hinged at the bottom, and as the desk is raised the legs fall forward, resting against the cleat upon the bottom of the top board, which holds it in the position shown by the diagram. Many other little conveniences may be added, such as a small cooking-stove, book-shelves, gun-racks, etc., but I shall not go into further details, my aim being only to suggest how it may be done, as every boy who is smart enough to build a flat-boat will have his own peculiar ideas about the manner in which it should be fitted up inside. The interior construction depends, in a measure, upon the number of persons who are to occupy the cabin, and whether it is to be used by a party of young naturalists upon a collecting tour, or for fishing and shooting excursions, or simply as a sort of picnic boat for a few days' enjoyment, such as most boys in the country are quite well able to plan and carry out unaided.

Although a rude home-made flat-boat does not possess speed, yet with a square sail rigged on the jack-staff, and with a good wind over the stern, it will make good time ; and as this sort of craft draws only a few inches of water, it can float in creeks and inlets where a well-loaded row-boat would drag bottom.

The advantages of a flat-boat consist in the fact that it is a comfortable, cosey little house in which one could spend a month very pleasantly hunting or fishing, or visiting the various points of interest along the shores of the river and inlets, and, whenever the floating home drifts in sight of a pleasant place to stop, all that is necessary is to make fast to the bank, thus escaping the nuisance of moving bag and baggage.

During a cruise the members of the party will have frequent occasion to put in practice all manner of devices for saving labor, and making the hunter as far as possible independent of a mate when, as often happens, two boys cannot be spared from the boat to go foraging together. One of these " wrinkles," as they are termed, is a floating fish-car, adapted for minnows or large fish, which being fastened to the fisherman's

waist, floats behind as he wades. This arrangement not only
saves much weariness in carrying finny spoils to camp after,

A New Wrinkle.

perhaps, a long and trying day, but it helps to keep the fish
fresh; and when not in active use it may be towed behind
" The Ark."

Many hints of this same kind might be given, but this one will suffice to show that a boy with his wits about him can lighten very materially the fatigues inseparable from camping out and flat-boating. Endurance of hardship is noble in itself, and there is call enough for it in this rough-and-tumble world; but the fellow who most enjoys " roughing it " in a trip outdoors is he who is quickest to save himself unnecessary exertion by using the simplest means at hand.

The Yankee Pine.

From the saw-mills away up among the tributaries of the Ohio River come floating down to the towns along the shore great rafts of pine lumber. These rafts are always objects of interest to the boys, for the youngsters know that when moored to the shore the solidly packed planks make a splendid platform to swim from. Fine springing-boards can be made of the projecting blades of the gigantic sweeps which are used to guide the mammoth rafts, and, somewhere aboard, there is always to be found a " Yankee Pine." Just when or why this style of skiff was dubbed with such a peculiar name I am unable to state; but this I know, that when a raft is to be broken up and carted away to the lumber yards there is, or always used to be, a good, light skiff to be had cheap.

However, all boys do not live on the bank of the river, and if they did there would hardly be " Yankee Pines " enough to go round; so we will at once proceed to see how to build one for ourselves. Although my readers may find the " Yankee Pine " a little more difficult to build than the blunt-ended, flat-bottomed scow, it really is a comparatively simple piece of work for boys familiar with the use of carpenters' tools.

For the side pieces select two straight-grained pine boards free from knots. These boards should be about 13 or 14 feet long,

8

a couple of inches over a foot in width, and as nearly alike
as possible in texture.   Besides these, there should be in the
neighborhood of a dozen other ¾-inch planks, an inch or two
over a half foot in width.   A small piece of 2-inch plank for

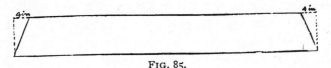

FIG. 85.

the stern piece is also necessary.   Upon the bottom edge of
the side board measure off from each end toward the centre 4
inches, mark the points, and saw off the corners shown by the
dotted line in Fig. 85.   Next take a piece of board 4 feet long
and a foot wide, saw off the corners as you did on the side
board, making it 4 feet on the top and 3 feet 4 inches on
the bottom.   This board is to be used only as a centre brace
while modelling the boat.

Out of the 2-inch plank make a stern piece of the same
shape as the centre brace; let it be 1 foot wide, 14 inches long
on the bottom, and 20 inches long on top.   Set the side boards
on their shorter or bottom edges, and place the centre brace in
the middle, as shown by Fig. 86 ; nail the side boards to it, using

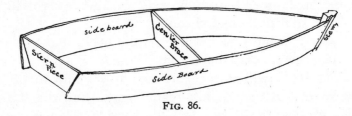

FIG. 86.

only enough nails to hold temporarily.   Draw the side boards
together at the bow, and against the stern board at the stern
(Fig. 86).   Hold the side pieces in position by the means of
ropes.   A stem should be ready to fix in the bow (Fig. 87).

This had better be a few inches longer than the sides are broad, as it is a simple matter to saw off the top after it is fitted. Make the stem of a triangular piece of timber, by planing off the front edge until a flat surface about ½ inch broad is obtained ; 2 inches from the front, upon each side, cut a

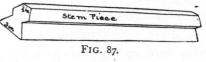

FIG. 87.

groove just the thickness of the side boards (¾ inch). Trim the stem so that the side pieces at the bow fit the grooves snugly, and nail the side boards to the stem and to the stern piece (Fig. 86).

Turn the boat upside down, and it will be discovered that the outlines of the bottom form an arch from stem to stern. If left in this shape the boat will sink too deep amidships. Remedy the defect by planing the bottom edge of both side pieces, reducing the convex form to straight lines in the middle. This will allow the bow and stern to sheer, but at the same time will make the central part of the bottom flat, and by having less to drag through the water make it easier to row. Nail the bottom boards on crosswise, and as, on account of the form of the boat, no two boards will be of the same size, they must be first nailed on and the projecting ends sawed off afterward. The centre brace may now be taken out and a long bottom board nailed to the centre of the bottom upon the inside of the boat (Fig. 88). Cut a small cross piece (B, Fig. 88) so that it will fit across the bow 3 inches below the top of the side boards. Nail it in place, driving the nails from the outside of the side-board through and into the end of the stick B. Saw out a bow seat, and, allowing the broad end to rest on the cross stick B, fit the seat in and secure it with nails (Fig. 88) ; 3 inches below the top of the stern piece nail a cleat across. At the same distance below the side board put a cross stick similar to the one in the bow. This and the cleat on the stern piece form rests for the stern seat. Five feet from the stern, saw a notch 2 inches deep and 1½ inch long in each side board (A, A′, Fig. 88). Saw two more notches of the same size 3 inches from the first; these will make the rowlock when the side strips have been fastened on.

These strips should each be made of 1-inch plank, 2 inches wide and an inch or two longer than the side boards. Nail the strips on the outside of the boat flush with the top of the side boards, making a neat joint at the stern piece, as shown in the illustration (Fig. 88). Cut two short strips to fit upon the inside

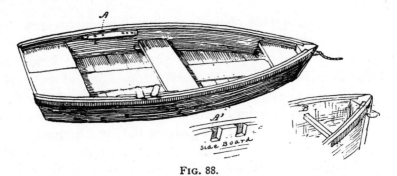

FIG. 88.

at the rowlocks, and fasten them firmly on with screws (Fig. 88, A). Next cut two cleats for the oarsman's seat to rest upon. Nail them to the side boards amidship a little nearer the bottom than the top, so that the seat, when resting upon the cleats, will be about half the distance from the top edge to the bottom of the side boards. Let the aft end of the cleats be about 6 feet 2 inches from the stern. Make thole-pins of some hard wood to fit in the rowlocks, like those heretofore described and illustrated by Fig. 77, B, page 104.

The Yankee Pine now only needs a keel board to complete it. This must be placed exactly in the centre, and is fastened on by a couple of screws at the thin end and nails from the inside of the boat. It is also fastened to the upright stick at the stern by screws (Fig. 89).

If the joints have been carefully made, your Yankee Pine is now ready for launching. Being made of rough lumber it needs no paint or varnish, but is a sort of rough-and-ready affair, light to row ; and it ought to float four people with ease. By using planed pine or cedar lumber, and

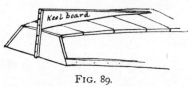

FIG. 89.

with hard-wood stem and stern, a very pretty row-boat can be made upon the same plan as a Yankee Pine, or by putting in a centre-board and " stepping " a mast in the bow, the Yankee Pine can be transformed into a sail-boat. But before experimenting in this line of boat building, the beginner had better read the following chapter on how to rig and sail small boats.

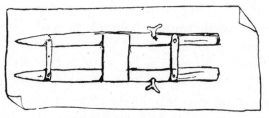

Top View of " Man Friday."

CHAPTER XIII.

HOW TO RIG AND SAIL SMALL BOATS.

To have the tiller in one's own hands and feel competent, under all ordinary circumstances, to bring a boat safely into port, gives the same zest and excitement to a sail (only in a far greater degree) that the handling of the whip and reins over a lively trotter does to a drive.

Knowing and feeling this, it was my intention to devote a couple of chapters to telling how to sail a boat; but through the kind courtesy of the editor of *The American Canoeist*, I am able to do much better by giving my readers a talk on this subject by one whose theoretical knowledge and practical experience renders him pre-eminently fit to give reliable advice and counsel. The following is what Mr. Charles Ledyard Norton, editor of the above-mentioned journal, says:

"Very many persons seem to ignore the fact that a boy who knows how to manage a gun is, upon the whole, less likely to be shot than one who is a bungler through ignorance, or that a good swimmer is less likely to be drowned than a poor one. Such, however, is the truth beyond question. If a skilled sportsman is now and then shot, or an expert swimmer drowned, the fault is not apt to be his own, and if the one who is really to blame had received proper training, it is not likely that the accident would have occurred at all. The same argument holds good with regard to the management of boats, and the author is confident that he merits the thanks of mothers, whether he receives them or not, for giving their boys a few hints as to practical rigging and sailing.

" In general, there are three ways of learning how to sail boats. First, from the light of nature, which is a poor way ; second, from books, which is better ; and third, from another fellow who knows how, which is best of all. I will try to make this article as much like the other fellow and as little bookish as possible.

" Of course, what I shall say in these few paragraphs will be of small use to those who live within reach of the sea or some big lake, and have always been used to boats ; but there are thousands and thousands of boys and men who never saw the sea, nor even set eyes on a sail, and who have not the least idea how to make the wind take them where they want to go. I once knew some young men from the interior who went down to the sea-side and hired a boat, with the idea that they had nothing to do but hoist the sail and be blown wherever they liked. The result was that they performed a remarkable set of manœuvres within sight of the boat-house, and at last went helplessly out to sea and had to be sent after and brought back, when they were well laughed at for their performances, and had reason to consider themselves lucky for having gotten off so cheaply.

" The general principles of sailing are as simple as the national game of ' one ole cat.' That is to say, if the wind always blew moderately and steadily, it would be as easy and as safe to sail a boat as it is to drive a steady old family horse of good and regular habits. The fact, however, is that winds and currents are variable in their moods, and as capable of unexpected freaks as the most fiery of unbroken colts ; but when properly watched and humored they are tractable and fascinating playmates and servants.

" Now, let us come right down to first principles. Take a bit of pine board, sharpen it at one end, set up a mast about a quarter of the length of the whole piece from the bow, fit on a square piece of stiff paper or card for a sail, and you are ready for action. Put this in the water, with the sail set squarely across (A, Fig. 90), and she will run off before the wind—which

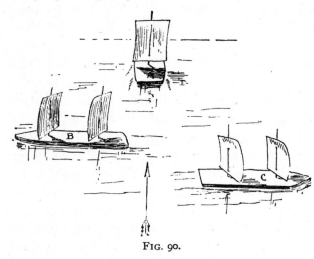

is supposed to be blowing as indicated by the arrow—at a good rate of speed. If she does not steer herself, put a small weight near the stern, or square end; or, if you like, arrange a thin bit of wood for a rudder.

FIG. 90.

"Probably the first primeval man who was born with nautical instincts discovered this fact, and, using a bush for a sail, greatly astonished his fellow primevals by winning some prehistoric regatta. But that was all he could do. He was as helpless as a balloonist is in mid-air. He could go, but he could not get back, and we may be sure that ages passed away before the possibility of sailing to windward was discovered.

"Now, put up, or 'step,' another mast and sail like the first, about as far from the stern as the first is from the bow. Turn the two sails at an angle of forty-five degrees across the boat (B or C, Fig. 90), and set her adrift. She will make considerable progress across the course of the wind, although she will at the same time drift with it. If she wholly refuses to go in the right direction, place a light weight on her bow, so that she will be a little 'down by the head,' or move the aftermost mast and sail a little nearer to the stern.

" The little rude affair thus used for experiment will not actually make any progress to windward, because she is so light that she moves sidewise almost as easily as she does forward. With a larger, deeper boat, and with sails which can be set at any angle, the effect will be different. So long as the wind presses against the after side of the sail, the boat will move through the water in the direction of the least resistance, which is forward. A square sail, having the mast in the middle, was easiest to begin with for purposes of explanation ; but now we will change to a 'fore-and-aft' rig—that is, one with the mast at the forward edge or 'luff' of the sail, as in Fig. 91.

Suppose the sail to be set at the angle shown, and the wind blowing as the arrow points. The boat cannot readily move sidewise, because of the broadside re-

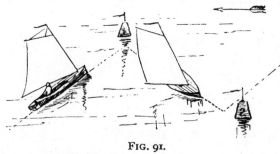

FIG. 91.

sistance ; she does not move backward, because the wind is pressing on the aftermost side of the sail. So she very naturally moves forward. When she nears buoy No. 1, the helmsman moves the 'tiller,' or handle of the rudder, toward the sail. This causes the boat to turn her head toward buoy No. 2, the sail swings across to the other side of the boat and fills on that side, which now in turn becomes the aftermost, and she moves toward buoy No. 2 nearly at right angles to her former course. Thus, through a series of zig-zags, the wind is made to work against itself. This operation is called 'tacking,' or 'working to windward,' and the act of turning, as at the buoys No. 1 and No. 2, is called 'going about.'

"It will be seen, then, that the science of sailing lies in being able to manage a boat with her head pointing at any possible angle to or from the wind. Nothing but experience can teach one all the niceties of the art, but a little aptitude and address will do to start with, keeping near shore and carrying little sail.

Simplest Rig Possible.

"I will suppose that the reader has the use of a broad, flat-bottomed boat without any rudder. (See Fig. 92.) She can-

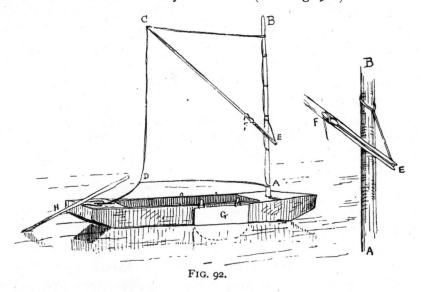

FIG. 92.

not be made to work like a racing yacht under canvas, but lots of fun can be had out of her.

"Do not go to any considerable expense at the outset. Pro-cure an old sheet, or an old hay-cover, six or eight feet square, and experiment with that before spending your money on new material. If it is a sheet, and somewhat weakly in its texture, turn all the edges in and sew them, so that it shall not give way at the hems. At each corner sew on a few inches of strong twine, forming loops at the angles. Sew on, also, eyelets or small loops along the edge which is intended for the luff of the sail, so that it can be laced to the mast.

"You are now ready for your spars, namely, a mast and a 'sprit,' the former a couple of feet longer than the luff of the sail, and the latter to be cut off when you find how long you want it. Let these spars be of pine, or spruce, or bamboo—as light as possible, especially the sprit. An inch and a half diameter will do for the mast, and an inch and a quarter for the sprit, tapering to an inch at the top. To 'step' the mast, bore a hole through one of the thwarts (seats) near the bow, and make a socket or step on the bottom of the boat, just under the aforesaid hole—or if anything a trifle farther forward—to receive the foot of the mast. This will hold the mast upright, or with a slight 'rake' aft.

"Lace the luff of the sail to the mast so that its lower edge will swing clear by a foot or so of the boat's sides. Make fast to the loop at D a stout line, ten or twelve feet long. This is called the 'sheet,' and gives control of the sail. The upper end of the sprit, C, E, is trimmed so that the loop at C will fit over it but not slip down. The lower end is simply notched to receive a short line called a 'snotter,' as shown in the detailed drawing at the right of the cut (Fig. 92). It will be readily understood that, when the sprit is pushed upward in the direction of C, the sail will stand spread out. The line is placed in the notch at E and pulled up until the sail sets properly, when it is made fast to a cleat or to a cross piece at F. This device is in common use and has its advantages, but a simple loop for the foot of the sprit to rest in is more easily made and will do nearly as well. H is an oar for steering. Having thus de-

scribed the simplest rig possible, we may turn our attention to
more elegant and elaborate but not always preferable outfits.

Leg-of-Mutton Rig.

" One of the prettiest and most convenient rigs for a small
boat is known as the 'leg-of-mutton sharpie rig' (Fig. 93).
The sail is triangular, and the sprit, instead of reaching to its
upper corner, stands nearly at right angles
to the mast. It is held in position at the
mast by the devices already described. This
rig has the advantage of keeping the whole
sail flatter than any other, for the end of
the sprit cannot ' kick up,' as the phrase
goes, and so the sail holds all the wind it
receives.

FIG. 93.

" Fig. 94 shows a device, published for
the first time in the *St. Nicholas Magazine*
for September, 1880, which enables the sail-
or to step and unstep his mast, and hoist or lower his sail without leaving his seat—a matter of great importance when the
boat is light and tottlish, as in the case of that most beautiful
of small craft, the modern canoe, where the navigator sits habitually amidships. The lower mast (A, B, Fig. 94) stands about
two and a half feet above the deck. It is fitted at the head
with a metal ferrule and pin, and just above the deck with two
half-cleats or other similar devices (A). The topmast (C, D)
is fitted at F with a stout ring, and has double halyards (E)
rove through or around its foot. The lower mast being in position (see lower part of Fig. 94), the canoeist desiring to make
sail brings the boat's head to the wind, takes the top-mast with
the sail loosely furled in one hand, and the halyards in the
other. It is easy for him by raising this mast, without leaving

his seat, to pass the halyards one on each side of the lower mast and let them fall into place close to the deck under the half-cleats at A. Then, holding the halyards taut enough to keep them in position, he will hook the topmast ring over the pin in the lower mast-head and haul away (see top part of Fig. 94). The mast will rise into place, where it is made fast. A collar of leather, or a knob of some kind, placed on the topmast just below the ring, will act as a fulcrum when the halyards are hauled taut, and keep the mast from working to and fro.

"The advantages of the rig are obvious. The mast can be raised without standing up,

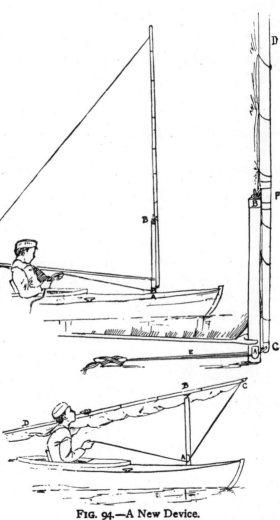

FIG. 94.—A New Device.

and in case of necessity the halyards can be let go and the mast and sail unshipped and stowed below with the greatest ease and expedition, leaving only the short lower mast standing. A leg-of-mutton sail with a common boom along the foot is shown in the cut as the most easily illustrated application of the device, but there is no reason why it may not be applied to a sail of different shape, with a sprit instead of a boom, and a square instead of a pointed head.

"The Latteen Rig

is recommended only for boats which are 'stiff'—not tottlish, that is. The fact that a considerable portion of the sail projects forward of the mast renders it awkward in case of a sudden shift of wind. Its most convenient

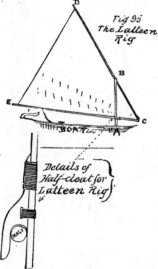

form is shown in Fig. 95. The arrangement for shipping and unshipping the yard is precisely like that shown in Fig. 94—a short lower mast with a pin at the top and a ring fitted to the yard. It has a boom at the foot which is joined to the yard at C by means of a hook or a simple lashing, having sufficient play to allow the two spars to shut up together like a pair of dividers. The boom (C, E) has, where it meets the short lower mast, a half-cleat or jaw, shown in detail at the bottom of the cut (Fig. 95), the circle representing a cross section of the mast. This should be

FIG. 95.—The Latteen Rig.

lashed to the boom, as screws or bolts would weaken it. To take in sail, the boatman brings the boat to the wind, seizes the boom and draws it toward him. This disengages it from the mast. He then shoves it forward, when the yard (C, D) falls of its own weight into his hands, and can be at once lifted clear of the lower mast. To keep the sail flat, it is possible to arrange a collar on the lower mast so that the boom, when once in position, cannot slip upward and suffer the sail to bag.

" The Cat-Rig,

so popular on the North Atlantic coast, is indicated in Fig. 91. The spar at the head of the sail is called a ' gaff,' and, like the boom, it fits the mast with semicircular jaws. The sail is hoisted and lowered by means of halyards rove through a block near the mast-head. The mast is set in the bows—' chock up in the eyes of her,' as a sailor would say. A single leg-of-mutton sail will not work in this position, because the greater part of its area is too far forward of amidships. No rig is handier or safer than this in working to windward ; but off the wind—running before, or nearly before it, that is— the weight of mast and sail, and the pressure of the wind at one side and far forward, make the boat very difficult and dangerous to steer. Prudent boatmen often avoid doing so by keeping the wind on the quarter and, as it were, tacking to leeward.

" This suggests the question of ' jibing,' an operation always to be avoided if possible. Suppose the wind to be astern, and the boat running nearly before it. It becomes necessary to change your course toward the side on which the sail is drawing. The safest way is to turn at first in the opposite direction, put the helm ' down' (toward the sail), bring the boat up into the wind, turn her entirely around, and stand off on the new tack. This, however, is not always possible. Hauling in the sheet until the sail fills on the other side is ' jibing ; ' but when this happens it goes over with a rush that sometimes carries mast and sheet or upsets the boat ; hence the operation should be first undertaken in a light wind. It is necessary to know how to do it, for sometimes a sail insists upon jibing very unexpectedly, and it is best to be prepared for such emergencies.

How to Make a Sail.

" For the sails of such boats as are considered in this paper, there is no better material than unbleached twilled cotton sheeting. It is to be had two and a half or even three yards wide. In cutting out your sail, let the selvedge be at the 'leech,' or aftermost edge. This, of course, makes it necessary to cut the luff and foot 'bias,' and they are very likely to stretch in the making, so that the sail will assume a different shape from what was intended. To avoid this, baste the hem carefully before sewing, and 'hold in' a little to prevent fulling. It is a good plan to tack the material on the floor before cutting, and mark the outline of the sail with pencil. Stout tape stitched along the bias edges will make a sure thing of it, and the material can be cut, making due allowance for the hem. Better take feminine advice on this process. The hems should be half an inch deep all around, selvedge and all, and it will do no harm to reinforce them with cord if you wish to make a thoroughly good piece of work.

" For running-rigging, nothing is better than laid or braided cotton cord, such as is used for awnings and sash-cords. If this is not easily procured, any stout twine will answer. It can be doubled and twisted as often as necessary. The smallest manila rope is rather stiff and unmanageable for such light sails as ours.

" In fitting out a boat of any kind, iron, unless galvanized, is to be avoided as much as possible, on account of its liability to rust. Use brass or copper instead.

Hints to Beginners.

" Nothing has been said about reefing thus far, because small boats under the management of beginners should not be afloat in a 'reefing breeze.' Reefing is the operation of reducing the spread of sail when the wind becomes too fresh. If you will look at Fig. 95 you will see rows of short marks on the sail above the boom. These are ' reef-points '—bits of line about a foot long passing through holes in the sail, and knotted so that they will not slip. In reefing, the sail is lowered and that portion of it between the boom and the reef-points is gathered together, and the points are tied around both it and the boom. When the lower row of points is used it is a single reef. Both rows together are a double reef.

" Make your first practical experiment *with a small sail and with the wind blowing toward the shore.* Row out a little way, and then sail in any direction in which you can make the boat go, straight back to shore if you can, with the sail out nearly at right angles with the boat. Then try running along shore with the sheet hauled in a little, and the sail on the side nearest the shore. You will soon learn what your craft can do, and will probably find that she will make very little, if any, headway to windward. This is partly because she slides sidewise over the water. To prevent it you may use a ' lee-board '—namely, a broad board hung over the side of the boat (G, Fig. 92). This must be held by stout lines, as the strain upon it is very heavy. It should be placed a little forward of the middle of the boat. It must be on the side away from the wind—the lee side—and must be shifted when you go about. Keels and centre-boards are permanent contrivances for the same purpose, but a lee-board answers very well as a makeshift, and is even used habitually by some canoeists and other boatmen.

" In small boats it is sometimes desirable to sit amidships, because sitting in the stern raises the bow too high out of water; steering may be done with an oar over the lee side, or with ' yoke-lines ' attached to a cross piece on the rudder-head, or even to the tiller. In this last case, the lines must be rove through rings or pulleys at the sides of the boat opposite

9

the end of the tiller.　When the handle of the oar (H, Fig. 92)
—or the tiller (F, Fig. 95) if a rudder is used—is pushed to the
right, the boat will turn to the left, and *vice versâ.*　The science
of steering consists in knowing when to push and how much to
push—very simple, you see, in the statement, but not always
so easy in practice.

"The sail should be so adjusted in relation to the rest of the
boat that, when the sheet is hauled close in and made fast, the
boat, if left to herself, will point her head to the wind like a
weather-cock, and drift slowly astern.　If it is found that the
sail is so far forward that she will not do this, the fault may be
remedied by stepping the mast further aft, or by rigging a
small sail near the stern.　This is called a 'dandy,' or 'steer-
ing-sail,' and is especially convenient in a boat whose size or
arrangement necessitates sitting amidships.　It may be rigged
like the mainsail, and when its sheet is once made fast will ordi-
narily take care of itself in tacking.

"Remember that, if the wind freshens or a squall strikes you,
the position of safety is with the boat's head to the wind.

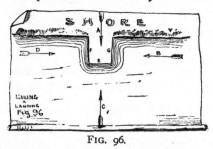

FIG. 96.

When in doubt what to do,
push the helm down (toward
the sail) and haul in the slack
of the sheet as the boat comes
up into the wind.　If she is
moving astern, or will not mind
her helm—and of course she
will not if she is not moving—
pull her head around to the wind with an oar, and experiment
cautiously until you find which way you can make her go.

"In making a landing, always calculate to have the boat's
head as near the wind as possible when she ceases to move.
This whether you lower your sail or not.

"Thus, if the wind is off shore, as shown at A, Fig. 96, land at F or G, with the bow toward the shore. If the wind is from the direction of B, land at E with the bow toward B, or at F; if at the latter, the boom will swing away from the wharf and permit you to lie alongside. If the wind is from D, reverse these positions. If the wind comes from the direction of C, land either at F or G, with the bow pointing off shore.

"If you have no one to tell you what to do, you will have to feel your way slowly and learn by experience; but if you have nautical instincts you will soon make your boat do what you wish her to do as far as she is able. *But first learn to swim before you try to sail a boat.*"

Volumes have been written on the subject treated in these few pages, and it is not yet exhausted. The hints here given are safe ones to follow, and will, it is hoped, be of service to many a young sailor in many a corner of the world.

CHAPTER XIV.

NOVELTIES IN SOAP-BUBBLES.

Every Boy His Own Bubble Pipe.

Every Boy his own Bubble Pipe.

"A SOAP-BUBBLE" is an uncouth, inelegant name for such an ethereal, fairy sphere. It is such a common, every-day sight to us that we seldom give it much attention or realize how wonderful and beautiful is this fragile, transparent, liquid globe. Its spherical form is typical of perfection, and the ever-changing, prismatic colors of its iridiscent surface charm the eye.

It is like a beautiful dream; we are entranced while it lasts, but in an instant it vanishes and leaves nothing to mark its former existence except the memory of its loveliness.

Few persons can stand by and watch another blowing bubbles without being seized with an uncontrollable desire to blow one for themselves. There is a peculiar charm or pleasure in the very act which not many who have known it ever outgrow. At the present time "soap-bubble parties" are becoming quite fashionable. At one of these gatherings the guests, old and young, furnished with clay pipes, stand around a table, in the centre of which is placed a fancy punch bowl filled—not with a mixture of ardent spirits, but soapsuds. Prizes are awarded to those among the guests who successfully launch in air the largest bubble, and to those who keep theirs flying for the greatest length of time or send them the highest. As may be imagined, these parties are very amusing, and everybody at first tries to prevent his or her neighbor from succeeding, until, amid great merriment and confusion, the hostess announces that if her guests expect the prizes to be awarded, a rule must be enacted compelling them to pay more attention to their own efforts and not allowing them to molest each other.

It is generally known that a bubble will burst if it touch any hard or smooth surface, but upon the carpet or a woollen cloth it will roll or bounce merrily.

If you take advantage of this fact you can with a woollen cloth make bubbles dance and fly around as lively as a juggler's gilt balls, and you will be astonished to find what apparently rough handling these fragile bubbles will stand when you are careful not to allow them to touch anything but the woollen cloth.

It may be worth remarking that the coarser the soap the brighter the bubbles will be. The compound known as " soft soap" is by some persons considered the best for the purpose.

In the accompanying illustrations are shown two kinds of soap-bubbles.

One of the pictures shows how to transform your bubble into an aërial vapor balloon.

If you wish to try this pretty experiment, procure a rubber tube, say a yard long, and with an aperture small enough to require considerable stretching to force it over the gas-burner. After you have stretched one end so as to fit tightly over the

burner, wrap the stem of a clay pipe with wet paper and push
it into the other end of the tube, where it must fit so as to allow no gas to escape.   Dip the bowl of your pipe into the suds
and turn the gas on ; the force of the
gas will be sufficient to blow the bubble for you, and, as the gas is lighter
than the air, the bubble, when freed
from the pipe, will rapidly ascend and
never stop in its upward course until
it perishes.

Gas-bubble.

Old Uncle Cassius, an aged negro
down in Kentucky, used to amuse the
children by making smoke-bubbles.

Did you ever see smoke-bubbles ?
In one the white-blue smoke, in beautiful curves, will curl and circle under
its crystal shell. Another will possess a
lovely opalescent, pearly appearance,
and if one be thrown from the pipe
while quite small and densely filled
with smoke, it will appear like an opaque polished ball of milky
whiteness.   It is always a great frolic for the children when
they catch Uncle Cassius smoking his corn-cob pipe.   They
gather around his knee with their bowl of soapsuds and bubble pipes, and while the good-natured old man takes a few lusty
whiffs from his corn-cob and fills his capacious mouth with
tobacco smoke, one of the children dips a pipe into the suds,
starts the bubble and passes it to Uncle Cassius.   All then stoop
down and watch the gradual growth of that wonderful smoke-
bubble ; and when " Dandy," the dog, chases and catches one
of these bubbles, how the children laugh to see the astonished
and injured look upon his face, and what fun it is to see him
sneeze and rub his nose with his paw !

The figure at the head of this chapter shows you how to make a giant bubble. It is done by first covering your hands well with soapsuds, then placing them together so as to form a cup, leaving a small opening at the bottom. All that is then necessary is to hold your mouth about a foot from your hands and blow into them. I have made bubbles in this way twice the size of my head. These bubbles are so large that they invariably burst upon striking the floor, being unable to withstand the concussion.

Although generally considered a trivial amusement, only fit for young children, blowing soap-bubbles has been an occupation appreciated and indulged in by great philosophers and men of science, and wonderful discoveries in optics and natural philosophy might be made with only a clay-pipe and a bowl of soapsuds.

CHAPTER XV.

FOURTH OF JULY BALLOONS WITH NEW AND NOVEL ATTACHMENTS.

DID you ever, while watching a beautiful soap-bubble dance merrily through the air, think how closely it resembled the immense silken bubble beneath which the daring aëronaut goes bounding among the clouds?

Especially is this true of the gas-bubble described in the foregoing chapter. When a boy, the author's ambition naturally led him from these vapor balloons to experimenting in more lasting material than soap-suds. He then devoted his attention for some time to paper balloons, and, after numerous experiments and disasters, succeeded in building balloons of a style which is comparatively safe from accident and seldom the cause of a mortifying failure. If you do not want to disappoint the spectators by having a fire instead of an ascension, avoid models with small mouth-openings or narrow necks. Experience has also taught the writer that balloons of good, substantial, portly build go up best and make their journey in a stately, dignified manner, while the slim, narrow balloon, on the contrary, even if it suc-

Too long a neck (unsafe).

ceeds in getting a safe start, goes bobbing through the air,
turning this way and that, until the flame from the fire-ball

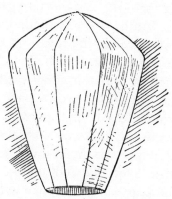

Too Square and Narrow (unsafe).

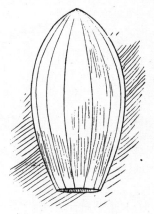

Too Narrow (unsafe).

touches and lights the thin paper, leaving only a handful of
ashes floating upon the summer breeze.

The reader can see here illustrated some of the objectionable

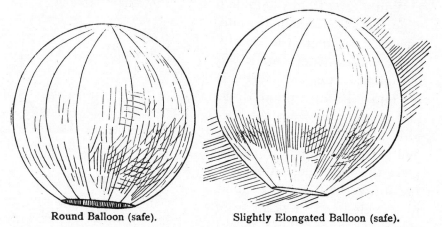

Round Balloon (safe).   Slightly Elongated Balloon (safe).

shapes as well as some of the safe styles. For large balloons,
strong manila-paper is best ; for smaller ones, use tissue-paper.

When you build a balloon, decide first what height you want it; then make the side pieces or gores nearly a third longer; a

Pumpkin-shaped Balloon (safe).

balloon of thirteen gores, each six feet long and one foot greatest width, when distended with hot air ready to ascend, is a little over four feet high. For such a balloon, first make a pattern of stiff brown paper by which to cut the gores. To make the pattern, take a strip of paper six feet long and a little over one foot wide; fold the paper in the centre lengthwise, so that it will be only slightly over a half foot from the edges to the fold. Along the bottom measure two inches from the fold and mark the point. At one foot from the bottom, at right angles from the folded edge, measure three inches and one-half, and mark the point; in the same manner mark off five inches from two feet up the fold. From a point three feet four inches from the bottom measure off six inches and mark the point; from this place the width decreases. At the fourth foot mark a point five inches and one-half from the fold; about three inches

Regular-shaped Balloon (safe).

and a third at the fifth foot; nothing, of course, at the sixth foot, or top, where the gore will come to a point. With chalk

or pencil draw a curved line connecting these points ; cut the
paper along this line and unfold it.

You will have a pattern the shape of a cigar, four inches

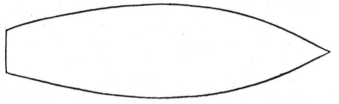

FIG. 97.—Single Gore.

wide at the bottom, one foot greatest width, and six feet long.
After pasting your sheets of manila or tissue-paper together
in strips of the required length cut out thirteen gores by the
pattern just made ; lay one of these gores flat upon the floor, as in

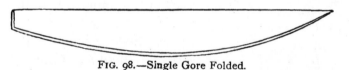

FIG. 98.—Single Gore Folded.

Fig. 97 ; fold it in the centre, as in Fig. 98 ; over this lay another
gore, leaving a margin of the under gore protruding from beneath (Fig. 99). With a brush cover the protruding edge with
paste, then turn it up and over upon the upper gore, and with

FIG. 99.—Folded Gore with a second Gore over it, ready for Pasting.

a towel or rag press it down until the two edges adhere. Fold
the upper gore in the centre as you did the first one, and lay
a third gore upon it ; paste the free protruding edge ; and so on

until all thirteen are pasted.   It will be found that the bottom gore and top gore have each an edge unpasted ; lay these two edges together and paste them neatly.

Next you must make a hoop of rattan or some light sub-

FIG. 100.

stance to fit the mouth opening, which will be about one foot and a half in diameter.   Fasten the hoop in by pasting the edges of the mouth opening around it.   In very large paper balloons it is well to place a piece of string along the edge of each gore and paste it in, letting the ends of the strings hang down below the mouth ; fasten the hoop in with these ends before pasting the paper over it. It will be found next to impossible to tear the hoop from a balloon, strengthened in this manner, with- out totally destroying the balloon.

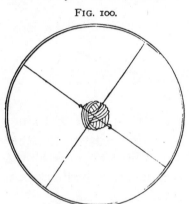

Top View of Hoop and Cross Wire.

Wick-ball.

Side View of Hoop showing Wick-
ball hung in place.

Should you discover an open- ing at the top of your balloon, caused by the points not joining exactly, tie it up with a string if it be small, but if it be a large

hole paste a piece of paper over it.   When dry, take a fan and fan the balloon as full of air as you can, and while it is inflated make a thorough inspection of all sides to see that there are no accidental tears, holes or rips.

Fig. 100 shows the cross wires that support the fire-ball. The latter is best made of old-fashioned lamp-wick wound, rather loosely, in the form of a ball, the size depending upon the dimensions of the balloon.   The sponge commonly used soon burns out and the balloon comes down in a very little while ; but the wick-ball here described seldom fails to propel the little air-ship upward and onward out of sight. A short, fine wire should next be run quite through the wick-ball, so that it can be attached to the mouth of the balloon in an instant by hooking the ends of this wire over the cross wires at the mouth.

If you use a little care you will have no difficulty in send-ing up the balloon. Place your wick-ball in a pan or dish, put the corked bottle of alcohol beside it, and about thirty feet away make a simple fire-place of bricks or stones, over which place a piece of stove-pipe. Fill the fire-place with shavings, twisted pieces of paper, or anything that will light readily and make a good blaze. In a loop of string fastened at the top of the bal-loon for that purpose let one of the party put the end of a smooth stick, and, with the other end in his hand, mount some elevated position and hold the balloon over the fire-place. Be-fore touching a match to the combustibles below, expand the balloon as much as possible by fanning it full of air ; then light the fire. Be very careful, in all the process that follows, to hold the mouth of the balloon directly above and not too near the stove-pipe, to prevent the blaze from setting fire to the paper, which will easily ignite. At this stage of the proceedings one person must take the bottle of alcohol, uncork it, and pour the contents over the wick-ball in the basin, and the ball must be made to soak up all it will hold of the spirits. The balloon will become more and more buoyant as the air becomes heated inside, and at length, when distended to its utmost, it will be-gin pulling to free itself. Holding the hoop at the mouth, walk to one side of the fire and with all speed have the ball at-tached securely in place. Touch a light to it, and it will blaze up. At the words " All right," let go. The same instant the stick must be slid from the loop on top, so as not to tear

the paper, and away will sail the balloon upon its airy
voyage.

Never attempt to send up a balloon upon a windy day, for
the wind will be sure, sooner or later, to blow the blaze aside
and set the paper on fire, and if once it catches up in the air
there is not much use in trying to save it.

After you have made a balloon like the one just described
and sent it up successfully, you can try other shapes. A very
good plan in experimenting is to make a small working model

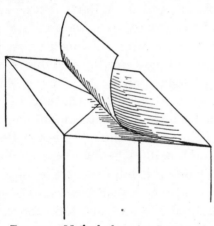

of light tissue-paper, fill it
with cold air by means of an
ordinary fan, and when it is
expanded any defect in form
or proportion can be readily
detected and remedied. If
it be too narrow, cut it open
at one seam and put in another gore, or *vice versâ*, until you are satisfied with the
result ; with this as a pattern,
construct your larger balloon.
Such a model, eighteen inches
high, lies upon the writer's

FIG. 101.—Method of pasting Paper and
Strings for Parachute.

table. He has sent it up in the house several times by holding it
a few moments over a burning gas-jet. The balloon rapidly fills
with heated air, and when freed soars up to the ceiling, where
it rolls along until the air cools, then falls gently to the floor.

The parachute shown in the tail-piece is simply a square
piece of paper with a string at each of the four corners, meeting
a short distance underneath, where a weight is attached. Fig.
101 shows how to make one that will not tear. It is made of
two square pieces of paper. Two pieces of string are laid diagonally across the first paper ; on top of this the second piece of

paper is pasted, enclosing the strings without disturbing them; the ends of the strings come out at the corners.

These parachutes are attached to a wire that hangs from the balloon in this manner: From the centre and top of the parachute is a string, we will say, a foot long; this is tied securely to one end of the large fuse from a pack of Chinese fire-crackers; a few inches from the other end of the fuse another string is tied and fastened to the wire. Just as the balloon starts the free end of the fuse is lighted (Fig. 102). When it has burned itself away past the point where the lower string has been fastened, it of course severs the connection between the parachute and the balloon, and the parachute drops, but does not go far, before the air beneath spreads it out, the weight at the bottom balances it, and it floats away slowly, settling lower and lower, but often travelling miles before finally reaching the earth.

All manner of objects may be attached to a parachute—notes addressed to possible finders, letters, or figures of men or animals. The latter look very odd in the air.

A real passenger balloon may be very closely imitated by painting crossed black lines upon the upper part of a paper balloon to represent the net-work. A pasteboard balloon-car, made after the manner shown in Fig. 103, and holding two pasteboard men cut out as shown in Fig. 104, may be hung on by hook-

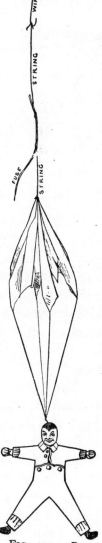

FIG. 102. — Parachute attached to the Fuse and Wire.

ing the wires attached to the car over the hoop at the mouth of the balloon. When the balloon and car are a little distance up in the air, it takes a sharp eye to detect the deception, because distance in the air cannot be easily judged.

FIG. 103.—The Car.

But so far we have dealt only with day balloons ; for night, you must attach some luminous object.

A lantern made like the one described in "Kite-time" (Fig. 29) may be fastened to the balloon by a long string and wire, and when it goes swinging after the larger light above, it has a curious appearance. In a similar manner, a long string of lanterns may be hung on to a large balloon, or packs of Chinese crackers may be exploded in mid-air by means of a fuse.

The writer has experimented in other fireworks, but found them very dangerous to handle. Mr. Stallknecht, of the *Hat, Cap and Fur Trade Review*, however, showed the author how to make a simple, safe, and beautiful pyrotechnic

FIG. 104.—A Couple of Aëronauts.

out of a Roman candle with colored balls, a piece of wire and a fuse. The fuse used can be bought in almost any city or town ;

Night Balloon.

it is sold to miners for setting off blasts. With the wire make a sort of wheel, with two or three spokes ; cut open the Roman candle and extract the powder and balls ; wrap up each ball with some of the powder loosely in a piece of tissue-paper and tie the paper at the ends upon the spokes or cross wires of the wheel, as shown in Fig. 105. Run the fuse spirally around, passing through each parcel containing a ball, and allow the long end of the fuse to trail down beneath from the centre or side (Fig. 106). To the rim of the wire wheel attach several wires of equal lengths with hooked ends ; hook these on to the hoop at the mouth of the balloon just before letting it go, and light the trailing end of the fuse. As the fire creeps slowly along, the balloon mounts higher and

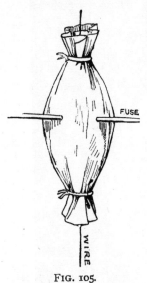

FIG. 105.

higher. Suddenly the whole balloon glows with a ruddy, lurid glare. The fire has reached the first ball. In another instant you see a floating globe of pale green light, then blue, and so on, until all the balls are consumed. Showers of pretty, jagged sparks are falling constantly during the illumination, caused by the burning powder. By the time all is over the tiny light of the solitary ball in the balloon looks like a star in the sky above,

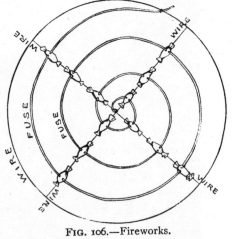

FIG. 106.—Fireworks.

travelling where the wind chooses to blow it. The most experienced aëronaut has but very little more command over the actions of his immense silken air-ship than has the young amateur who builds his balloon of tissue-paper and sends it skyward with a ball of fire for its motive power.

Through the Clouds.

CHAPTER XVI.

HOW TO CAMP OUT WITHOUT A TENT.

THE next best thing to really living in the woods is talking over such an experience. A thousand little incidents, scarcely thought of at the time, crowd upon my mind, and bring back with them the feeling of freedom and adventure so dear to the heart of every boy. Shall I ever enjoy any flavor earth can afford as we did our coffee's aroma ? The flapjacks—how good and appetizing ! the fish—how delicate and sweet ! And the wonderful cottage of boughs, thatched with the tassels of the pine—was there ever a cottage out of a fairy tale that could compare with it ?

In fancy I can see it now. There stands the little cot, flooded with the light of the setting sun ; those who built it and use it for a habitation are off exploring, hunting, fishing, and foraging for their evening meal, and the small, shy creatures of the wood take the opportunity to satisfy the curiosity with which they have, from a safe distance, viewed the erection of so large and singular a nest.

The boys will soon return, each with his contribution to the larder—a fish, a squirrel, a bird, or a rabbit, which will be cooked and eaten with better appetite and enjoyment than the most elaborate viands that home could afford. And although such joys are denied to me now, I can, at least, in remembering them, give others an opportunity to possess similar pleasures. It shall be my object to describe how these houses may be built and these dinners cooked, and that, too, where there are

FIG. 107.—Frame of Cottage.

neither planks, nor nails, nor stoves. To boys well informed in woodcraft, only a few hints need be given; but for the benefit of amateurs we will go more into detail.

Four persons make a good camping-party. Before arriving at their destination these persons should choose one of their number as captain.

The captain gives directions and superintends the pitching of the tent or the building of the rustic cottage. The site for the camp should be upon a knoll, mound, or rising ground, so as to afford a good drainage. If the forest abounds in pine trees, the young cottage-builder's task is an easy one. It often happens that two or three trees already standing can be made to serve for the corners of the proposed edifice, though trees for corners are not absolutely necessary.

Fig. 107 represents part of the framework of one of the simplest forms of rustic cottage. In this case, two trees serve for the two posts of the rear wall. The front posts are young trees that have been cut down and firmly planted at about four or five paces in front of the trees, as shown in the illustration. Enough of the branches have been left adhering to the trunks of the upright posts to serve as rests for the cross bars. To prevent complication in the diagram, the roof is not shown. To make this, fasten on an additional cross bar or two to the rear wall, then put a pole at each side, slanting down from the rear to the front, and cover these poles with cross sticks. When the framework is finished, the security and durability of the structure will be improved by fastening all the loose joints, tying them together with withes of willow, grass, or reeds. The next step is to cover the frame. This is done after the method shown in Fig. 108. From among some boughs, saved for this purpose, take one and hang it upon the third cross bar, counting from the ground up; bring the bough down, passing it inside the second bar and resting the end on the

ground outside the first bar; repeat this with other boughs until the row is finished. Then begin at the fourth bar, passing
the boughs down inside the third and outside the second bar,
so that they will overlap the first row. Continue in this man-

FIG. 108.—The way to Thatch.

ner until the four walls are closed in, leaving spaces open where
windows or doors are wanted. The roof is thatched after the
same method, beginning at the front and working upward and
backward to the rear wall, each row overlapping the preceding
row of thatch. The more closely and compactly you thatch
the roof and walls, the better protection will they afford from
any passing shower. This completed, the house is finished,
and you will be astonished to see what a lovely little green cot
you have built.

A cottage may be built differing from the one we have just
described by having the roof extended so as to form a sort of

verandah, or porch, in front; the floor of the porch may be covered with a layer of pine-needles. Should you find your house too small to accommodate your party, you can, by erecting a duplicate cottage four or five paces at one side, and roofing over the intervening space, have a house of two rooms with an open hall-way between.

Before going to housekeeping, some furniture will be necessary; and for this we propose to do our shopping right in the neighborhood of our cottage. Here is our cabinet and upholstery shop, in the wholesome fragrance of the pines.

After the labor of building, your thoughts will naturally turn to a place for sleeping. Cut four forked sticks, sharpen the ends, and drive them firmly into the ground at the spot where you wish the bed to stand in your room. Two strong poles, long enough to reach lengthwise from fork to fork, will serve for side boards; a number of short sticks will answer for slats; after these are fastened in place you have the rustic bedstead shown in Fig. 109. A good spring mattress is very desirable, and not difficult to obtain. Gather a lot of small green branches, or brush, and cover your bedstead with a layer of it about one foot

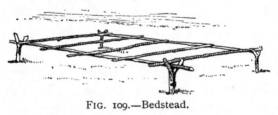

FIG. 109.—Bedstead.

thick; this you will find a capital substitute for springs. For your mattress proper, go to your upholstery shop under the pine tree and gather several armfuls of the dry pine-needles; cover the elastic brush *springs* with a thick layer of these needles; over this spread your India-rubber blanket, with the rubber side under, so that any moisture or dampness there may be in your mattress may be prevented from coming through. You may now make up your bed with what wraps or blan-

kets you have with you, and you have (Fig. 110) as complete
and comfortable a bed as any forester need wish for. In the
place of pine-needles, hay or grass may be used. I have slept
very comfortably
upon a brush mat-
tress covered with
iron-weed.*

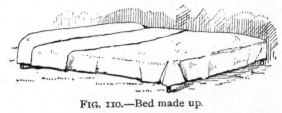

FIG. 110.—Bed made up.

I would suggest
to any boy who
means to try this
rustic cabinet-making, to select carefully for the bed-posts sticks
strong enough to support the weight he intends them to bear,
otherwise his slumbers may be interrupted in an abrupt and
disagreeable manner. My first experiment in this line proved
disastrous. I spent the greater part of one day in building and
neatly finishing a bed like the one described. After it was
made up, with an army blanket for a coverlid, it looked so soft,
comfortable, and inviting that I scarcely could wait for bed-
time to try it.

When the evening meal was over and the last story told
around the blazing camp-fire, I took off hat, coat, and boots
and snuggled down in my new and original couch, curiously
watched by my companions, who lay, rolled in their blankets,
upon the hard ground. It does not take a boy long to fall
asleep, particularly after a hard day's work in the open air, but
it takes longer, after being aroused from a sound nap, for him
to get his wits together—especially when suddenly dumped
upon the ground with a crash, amid a heap of broken sticks
and dry brush, as I happened to be on that eventful night.
Loud and long were the shouts of laughter of my companions

* Iron-weed ; flat-top (Vernonia noveboracensis) ; a common Kentucky weed,
with beautiful purple blossoms.

when they discovered my misfortune. Theoretically, the bed was well planned, but practically it was a failure, because it had rotten sticks for bed-posts.

Having provided bed and shelter, it is high time to look after the inner boy ; and while the foragers are off in search of provisions, it will be the cook's duty to provide some method of cooking the food that will be brought in.

One of the simplest and most practical forms of bake-oven can be made of clay and an old barrel. Remove one head of the barrel, scoop out a space in the nearest bank, and fit the barrel in (Fig. 111). If the mud or clay is not damp enough,

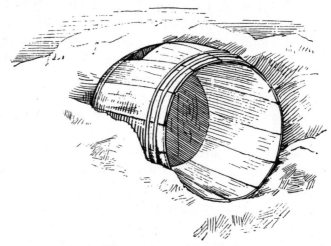

FIG. 111.—Barrel in Bank.

moisten it and plaster it over the barrel to the depth of a foot or more, leaving a place for a chimney at the back end, where part of a stave has been cut away ; around this place build a chimney of sticks arranged log-cabin fashion and plastered with mud (Fig. 112). After this, make a good, rousing fire in the barrel, and keep adding fuel until all the staves are burned out and the surrounding clay is baked hard. This makes an oven

that will bake as well, if not better, than any new patented
stove or range at home. To use it, build a fire inside and let
it burn until the oven is thoroughly heated, then rake out all
the coal and embers, put your dinner in and close up the front

FIG. 112.—Heating the Oven.

with the head of the barrel preserved for this purpose. The
clay will remain hot for several hours and keep the inside of
the oven hot enough to roast meat or bake bread.

If there be no bank convenient, or if you have no barrel
with which to build this style of oven, there are other methods
that will answer for all the cooking necessary to a party of boys
camping out. Many rare fish have I eaten in my time. The

delicious pompano at New Orleans, the brook-trout and gray-ling, fresh from the cold water of Northern Michigan, but never

FIG. 113.—A Stone Stove.

have I had fish taste better than did a certain large cat-fish that we boys once caught on a set-line in Kentucky. We built a fire-place of flat stones, a picture of which you have in Fig. 113, covered it with a thin piece of slate, cleaned the fish and with its skin still on, placed it upon the slate. When it was brown upon one side we turned it over until it was thoroughly cooked. With green sticks we lifted off the fish and placed it

FIG. 114.—A Butter-Knife.

upon a piece of clean bark ; the skin adhered to the stone, and the meat came off in smoking, snowy pieces, which we ate with the aid of our pocket-knives and rustic forks made of small green twigs with the forked ends sharpened.

If stones cannot be had to answer for this stove, there still remains the old, primitive camp-fire and pot-hook. The very sight of this iron pot swing-ing over a blazing fire sug-gests soup, to eat which with any comfort spoons are necessary. These are quickly and easily made by thrusting clam or mussel shells into splits made in the ends of sticks. A splendid butter-knife can be made from the shell of a razor-oyster with a little care in a similar manner (see Fig. 114).

FIG. 115.—Frame of Rustic Chair.

If you stay any time in your forest home you can, by a lit-tle ingenuity, add many comforts and conveniences. I have drawn some diagrams, as hints, in this direction. For instance, Fig. 115 shows the manner of making an excellent rustic chair of two stout poles and two cross poles, to which are fastened the ends of a piece of can-vas, carpet or leather (Fig. 116), which, swinging loose, fits itself exactly to your form, making a most com-fortable easy-chair in which to rest or take a nap after a hard day's tramp. It of-

FIG. 116.—The Rustic Chair Finished.

ten happens that the peculiar formation of some stump or branch suggests new styles of seats. A table can be very readily made by driving four forked sticks into the ground for legs, and covering the cross sticks upon the top with pieces of birch or other smooth bark. Fig. 117 shows a table made in

this manner, with one piece of bark removed to reveal its construction.

As a general rule, what is taught in boys' books, though correct in theory, when tried

FIG. 117.—A Camp Table.

proves impracticable. This brings to mind an incident that happened to a party of young hunters camping out in Ohio. Early one morning one of the boys procured from a distant farm-house a dozen pretty little white bantam eggs. Having no game, and only one small fish in the way of fresh meat, the party congratulated themselves upon the elegant breakfast they would make of fresh eggs, toasted crackers, and coffee. How to cook the eggs was the question. One of the party proposed his plan.

" I have just read a book," said he, " which tells how some travellers cooked fowls and fish by rolling them up in clay and tossing them into the fire. Shall we try that plan with the eggs ? "

The rest of the party assented, and soon all were busy rolling rather large balls of blue clay, in the centre of each of which was an egg. A dozen were placed in the midst of the hottest embers, and the boys seated themselves around the fire, impatiently waiting for the eggs to cook. They did cook—with a vengeance ! Zip, bang ! went one, then another and another, until, in less time than it takes to tell it, not an egg remained unexploded ; and the hot embers and bits of clay that stuck to

the boys' hair and clothes were all that was left to remind them
of those nice, fresh bantam eggs. It was all very funny, but
ever after the boys of that party showed the greatest caution in
trying new schemes, no matter how well they might seem to be
endorsed.

Hints to Amateur Campers.

From time immemorial it has been the custom of the city
fellows to laugh at their country cousins, and to poke all manner of fun at them on account of their verdancy in regard to
city manners and customs. This is hardly fair, for if a real
city fellow be placed on a farm, or in the woods, his ignorance
is just as laughable and absurd. It was only the other day I
saw a young New York artist refuse to drink from a spring
because something *was bubbling up at the bottom.* Experience
is a great teacher. Even the artist just mentioned, after making himself sick upon stagnant water, would, no doubt, learn to
select bubbling springs in the future. A few timely hints may,
however, prevent many mishaps and unpleasant accidents.

Provisions.

It is always desirable to take as large a stock of provisions
as can be conveniently transported. In these days of canned
meats, soups, vegetables, and fruits, a large amount of provisions may be stored in a small space. Do not fail to take a
plentiful supply of salt, pepper, and sugar ; also bacon, flour,
meal, grits, or hominy, tea, coffee, and condensed milk. If
you have any sort of luck with your rod, gun, or traps, the
forest and stream ought to supply fresh meat, and with the appetite only enjoyed by people who live out doors you can "live
like a king."

Shelter.

Because I have described but one sort of shelter my readers must not suppose that it is absolutely necessary to build a

cottage like the one described. On the contrary, there are a thousand different plans that will suggest themselves to fellows who are accustomed to camping out. The huts, or sheds, built of "slabs" by some of the Adirondack hunters are very convenient, but unless the open ends are protected, in time of a storm, the rain is apt to drive in and soak the inmates. The two sheds face each other, and in the middle of the space between the camp-fire blazes, throwing a ruddy light at night into both compartments.

By taking advantage of a rock, a fallen or uprooted tree, the work of building a hut is ofttimes materially lessened.

Tents, of course, are very handy and comfortable, and if obtainable should by all means be used. At least one or two good sharp hatchets should form a part of the equipment of every camp; it is astonishing, with their aid and a little practice, what a comfortable house may be built in a very short time.

Choosing Companions.

Never join a camping party that has among its members a single peevish, irritable, or selfish person, or a "shirk." Although the company of such a boy may be only slightly annoying at school or upon the play-ground, in camp the companionship of a fellow of this description becomes unbearable. Even if the game fill the woods and the waters are alive with fish, an irritable or selfish companion will spoil all the fun and take the sunshine out of the brightest day. The whole party should be composed of fellows who are willing to take things as they come and make the best of everything. With such companions there is no such thing as "bad luck;" rain or shine everything is always jolly, and when you return from the woods, strengthened in mind and body, you will always remember with pleasure your camping experience.

CHAPTER XVII.

BIRD SINGERS, ETC.

VERY many amusing contrivances can be made of the most simple materials. I have seen boys pluck a blade of grass, and, by simply stretching it edgewise between their thumbs, make a musical instrument with which they could imitate the notes of a singing bird so closely as to perfectly deceive persons not in the secret. After placing the blade of grass, as shown by the illustration, put your lips to your thumbs at the hollow between the joints and blow. The result will be a shrill noise which, with very little practice, can be made to resemble the notes of different wild birds.

The Block Bird Singer.

The illustration (Fig. 118) shows an instrument made upon the same principle as the "bird singer" just described. The 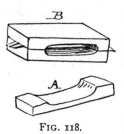 "block bird singer" consists of two blocks of pine small enough to fit between the front teeth of the operator. The blocks are hollowed out in the middle, as shown by A, Fig. 118.

Stretch a blade of grass across the hollow of one of the blocks and place the other block on top of it, as shown by B, Fig. 118.

FIG. 118.

Place the blocks between your teeth, and by drawing in and expelling your breath you can produce a series of shrill

11

noises which, with practice, may be made to imitate the notes of a singing bird. A thin strip of writing-paper may be substituted for the blade of grass where the latter is hard to procure.

The Corn-stalk Fiddle.

The writing of the above title has sent me back to my boyhood with one great leap over the intervening years. In imagination I am again a barefooted youngster, with straw hat, short pants, and checked apron. Again I can experience the feeling of pride and importance as from my pocket comes the well-remembered jack-knife, with a great shining blade that

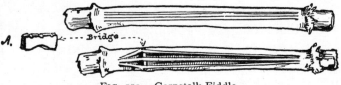

FIG. 119.—Cornstalk Fiddle.

opens, like any *man's* knife, with a snap! If I were this moment placed in a particular barn-yard in company with my reader, I could take him to the exact spot where a pile of corn-stalks used always to be heaped up in the corner of the fence. Let us suppose we are there. Select a good straight corn-stalk, and with the "shiny" blade of the jack-knife cut four slits from joint to joint, as shown by the top diagram, Fig. 119. Now out of that chip at your feet make a wooden bridge like the one shown by A, Fig. 119. With the point of the jack-knife lift up the three strings of the fiddle and slide the bridge under them edgewise; then gently, but firmly, raise it to an upright position and spread the strings apart, allowing them to fit into the notches cut for the purpose in the bridge (see lower diagram, Fig. 119). Make the bow of a smaller corn-stalk than that used for the fiddle. No tune can be played upon this instrument, but a funny squeaking noise can be produced.

The squeak of the corn-stalk fiddle brings to my mind another rustic instrument.

The Pumpkin-vine Fife.

Cut a good thick, straight pumpkin-stem and make holes in it like those in a fife. If you know how to blow on a fife you may not only produce a noise with the pumpkin-stem, but a tune may be played upon this simple instrument which, even if only partially successful, will amuse your hearers to that degree that you will feel yourself amply repaid for the trouble.

A Pumpkin-vine Flute.

Cut off a long leaf-stem like the one shown in the illustration (Fig. 120). With the blade of your knife make a slit (A, B) through both sides of the stem. Then at the base of the leaf, in the solid part just beyond the end of the hollow in the stem, cut off the stem at C, D. By putting this end in the mouth and blowing, a noise will be produced, deep and sonorous, sounding like a distant steamboat's whistle. Holes may be cut for the fingers similar to those just described for the fife.

If one stem fails to work, cut another and try it until you succeed. The pumpkin-vine flute, like the corn-stalk fiddle, will amuse small boys, but if my reader does not belong to that class he may make of a piece of fishing-cane a first-rate fife.

FIG. 120.—A Pumpkin - vine Flute.

Cane Fife.

The fishing-pole being much harder material than the succulent pumpkin-vine stem, is proportionally more difficult to cut.

If you can, borrow a real fife ; select a piece of cane of about the same size, and cut the holes in one side of the cane, at the same distance apart as those in the real fife. Any hollow stick of the proper size will answer as a substitute for the piece of fishing-pole.

The Voice Disguiser

is made of a piece of corn-stalk about three inches long. After removing the pith cut a notch near each end, as shown in the illustration, upon opposite sides of the corn-stalk; upon the

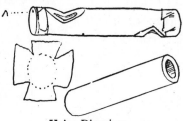

ends stretch a piece of fish-bladder, or any thin membrane; a piece of thin tracing-paper will answer. With a large pin make a hole in each piece of membrane, as shown at A in the illustration. Now cover the notch, cut into the corn-stalk,

Voice Disguiser.

with your mouth and laugh ; the noise you produce will set you laughing in earnest. By placing your mouth over either of the notches and talking or singing, the voice is so changed as to be perfectly disguised, and if you sing a song through this instrument it sounds like some one playing on a comb covered with paper. The voice disguiser is very handy in Punch and Judy or puppet shows.

The Locust Singer.

This little instrument, simple as it is, is calculated to afford considerable amusement.

With one of these toys can be made not only a loud noise, which in itself pleases most boys, but it reproduces exactly the sound of the *cicada*, or " locust," as the harvest-fly is commonly but improperly called. The " locust singer," as may be seen by reference to the illustration, consists of a horse-hair with a

The Locust Singer.

loop at one end and a weight attached to the other end. A pine stick, with a groove cut around it near the top, is thrust through the loop of horse-hair, and the groove in the stick thickly covered with powdered rosin.

When the weight is swung rapidly around, the horse-hair, in sliding over the rosined stick, produces a noise which closely resembles the well-known song of the harvest-fly. If a tin pill-box is used for a weight and the hair run through a hole in the lid and fastened by a knot upon the inside, the lid of the box acts as a sort of sounding-board. A piece of parchment or paper is sometimes pasted over the box tightly, like a drum-head, and the hair attached to this ; but a little stone wrapped in a piece of cloth answers every purpose.

A piece of kid, from a discarded glove, tied tightly over the top of a bottle-head, makes a loud-voiced locust singer. The head of the bottle may easily be removed, by striking repeated blows with a case-knife on the neck of the bottle, at the desired point of separation.

The Hummer.

This is somewhat similar to the toy just described, but even more simple in construction. It consists of a piece of shingle about an inch and one-half wide and five or six inches long, with a string attached to one end. When the hummer is swung around the head it makes a loud, buzzing noise.

CHAPTER XVIII.

BIRD NESTING.

How to Collect and Preserve Eggs.

As regular as the seasons, is the flight of our feathered summer visitors ; and their wonderful little nests can be found, by those who choose to look for them, in all manner of situations—in the grass, in the shrubs, in the trees, on the barren moor, on the face of the rocky cliff, in the sand banks, high up in the church steeple, under the low, overhanging eaves of the farmhouse or among the rafters of the hay-loft. Even the very chimneys of the dwellings are invaded by birds in search of a safe retreat where they can rear their little families undisturbed. Professor Rennie, in speaking of the apparent mechanical knowledge displayed by birds in the construction of their nests, says : " This work is the business of their lives—the duty which calls forth that wonderful ingenuity which no experience can teach and which no human skill can rival. The infinite variety of modes in which nests of birds are constructed, and the exquisite adaptation of the nests to the peculiar habits of the individual, offer a subject of almost exhaustless interest." I trust not one of my readers belong to that class of boys who wantonly destroy and pillage birds' nests, for which offence against good taste and good sense it is hard to find language strong enough to use in condemnation. Nor is it proper to start a collection of birds' eggs as the fancy seizes you, to amuse yourself for a time, afterward allowing the eggs to become broken and forgotten. If you really wish to make a collection of eggs for the purpose of study, there is no harm in taking a few nests and eggs for your cabinet. There are clauses in the game laws of most, if not all, of the States, which grant exceptional privileges to collectors for scientific purposes.

Eggs should be "blown," or emptied of their contents, as soon as collected, the empty shells being much less liable to break than the unblown egg. To blow eggs you should have an egg-drill and blow-pipe, but if such instruments are out of your reach a pin will answer for a drill and your lips for the blow-pipe. Make a very small hole in each end of the egg, and taking it gently between the thumb and forefinger, place one hole to the lips ; then blow, not too hard, but steadily, until the contents come out of the hole at the other end.

The use of the blow-pipe and drill not only simplifies the operation and lessens the chances of breaking the eggs, but it also makes much neater specimens. Hold the egg firmly, but gently, with its ends between the thumb and forefinger of the left hand. Apply the point of the drill to the middle of one side, and, by imparting a twirling motion to the instrument, drill a hole in the egg-shell, filing away the shell gradually until the opening is large enough to admit the end of the blow-pipe, which should fit in the hole loosely, so that when the egg is "blown" the contents of the shell may escape around the end of the pipe. Hold the egg in the left hand, with the hole downward ; insert the small end of the blow-pipe into the hole just drilled. It is often a good plan to force water into the shell through the blow-pipe, and after all the contents have been ejected to thoroughly rinse out the shell.

The drying is an important part of the proceeding ; for this purpose the egg is usually placed in sand, bran or meal. Some authorities claim that this is wrong, as the substances are apt to cake around the hole, where they become damp from the moisture absorbed. I have often found it difficult to remove the caked meal without injuring the shell. A recent writer suggests setting the eggs, hole downward, upon a piece of blot-ting-paper or a soft cloth. The paper or cloth not only absorbs the moisture without sticking to the shell, but, being soft and yielding, the eggs may be rolled about with no fear of breaking, and they may be dried in this manner thoroughly, without rubbing off the color or destroying the "bloom" peculiar to nicely preserved specimens.

A cabinet of eggs is not only an interesting object, but if the owner has collected them himself, he must necessarily acquire an amount of scientific knowledge that will not only at once make him an authority upon ornithology, even among learned men, but at the same time put him ahead of all the boys in wood-craft.

Eggs may be kept in boxes filled with bran or cotton, or they may be gummed on cards and the name of the bird and date of the collection written underneath ; but probably the best way is to keep them in a chest of shallow drawers made for the purpose.

As soon as an egg is collected, number it with a lead pencil, and under a duplicate figure in a note-book write the number of eggs that were in the nest, the date of the collection, name or supposed name of the bird, with any and all other remarks of interest.

Birds' Nests.

A collection of nests makes an ornamental and interesting addition to a cabinet, and some very curious nests may be found. The two-story nest of the summer yellowbird is always an ad-dition, especially if both compartments contain eggs.

The summer yellowbirds, though confiding little creatures, are not readily duped or imposed upon. Their instinct is suffi-ciently near reason for them to detect the difference between their own little fragile, prettily marked, greenish-colored eggs and the great dark-colored ones the vagabond cow blackbird has surreptitiously smuggled into the cosey nest. The domestic little couple cling to the spot selected for their house and will not leave it; neither will they hatch the obnoxious eggs, which they are apparently unable to throw out; but the difficulty is soon surmounted, and so are the gratuitous eggs, for the yellowbirds proceed at once to cover up the cow blackbird's eggs, constructing a new nest on top of the old one, building a second story to their house.

. Last summer Mr. Lang Gibson brought me one of these two-story nests which he found at Flushing, L. I. ; the lower nest contained two cow blackbird's eggs, and the upper one three eggs of the summer yellowbird. Gibson watched the construction of the nest. Visiting it again after it was finished, he discovered the egg of a cow blackbird. Next day two of these eggs occupied the nest. Some time afterward, to his surprise, he found the nest contained three eggs of the yellowbird and no signs of the existence of those deposited by the blackbird, but the nest had the appearance of being much taller than at first, and an examination disclosed it to be a two-story nest, the lower compartment containing two cow-birds' eggs, and the upper part three yellowbirds' eggs. Since writing the above, the same young collector presented me with another double nest. This time both nests were inhabited and contained eggs ; the lower story is a meadow wren's nest with an entrance on one side, and the upper one is the nest of the red-winged or swamp blackbird. The eggs in both compartments were warm when discovered, which proves that they were fresh and that the old birds had not long been absent.

Preserving Nests.

Nests made of woollen fibres must be dusted with fine tobacco, snuff, or camphor, to keep the moths out. Nests made of sticks, straws, etc., will not be attacked by insects, and need no preparation to preserve them.

CHAPTER XIX.

HOW TO REAR WILD BIRDS.

Robins, Thrushes, Wrens, and other Small Birds.

Learn the habits of any creature, and give it a chance to follow them, and you will find but little difficulty in keeping it healthy in confinement.

It is a mistake to suppose that it is a sin to keep wild birds in confinement; for when their wants are understood and attended to with any degree of care, the little creatures soon learn to love their cage, and will, more than likely, return to it of their own free will, if by accident or design they are set at liberty. When you hear it said that it is impossible to domesticate this or that bird, remember that the staid old barn-yard fowl is descended from a bird as wild and shy as any that inhabits the far Western forests. You need not hesitate to attempt to rear and tame any bird that runs or flies, provided that you are thoroughly acquainted with its habits when in a wild state.

Care should be taken to observe the food with which the parent birds feed their young, and if the natural food is difficult to obtain, a healthy substitute can often be discovered by experiment. Do not try, however, to force a young bird to eat that which appears distasteful to it, nor must it be forced to eat when not hungry. The feathered babies, as a rule, are very greedy, and will open wide their mouths as soon as they hear any one approach, so that it is only necessary to drop the food between the widespread bills as often as they are opened.

Squabs.

Doves and pigeons, when young, do not open their mouths like other birds, but they will keep their bills firmly closed and run them between your fingers, flapping their wings and making a whistling noise.

To feed a squab, its mouth must be opened by taking the sides of the bill between the thumb and forefinger of the left hand, and gently pinching it at the base until the mouth opens; then push an oblong pellet of bread softened with milk between the mandibles. You will always be successful in rearing squabs in this manner. Bread softened with sweet milk, or boiled potatoes mixed with eggs, is a healthy diet for many young birds.

The prepared food sold at bird-stores under the name of mocking-bird food I have discovered to be almost universally relished by insectivorous birds after they are old enough to feed themselves. As soon as a young bird can hop around, supply it with plenty of water to bathe in, at least once or twice a day; if you keep your pet's surroundings neat, the bird will not fail to keep its little person tidy and trim. The ground or grass finch will not bathe in water, but performs his ablutions in dust or fine sand, and a supply of sand should be provided.

The Cow Blackbird.

There is often a third party interested in the construction of all small birds' nests—a homeless, happy-go-lucky Bohemian bird, who has a sort of tramp's interest in the housekeeping arrangements of most of the smaller feathered denizens of copse and wood. This is the well-known cow blackbird, who disdains to shackle her freedom with the care of a family, and shifts a mother's responsibility by farming her progeny out, while she seeks the incongruous but apparently congenial companionship of the cattle, with whom she appears to be on the most intimate terms.

The cow-bird deposits its eggs indiscriminately among the nests of smaller birds. The blackbird's eggs generally hatch out a day or two before the adopted mother's own eggs, so when the legitimate members of the family do come, it is to find their nest already occupied by the strong, lusty interlopers, who, on account of their superior size and strength, come in for the lion's share of all the food brought to the nest. Thus the innocent parents rear the aliens, while their own young starve. It is really a pitiable sight to see a couple of little greenlets anxiously searching from daybreak till evening for food to fill the capacious crop of one or more young cow blackbirds considerably larger than the greenlets themselves.

As might be expected, the young cow-bird is an inveterate gormandizer, and you cannot supply it with enough food to stop its cries for more. True to its instinct, when its craw is crammed to its utmost extent, the young pauper will still cry for more and open wide its mouth, for fear its foster brothers and sisters should receive some share of the food. The blackbird wastes all it cannot eat, deliberately throwing the food away by a sudden jerk of the head.

Wrens, Sparrows, and Finches.

Feed young wrens, sparrows, and finches upon chopped worms and the soft parts of grasshoppers. As soon as their bills become hard enough the finches and sparrows may be fed upon bird seed that can be procured at any bird store.

The Bobolink.

Feed young bobolinks upon the soft parts of grasshoppers, and as they grow older and become inclined to corpulency, do not let them have too much to eat, or they will kill themselves.

The Catbird.

The catbird resembles the mocking-bird so closely in its habits that it may be reared upon exactly the same food. I have made several successful attempts at rearing catbirds, and find them amusing and lively pets. One bird, that bore the name of " Greedy," would when called fly from the top of the tallest tree and alight upon my head or shoulder. The catbird will attempt to mimic almost every sound it hears. There is at present a couple of these birds which have a nest near my window. Here they build year after year, they have become quite tame, and the male bird has learned the first two notes of a bugle-call; it is very amusing to hear him struggle to master the rest of the call. When I whistle it to him, he sits on his favorite perch, a low limb of a peach-tree, and holding his head to one side, patiently waits until the call is finished; then filling his lungs, he gives the first two notes with remarkable clearness, hesitates a moment as if undecided what to do next, and ends in a wild burst of song. Often the bird will practise in a low key for ten minutes at a time, but as soon as he sees that he is observed he will commence the scolding cat-cry from which these birds derive their name. The catbird or black-capped thrush requires a large cage and plenty of water for bathing purposes. A food preparation, published first, I think, in *Harper's Bazar*, consists of two-fifths pounded cracker, two-fifths oatmeal, and one-fifth hard-boiled egg; to be thoroughly mixed with equal proportions of milk and water until it is of the consistency of fresh bread.

Robins

are as easily domesticated as the catbird, and can be fed upon almost the same food. Fruit in season is always relished by Bob, and he will kill himself eating it if the quantity is not restricted. A robin that the writer once owned would eat a large slice of watermelon down to the green rind in a single day. Feed the young birds upon the soft parts of the grasshopper, white grub worms, and chopped angle-worms, or if such food cannot be obtained, use the yolk of hard-boiled eggs mixed with stale wheat bread made into a paste with a little milk or water. When the bird grows older the following preparation may be given: One-third stale wheat bread well soaked in water and pressed, one-third dry grated carrot, one-sixth of hard-boiled egg, and one-sixth of bruised hemp-seed. Mix well into a paste.

Robins will acquire a taste for many dishes which in their wild state they could never have eaten. One bird described by a writer in the *Science News* became very fond of hot doughnuts and other equally strange diet.

The Brown Thrush, or Thrasher.

Every country boy is familiar with " the long-tailed thrush," as they call this bird, and all of them know what a graceful bird he is, while, strange to say, but few know that he is an excellent song bird, little inferior to the mocking-bird in that respect. The brown thrush makes a good cage bird, and can be reared and kept upon the same food as that just described for the robin ; their nests are generally found in low bushes among the thickets skirting cultivated ground.

The Wood Thrush

is of a bright brown upon the back, with a light speckled breast and a much shorter tail than the thrasher. Why this bird is called the wood thrush, is a question ; around Flushing, L. I., it is seldom, if ever, seen in the woods proper, but in the ornamental trees on the lawns and the shade trees in the streets of the village this bird makes his home. His song, though rich and full, is short. The wood thrush is easily kept in captivity, and makes a valuable addition to an aviary. The young may be reared upon the same food as that described for the catbird.

Bluebirds

are pretty little creatures, making their appearance in the early spring. They build their nests in hollow trees, knot-holes, or bird-houses erected for that purpose, and have been known to build in a dove-cot, but since the introduction of that noisy little street gamin, the English sparrow, the bluebirds have mostly deserted the immediate neighborhood of the dwellings, and may be found in the orchards and other safe retreats. The bluebird makes an excellent pet, is of a lovable disposition, and will not associate with other birds except of its own kind.

Use about the same food as that described for robins.

The Summer Yellowbird.

While the expanding leaves of tree and shrub retain the tender tints of pink, and the broad lily-pads commence to mosaic the surface of the ponds with green, in perfect harmony with the bursting bud and opening flower comes the summer yellowbird, and from hedge and bush may be heard his song, as simple and pleasing as the tasteful but modest plumage that covers his little person. Almost immediately after the first appearance of these industrious little birds they commence their preparations for housekeeping. The male bird flies busily about selecting such material as feathers, plants, fibres, the furze from ferns, the catkins from willows, and other similar objects, all of which he brings to his mate, who arranges and fashions their delicate nest. So quickly and deftly does this little couple labor that they build the greater part of their house in a single day.

The author has never attempted to rear the summer yellow-bird, nor has he ever seen one in confinement ; but there is no reason why this beautiful warbler should not make as good a cage-bird as any other feathered songster. You may feed the young upon the soft parts of grasshoppers and soft grubs. This much can be learned by watching the parent birds attending to the wants of their tiny offspring.

The Bluejay

is a noisy, showy bird of brilliant plumage, with a pretty crest upon its head ; the bill is black ; the back and wings different shades of blue, with black stripes ; throat, cheeks, and breast light gray ; a black ring around his neck extends like a collar down to his chest.

Although the jay is no musician he is an excellent mimic, and can be taught to crow like a cock, bark like a dog, and to whistle a tune ; he is a large, handsome bird, and looks well in a cage. The only young one the writer ever had was one that had just left its nest. It was caught in an orchard, and thrived upon grubs and worms of all sorts. Either the food described for the robin or the catbird ought to answer also for the blue-jay; an occasional spoonful of raw egg is relished by a young jay.

Want of space will prevent the enumeration of all the feath-ered creatures that make their home in our forests and orchards ; but this chapter will be incomplete if it contains no mention of that most lovely of all American birds, the little feathered mite called a

Humming-Bird.

Even if captured when full grown, this delicate little crea-ture can be tamed in a remarkably short time.

12

Although the writer has been fortunate enough to find several little bunches of the cotton-like substance which forms the nest of the humming-bird, he has captured but one young bird; that one was discovered disconsolately peeping as it sat upon a smooth stone in the middle of a Kentucky stream.   Upon the overhanging branch of a button-wood tree there was a little lump which was at once recognized as a humming-bird's nest, but so closely did it approach the branch in texture and color, that it might have been passed by unobserved had it not been for the otherwise unaccountable appearance of the little feathered midget upon the stone directly under it.   The young bird, when picked up, did not offer to fly, but opened its long, slender bill and made a peeping noise, eagerly swallowing some little insects that were put into its mouth.   It was not long before the parent birds commenced buzzing around the author's head like enraged bumble-bees; they even flew against his face, nor did they leave him until he had set their offspring free.

A writer in *Chambers's Journal* upon this subject says:

"It was long thought that humming-birds would not live in confinement; and this idea is so far correct that, although easily tamed, they will not live long in captivity if fed only on syrup.   If confined to this food they die in a month or two, apparently starved; whereas, if kept in a small room, the windows of which are covered with fine net, so as to allow insects to enter, they may be preserved for a considerable time in health and beauty.   Their nests are very curious; many of them are cup-shaped and very small, sometimes no larger than the half of a walnut shell; and they are often beautifully decorated on the outside with lichens, so as exactly to resemble the branch in the fork of which they are placed.   They are formed of cottony substances, and are lined inside with fibres as fine and soft as silk.   The nests of other species are hammock-shaped, and are suspended to creepers; the Pichincha humming-bird has been known to attach its nest to a straw-rope hanging in a shed; their eggs are white, and they never lay more than one or two. Once, when on the Amazon, Mr. Wallace had a nest of young humming-birds brought to him, which he tried to feed on syrup, supposing that they would be fed on honey by their parents. To his surprise, however, they not only would not swallow the liquid, but nearly choked themselves in their efforts to eject it. He then caught some very small flies, and dropped one into the wide-open mouth of the poor little orphan humming-bird; it closed instantly with a satisfied gulp, and opened again for more. The little creatures, he found, demanded fifteen or twenty flies each in succession before they were satisfied; and the process of feeding and fly-catching together required so much time that he was reluctantly compelled to abandon them to their fate."

The Illustration has been drawn by the writer from a compound yellowbird's nest. The upper story or nest is partly lifted so as to show the cow blackbird's eggs in the nest below.

CHAPTER XX.

HOW TO REAR WILD BIRDS—Continued.

The Crow, Hawk, and other Large Birds.

"I want my Ma!"

A FUZZY topknot surmounting a head too heavy for the slender neck to hold upright; large, protruding eyes protected by lids that are tightly gummed together; a bluish black skin, with no feathers to hide the wrinkles; a large paunch like an alderman. Such is the appearance of a very young crow; and after a glance at the accompanying sketch, drawn from nature, the reader will no doubt agree with the writer in calling it the worst looking "baby in the woods," and if mischief be a sign of badness, then "Jim Crow" does not belie his looks. He is especially comical when his great blood-red mouth is expanded to its utmost dimension in expectancy as he awaits a morsel of food.

Of all our native birds the crow is probably the hardiest, and the least trouble to bring up by hand. Almost any kind of soft food, bread and milk, corn meal mush, grub worms, raw lean meat, or raw liver is devoured with relish by the black baby ; any of the foods described in the preceding chapter may be fed to the crow. As soon as he is able to walk " Jim " will begin to learn to eat without help. The feathers will by this time have grown, covering the body with a suit of glossy black, which gives the bird a very genteel and respectable appearance. The crow ought never to be confined in a cage, but allowed to wander around at will.

The first crow that came into the author's possession had scarcely escaped from its egg-shell prison before it was taken from the cradle of rough sticks that the parent birds had built near the top of a pine tree.

The bird was christened Billy, and from morn until night the neighbors could hear him as he loudly clamored for food. Before school-time in the morning an egg was broken and the contents of the shell dropped into William's great red mouth ; with a gobbling noise the egg would be swallowed ; then as if sat-isfied for the present he would settle down for a nap. During the noonday recess, Billy, with his red mouth wide open, was always loudly calling for his noontime meal, which consisted of the same material as his breakfast and supper. Three eggs a day kept the little black rascal fat and healthy, and it was not long before the naked little body was covered with a coating of glossy black feathers, and Billy, abandoning the old basket which had served him for a nest, now awaited his master's return from school, perched upon the iron railing fence of the front yard. From eggs to fresh liver was an easy step, and one that the bird gladly took. Corn he never ate unless it was in the form of " Johnny-cake " or mush ; stale meat was his detestation ; in fact, a cleaner or more dainty bird in regard to his food was never reared. Billy was not long in making a name and reputation for himself ; a more affectionate and mischievous imp never

wore a coat of black or buried silver thimbles in a flower bed.
Although his pranks were often very annoying, they were always
amusing, and no one ever thought the less of the bird for stealing
all the fish from the miniature pond, nor did his master's anger,
though great, cause him to administer severe punishment to the
black culprit when he discovered the fish all neatly stowed away
under the shingles of the rabbit house. When the young rabbits were discovered nicely pressed between the leaves of some
books of travel just purchased, the gentleman to whom the books
belonged declared war. He went to the lawn to search for
Billy, and the bird flew to him, and, alighting upon his shoulder
in the most fearless and confident manner, commenced a long
explanation of his misdeeds in the crow language. What he
said was unintelligible; but the gentleman's anger was not only
mollified but changed to mirth, for he came back to the house
laughing heartily. Billy, still perching upon his shoulders,
seemingly enjoyed the situation.

Since the writer's first experiment he has brought up several

other crows successfully upon a diet
of fresh meat, bread and milk, and
boiled potatoes mixed with eggs.

The Hawk.

Naturally possessed of a wild,
fierce nature, loving the open air and
the wide, blue sky, the hawk is a

Strap for Hawk's Leg.   born freebooter; but wild and fierce
as he is, he may nevertheless be perfectly tamed if taken from
the nest when quite young.

After you have obtained a young hawk, make it a rule
to always feed it yourself and never allow any one else to do
so. Give a peculiar whistle (in the same manner) each time
you feed it, and the bird will learn to know the signal and come

at the call. Keep the hawk in your company as much as possible, and when you can, set its perch where it will see the people around the house, and become accustomed to their presence ; by this means the bird may be taught not to fear man, and it will soon become as harmless as any small cage-bird.

Feed young hawks upon fresh lean meat of any kind. When they grow older they develop a fondness for rats, mice, and small birds. Do not trouble yourself about their drinking-water, as they do not need it.

The Hawk as a " Scare-crow."

A tame hawk is very useful in keeping the chickens out of the garden. Whenever the writer has placed the perch with his pet hawk upon it in the garden, not a chicken has dared to enter the enclosure ; they all seem to know their enemy by instinct, and give it a wide berth.

The hawk himself seems to know when he is doing guard duty, and will sit as motionless as a statue, his head sunk down upon his shoulders, but the keen, bright eyes survey the whole field, and not an object moves that they do not see.

The Hawk as a Decoy.

If you want to trap other birds a tame hawk is a very valuable assistant. At any convenient spot set your bird traps, near by fasten the hawk, and retire a little distance ; it will not be many minutes before the small birds will discover their dreaded enemy, and from bush and tree the spunky little feathered warriors will come to give battle. In a few moments the ground and air around the hawk will be filled with robins, catbirds, blackbirds, sparrows, yellowbirds, thrushes, wrens, and even the tiny humming-bird, making up in grit what he lacks in size, will join the other birds in their war against a common foe. In the confusion and bustle that ensues some of the small birds are sure to enter a trap or become entangled in a snare, and must be removed before they injure themselves in struggling to regain their freedom. As soon as you retire a little distance the small birds will again commence their war upon the pet hawk, who is thoroughly competent to take care of himself, so you can devote your whole attention to your traps. As a pet the hawk is a pretty bird, and always charms spectators by his bold, military bearing and his bright, clear eyes.

Owls

the author has found inclined to be more wild and untamable than hawks and not so interesting. Even the little screech-owls are vicious and treacherous, snapping their small bills in a savage way whenever they are approached. A friend sends word that he has been more successful, and has even succeeded in taming the great Virginia horned owl, which was allowed to fly around with perfect freedom. "Bubo" would fly all over the village but return at meal times ; he would come at a call and knew his master, obeying him even to the extent of letting go his hold of a pet bobolink when commanded to do so. The bobolink, though a little bruised, was otherwise unhurt, and soon recovered from the effects of being caught in the dreaded talons of "Bubo."

Sea Birds.

Any of the guillemot tribe will do well if kept in an enclosure where there is room for them to run about. The author has seen numbers of tame sea birds, although he never attempted to rear one himself, and would advise the reader not to try unless he has plenty of room. Sea birds are strange creatures, and their characteristics are so well portrayed by a writer for *The London Field* that part of the amusing article is here given in the writer's own words :

" I have been forced to banish a couple of herring gulls, as they persist in tearing up the grass by the roots. Some few years back I had a third of the same species, named 'Sims Reeves' (all the birds are named, so that I can give directions for special treatment to any particular individual during my absence) ; but he asserted his authority over the other two, 'Moody' and 'Sankey,' in such an overbearing manner— driving them round and round the pond, the two poor wretches meekly trotting in front of him, while he every now and then gave vent to the most melancholy and piercing screams—that, as I found they would not live peaceably to- gether, Sims Reeves was allowed to go with his wing unclipped, and in due course took his departure. No sooner had he gone than Moody at once became 'boss,' and the last state of poor Sankey was no better than the first. At times they were quiet and contented enough ; resting side by side on the grass, they appeared to be the best of friends. Without the slightest warning, however, Moody would arise, and when he had cleared his throat by a preliminary 'caterwaul,' the submis- sive Sankey, having learned by experience that it would not do to be caught, would be up and off. Then, with his head drawn back between his shoulders and his feathers slightly puffed out, Moody would follow in his wake. For an hour or so this mournful procession, round and round the pond, would con- tinue. At last Moody would stop, Sankey also pulling up at the distance of a yard or two. Moody leading, they would then commence a duet *à la* tomcat, when, suddenly dropping on their breasts on the ground, they would turn rapidly round several times, and at last attack the grass in the most excited manner, tearing it up by the roots and scattering the fragments in every direction. This proceeding is accompanied by the most melancholy cries and screams, and when it is stated that the voice of Grimalkin in his happiest, or rather his unhappiest

moods, is almost sweet and pleasing to the ear compared with
the discordant wailing of these infatuated birds, one may judge
of the nature of their performance. Whether these antics are
intended for courtship or defiance I am perfectly ignorant, but
I have observed pewits acting in much the same manner. At
first I imagined the bird was forming its nest (I was in a punt
at about ten yards' distance), but on examining the spot on the
following day I found no marks, and then came to the conclu-
sion that the bird was either showing himself off for the admi-
ration of the female, who was close by, or else bidding defiance
to another male, which I could plainly see indulging in the
same performance at a short distance. I have not the slightest
doubt that gulls, and every species of sea bird, might, with
proper attention and food, be so thoroughly reconciled to confinement that they would nest and rear their young."

Strange Domestic Fowls.

In a small town situated in the interior of Georgia there
lives a queer sort of sporting character, who has, or did
have a few years ago, the strangest collection of fowls in his
chicken-yard that it has ever been my fortune to see. I was
strolling along a side street in the town when my attention was
attracted by the sight of a large black bear chained to the
door-post of a small frame tavern. While watching the huge
beast, I was accosted by the proprietor, and invited into the
barn-yard to see his " chickens," which he was about to feed.
The invitation was accepted. At the first call of chick! chick!
there came flying and running a curious assortment of fowls,
tumbling over each other in their greedy haste. There were
ducks, geese, and chickens like those to be seen in any farm-
yard, but mingled with these were wild geese, mud hens, partridges, and beautiful little wood ducks; the latter seemed
tamer than the domestic species. Towering above all the other

fowls, flapping his wings, and making a loud metallic noise, was a great long-legged, red-headed crane.   I afterward learned that the wild geese and ducks had their wings clipped, for, although they may be perfectly tame, these birds are very liable to fly away in the autumn when they see or hear their wild "cousins" and their "aunts" flying overhead.   I give this little experience to show the boys that any bird may be domesticated if its habits and wants are understood ; of course, it is always best to take young birds for the purpose.

CHAPTER XXI.

HOME-MADE HUNTING APPARATUS, ETC.

Spearing Fish.

"I DON'T know! Shure I *niver tried*," is the answer reported to have been made by an Irishman, when asked if he could play the fiddle. No doubt there are many boys who would give a like reply if asked if they could spear a fish.

An amateur's first attempt at casting a spear will probably meet with about the same success as "Paddy" might be expected to achieve in his first trial of a fiddle; but almost anything can be accomplished by practice. The keen enjoyment of the fisher who by his skill and dexterity has succeeded in striking a fine fish, can only be compared to the pleasant triumph of his brother sportsman in the field who has just secured two birds by a difficult double-shot.

How to Make a Fish Spear.

Make the shaft or handle of any straight stick or pole seven or eight feet long; trim it down, and test the weight occasionally by balancing it in the hand. When the shaft seems to be about the proper weight, it should be let alone, and attention directed to the barbs for the head of the spear.

In place of the ordinary single point generally used as a spear head, the fishing spear may be supplied with two points, as shown in the illustration (Fig. 121, p. 189). Any hard, elastic material will do for the head, split bamboo or cane, two pieces of heavy iron wire, filed to a point and notched into barbs upon the inside, as shown in the diagram, or the points may be made of bone like the fish arrows used by the inhabitants of Vancouver's Island. Very hard wood will also answer for the spear head. After the head pieces are notched and pointed, they should be firmly bound to the spear at a point a few inches below the end of the shaft. A couple of small wedges driven in between the shaft and the points will diverge the latter, as in the illustration. After this is accomplished, lash the barbs firmly on up to the head of the shaft. If a fish be struck by one of these weapons, it will be next to impossible for it to escape. The elastic points at first suddenly spread apart as the spear strikes the fish's body; the next instant they violently contract, holding the fish a secure prisoner. The barbs upon the inside prevent the prey from slipping out, no matter how smooth and slimy his body may be.

A small instrument made upon a similar plan can be used for catching snakes or other reptiles that are not safe or pleasant to handle. Frogs may also be readily captured with a fish spear, and any boy who takes the time to make one of these weapons will find himself amply repaid for his trouble. The elder stick described and illustrated upon page 34 is made upon the same principle as the fish spear.

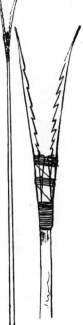

FIG. 121.—Fish Spear and Enlarged View of Spear Head.

Armed with fish spears and torches great fun can be had spearing fish from a row-boat at night. The torch illuminates the water and appears to dazzle the fish, at the same time disclosing their whereabouts to the occupants of the boat, who with poised spears await a favorable opportunity to strike the scaly game.

How to Make the Torches and Jack-Lights.

One way to make a torch is to wind lamp-wick upon a forked stick (Fig. 122). The ball of wick must be thoroughly saturated with burning fluid of some kind. The torches should all be prepared before starting upon the excursion.

Never take a supply of kerosene or any explosive oil with you in the boat, for, in the excitement of the sport, accidents of the most serious nature may happen. A safe light can be made with a number of candles set in a box. A glass front allows the light to shine through, and a piece of bright tin for a reflector behind adds brilliancy to the illumination. A box of this description is generally called a "jack-box;" it is much less trouble than the flaring pine-knot or wick-ball torches.

The candles in the "jack-box" should be replenished each time after it is used; in this manner the jack may be kept always ready for use. After the candles are lighted fasten the box in the bow of the boat; here it will throw a bright light ahead, illuminating the water, but casting a heavy, dark shadow in the boat, concealing the occupants from view. The boys in the boat can, of course, see all the better for being themselves in shadow.

FIG. 122.—Wick-torch.

The Boomerang.

We might expect strange weapons to come from a land that produces quadrupeds with heads like ducks, and other great beasts that go bounding over the plains like some immense species of jumping spiders, using their thick tails as a sort of spring to help them in leaping, and carrying their young in their fur-lined vest pockets! Nor will we be disappointed when, after viewing the duckbill and the kangaroo, we see the odd-looking clubs called boomerangs, or the simple but in-

genious throw-sticks by means of which the native Australians are enabled to cast their weapon, with the greatest accuracy, an astonishingly long distance.

The boomerang, or bommerang as it is sometimes called,
is one of the most mysterious weapons known. Evolved by
slow degrees from a simple war club by the ignorant and savage Australians, this instrument excites the interest and aston-
ishes the civilized man by its strange and apparently unaccountable properties. To all appearances it is a simple, roughly
hewn club, yet its movements when thrown by an expert hand
are so eccentric as to make it a curious anomaly even to persons educated in natural philosophy. Whatever is wonderful or
marvellous is always a subject of peculiar interest to mankind
generally, but to boys an inexplicable natural phenomenon is a
treasure-trove of immeasurable value.

How to Make a Boomerang.

With boiling water scald a piece of well-seasoned elm, ash,
or hickory plank that is free from knots. Allow the wood to
remain in the water until
it becomes pliable enough
to bend into the form
indicated by Fig. 123.
When it has assumed the
proper curve, nail on the
side pieces A, A (Fig.
123) to hold the wood in

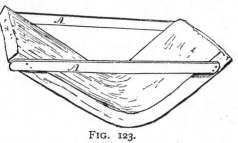

FIG. 123.

position until it is thoroughly dry; after which the side pieces
may be removed, with no fear that the plank will not retain the
curve imparted.

Saw the wood into as many pieces as it will allow (Fig. 124
B), and each piece will be a boomerang in the rough that only

needs to be trimmed up with a pocket-knife, and scraped smooth with a piece of broken glass to make it a finished weapon.

A large wood-rasp or file is of great assistance in shaping the implement. Fig. 124 C shows a finished boomerang. Fig.

124 D shows a cross section of the same. The curve in no two boomerangs is exactly the same; some come round with a graceful sweep, while others bend so suddenly in the middle that they have more the appearance of angles than curves. Just what the quality is that makes a good boomerang is hard to discover, although, as a rule, the one that appears to have the best balance and feels as if it might be thrown easily is the best.

FIG. 124.

To Throw a Boomerang,

grasp the weapon near one end and hold it as you would a club; be careful to have the concave side, or hollow curvature, turned from you and the convex side toward you. Take aim at a stone, tuft of grass or other object on the ground about a hundred yards in front of you, and throw the weapon at the object. The weapon will in all probability not go anywhere near the mark, but, soaring aloft, perform some of the most extraordinary manœuvres, then starting off again with apparently renewed velocity, either return to the spot from where it was thrown or go sailing off over the fields like a thing possessed of life. A boomerang cast by a beginner is very dangerous in a crowd, for there is no telling where it is going to alight, and when it does come down it sometimes comes with force enough to cut a small dog almost in two.* Select a large open field where the ground is soft and there is no one around to be hurt. In such a field you may amuse yourself by the day throwing these curious weapons, and you can in this manner learn how to make the boomerang go through all manner of the most indescribable movements seemingly at your bidding.

The Miniature Boomerang

here represented is supposed to be cut out of a card. The shape given in the illustration is a very good one, but it may be varied to an almost unlimited degree. Card boomerangs over an inch or so in length do not work well, but they may be made very much smaller.

One of these tiny instruments cannot be grasped by the hand, but when it is to be launched upon its eccentric journey the toy should be laid flat upon a card, allowing one end to project from the side as in Fig. 125. Take hold of the lower left hand corner of the card with the left hand, and with the forefinger of the right hand fillip the boomerang, striking it a quick, smart blow with the finger-nail, and the little missile will sail away, going through almost the same manœuvres that the large wooden boomerang does when thrown from the hand.

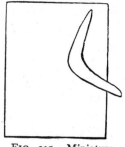

FIG. 125.—Miniature Boomerang.

Small boomerangs can be whittled out of a shingle with a pocket knife, and considerable amusement had with them ; these small affairs can be thrown on the crowded playground, where it would be exceedingly dangerous to experiment with the larger and heavier club before described.

---

* "I have seen a dog killed on the spot, its body being nearly cut in two by the boomerang as it fell."—Rev. J. G. Wood.

The Whip-Bow.

This graceful and powerful weapon is like an ordinary long-bow, with the exception that the bow-string is made fast to but one end, after the manner of a whip-lash ; where the whip-lash

Position Assumed when Casting the Arrow.

terminates in a "snapper," the bow-string ends in a hard, round knot (Fig. 126) ; the arrow is made like any other arrow, either with a blunt end or a pointed spear-point. In one side of the arrow a notch is cut (Fig. 126, A) ; the bow-string being slipped into this notch, the knot at the end of the string prevents the arrow from slipping off until thrown by the archer, who, taking the butt of the whip-bow in his right hand, holds the arrow at the notch with his left hand, as in the illustration ; then swaying his body from side to side, he suddenly lets go with his left hand, at the same time extending his right arm to its full length from his side ; this not only gives the arrow all the velocity it would acquire

FIG. 126.—Whip Bow.

from the bow, but adds the additional force of a sling, thus sending the projectile a greater distance. The only place that I have seen the whip-bow used is on the lake shore in Northern Ohio. In some parts of this section it used to be a great favorite among the boys, who would throw the arrows up per-pendicularly an amazing distance. Arrows can be bought in any city, but most boys prefer to make their own, leaving the "store arrows" for the girls to use with their pretty "store bows." The essential quality in an arrow is straightness. A spear-head can be made of an old piece of hoop-iron, a broken blade of a knife, or any similar piece of iron or steel, by grind-ing it down to the proper form and then binding it on to the shaft with fish line, silk, or a "waxed end," such as shoe-makers use, or the arrow may have a blunt end with a sharp-pointed nail in the head. These arrows should only be used in target practice or when after game ; they are dangerous on the play-ground. A simple whip-bow may be made by any boy in a few minutes out of an elastic sapling or branch, and an arrow cut out of a pine shingle with a pocket-knife. This can be improved upon as much as may be de-sired by substituting a piece of straight-grained, well-seasoned wood for the green branch, and regularly made Indian arrows for the crude pine ones.

Throw-Sticks.

The same race that invented the wonderful boomerang also originated the equally ingen-ious throw-stick illustrated by Fig. 127, page 196. Although any of my readers can, in a few

Using the Throw-Stick.

moments, fashion a throw-stick from a piece of wood by the aid of a pocket-knife, I doubt if they could use the instrument to any advantage without considerable practice.

Make the lance of cane or bamboo; use a straight piece and put an arrow-head upon one end; then holding the lance on a throw-stick, as shown by the accompanying illustration, cast it with all your might. The first trials will, doubtless, be failures, but nothing is gained without practice; and when you once "catch the hang of the thing"

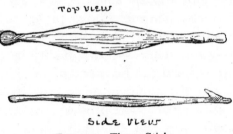

TOP VIEW

SIDE VIEW

FIG. 127.—Throw-Sticks.

you will be astonished to see what a distance a comparatively small boy can throw a spear. Any straight, thin stick may be used as a lance. Allow one end to rest against the point upon the throw-stick, which will hold it in place until the cast is made. The throw-stick acts as a sling, lending additional force to the arm, and sending the spear much further than the strongest man can cast it with his unaided hand.

The Bird-Bolas.

Probably all of my readers have read of that wonderful sling called a "bolas," used by some tribes of savages for the capture of game, but I doubt if any of them ever tried to manufacture one for themselves. Yet this curious missile can be made by a boy, and if he be inclined to field sports, he will find that a bird-bolas will do considerable execution.

Hunt for a half dozen round stones about the size of large marbles, or, better still, take six leaden musket-balls,

FIG. 128.—Bird-Bolas.

wrap each ball in a piece of an old kid glove, buckskin, or

cloth, as shown by the diagram (a, b, Fig. 128). Take three pieces of string each five feet long, double them in the centre, and bind the doubled parts together; a few small feathers may be bound in to add a finished and Indian look to the bolas. To the ends of the strings attach the bullets (Fig. 128). To cast the bolas, grasp it by the feathered part with the thumb and first finger, whirl it around your head as you would an ordinary sling. When you let go, the loaded ends of the strings will fly apart, so that the missile will cover a space in the air of five feet in diameter. If a string strike a bird it will instantly wrap itself round and round the body; if the loaded end strike the game it will, of course, stun or disable it. One of these instruments cast into a flock of birds is certain to bring down several.

For target practice, use in the place of the ordinary butt a number of reeds or sticks stuck upright in the ground about a foot apart; after measuring the distance for the marksman to stand and marking the spot, let him see how many reeds he can level at a single cast of the bolas. The one who makes the biggest score can assume the title of " Big Injun," and wear a feather in his hat, or an appropriate badge, until some more skilled hand beats the record and wins the title and the badge. No shots should count unless made in a regularly appointed match.

The Elastic Cross-Bow.

(A NEW KIND OF CROSS-BOW.)

Select a piece of thick pine or cedar plank and saw out a piece of the form shown by A, Fig. 129. Trim it down with a jack-knife until it becomes more finished and gun-like in appearance. With a gouge, such as may be borrowed at any carpenter or cabinet-maker's shop, cut a half round groove from the butt to the muzzle of the barrel. The groove must be perfectly straight and true (B, Fig. 129). Bore a hole in the piece (E), for the bow to fit in. The bow in this case should be made perfectly stiff, so as not to bend in the least when the line is drawn and the gun set. The bow may be bent into the proper form by steeping it in boiling water until the wood becomes pliable, and binding it firmly into the required position. After it

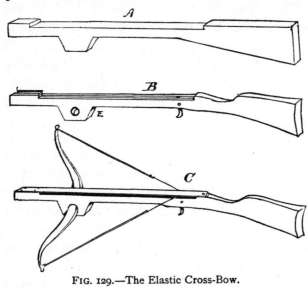

has become perfectly d r y t h e wood will retain the form and the bindings may be cut off. Trim the bow nicely into shape, and make it of such size that it will *not* *b e n d* when the string is drawn. Fit the bow into place, not like an ordinary cross-bow but in a re-

FIG. 129.—The Elastic Cross-Bow.

versed position, as shown by the diagram C, Fig. 129. It might be an improvement to set the bow back toward the stock an inch or two further than the one in the illustration. For a bow-line use two pieces of strong elastic, with a string for a centre piece. The centre cord prevents the bow-line from wearing out as soon as it would if it were all elastic (Fig. 129, C). Make the trigger in the manner described for the plunger pistol (Fig. 134, page 204), but instead of fastening it upon one side with a screw, set it in a slot cut for the purpose in the middle of the barrel near the stock, and let it move freely upon a pivot.

Cut a thin, smooth piece of pine just long and wide enough to cover the gun-barrel from stock to muzzle, and fasten it on with a couple of small brads at the muzzle and a screw at the stock (Fig. 129, C).

There is always a certain amount of danger attending the use of firearms which is avoided by the cross-bow, added to which advantage is the fact that the twang a bow-string makes is so slight a noise as not to alarm the game, and if the young sportsman be inexperienced he may shoot several times at the same bird or rabbit without frightening it away. With a little practice it is astonishing what precision of aim can be obtained with the cross-bow. I know boys who seldom

FIG. 130.—Elastic Sling.

miss a bird even with the simple elastic sling, consisting of two pieces of rubber bands attached to a forked or a straight stick (Fig. 130).

Hunter's Cabin.

CHAPTER XXII.

HOW TO MAKE BLOW-GUNS, ELDER GUNS, ETC.

THE fierce and savage head hunters of Borneo go to war armed with the same implements with which the school-boys shoot peas or pellets of clay at unsuspecting citizens as they pass the ambuscade of tree or fence. The blow-guns used by the Dyaks of Borneo are called sumpitans, and instead of clay balls they carry poisoned arrows. A spear is also attached to the side of one end of the sumpitan, after the manner of a bayonet on a modern rifle. In speaking of the sumpitan a recent writer says : " This curious weapon is about eight feet in length and not quite an inch in diameter, and is bored with the greatest accuracy, a task that occupies a long time, the wood being very hard and the interior of the sumpitan smooth and even polished. It is not always made of the same wood. The surface is of equal thickness from end to end." Among the South American Indians the sumpitan is represented by the long delicate " pucuna," or the heavy and unwieldy " zarabatana." All savages use poisoned arrows in their blow-guns instead of harmless pellets of clay or putty. Taking a few hints from the primitive warriors and hunters of Borneo and South America, any boy, with a little care and small expense, can construct for himself a blow-gun which will be handy to carry around and will shoot with great accuracy. Mr. W. Hamilton Gibson, the well-known artist, has acquired such skill with the blow-gun that he seldom misses the mark, and often brings home birds and other creatures brought down by a clay pellet blown from a glass sumpitan.

For twenty-five cents a glass tube, three or four feet long, can be purchased. With these tubes can be made the best of blow-guns, but they are objectionable on account of being liable to break at any moment from some accidental blow or jar. With some flannel or woollen cloth and an old piece of cane fishing-pole a cover and a case can be made to enclose the glass and prevent its being broken by anything short of a severe knock or fall.

To Make a Blow-Gun.

Select a good straight piece of glass tube about three or four feet long. To discover whether the glass tube is straight or not, hold it horizontally level with the eye and look through it, and any deviation will be quickly seen. Wrap the tube with strips of flannel or woollen cloth, as illustrated by Fig. 131, A. The

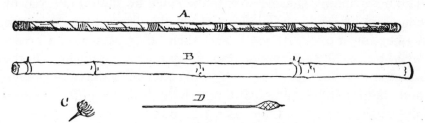

FIG. 131.—The Hunter's Blow-Gun.

cloth will make a soft covering or cushion for the outside of the glass and render it less liable to break. With a red-hot iron rod, or some similar instrument, enlarge the hollow in the centre of a piece of cane until the blow-gun can be slid inside the cane. With putty, shoemakers' wax or beeswax secure the tips of the tube in place. Trim off the ends of the cane until they are flush with the ends of the glass. You will then have a blow-gun that can be used to hunt with (B, Fig. 131). For missiles may be used arrows, tacks, peas, or clay. The arrows must be very small, and a pin with its head filed off makes a simple point ; some raw cotton bound on the butt end to make it fit the inside of the gun finishes the missile (Fig. 131, D). The tack is prepared by fastening short pieces of worsted or carpet ravellings to it just below the head with shoemakers' or beeswax (C, Fig. 131).

This not only fills up the space inside the blow-gun, making it fit, but the yarn also acts as a feather does upon an arrow and causes the tack to fly straight and point foremost. The worsted-headed tack is a " tip-top " missile for target practice. The clay pellet will bring down small birds, stunning them, but doing them no serious injury, so that if the birds are quickly picked up they can be captured alive.

Along the Mississippi River, from New Orleans to Nashville, there are still some remnants of the Indians that in olden times paddled their canoes up and down the Father of Waters. The boys among these tribes make splendid blow-guns out of cane. When the inside is bored out they straighten the cane by heating it over hot coals, and then, after attaching a heavy weight to one end, suspending it by a string attached to the other end. The heat from the hot coals makes the cane pliable, and before it becomes cold and hard, the weights make it almost as straight and true as a rifle-barrel.

Squirt-Guns.

Some time during the summer of each year a boy used to appear with a squirt-gun made of a piece of cane. Squirt-gun-time then commenced, next day four or five guns might be seen on the play-grounds, and before a week had passed the curb-stone in front of the little frame school-house presented a line of boys all busily engaged in seeing who could shoot the greatest distance ; the dusty macadamized street registered every drop of water by a muddy spot. I found that by adding a quill as a nozzle to my "squirt" it would throw water much further than the others. It is a very simple thing to make a good squirt-gun, and one may be manufactured in a few minutes.

First cut a joint from a piece of an old cane fishing-pole, being careful not to disturb the pithy substance that almost closes the hollow at the joints. Insert a quill for a nozzle at one of the joints and see that it fits tightly; leave the other end open. With your pocket-knife fashion from a piece of pine or cedar the plunger (B, Fig. 132); leave the wood

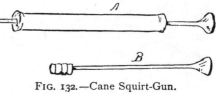

FIG. 132.—Cane Squirt-Gun.

a little thicker at both ends and wrap a rag around one end, making it just thick enough to fit snugly in the cane after wetting it. This completes the "squirt" (A, Fig. 132). To use it, immerse the quill in water, first push the plunger in, then draw it out slowly until the gun is filled with water. Take aim, and when you push the plunger back again the water will issue from the quill in a sudden stream, travelling quite a distance. One of these water-guns is quite useful in the garden; by its means the insects infesting the rose bushes and other shrubs may be knocked off in no time. When the owner of an aquarium finds dead animals or plants that should be removed, located in some crack or cranny that is difficult to reach, the squirt-gun is just the thing to dislodge the objects without disturbing the surrounding rocks or plants.

FIG. 133.—A Simple Elder-Gun.

Elder-Guns and Pistols.

When the author was a very small boy he was taught by some playmates to make an elder gun, a simple contrivance, made of a piece of elder or any other hollow stick. A long

notch cut in one side admits a spring made of whalebone (Fig.
133). By pushing the spring back the short arrow shown in
the illustration can be propelled quite a distance. If instead
of the awkward whalebone spring a piece of elastic be used, a

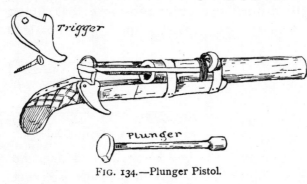

much neater gun
can be m a d e.
Fig. 134 shows
a pistol made
with an elder bar-
rel and a stock
of pine. A plun-
ger, similar in
many respects to
the one used in

FIG. 134.—Plunger Pistol.

the squirt-gun, is made with an edge to catch in the trigger.
An elastic band is bound to the barrel with string, and the
loop fastened to the butt end of the plunger. When the latter
is drawn back to the trigger it stretches the elastic. By pulling
the trigger toward you it loosens the plunger, which flies back
with a snap, sending the arrow out with considerable force.
The barrel of the pistol may be fastened to the stock by two
strips of tin or leather. The diagram shows the form of the trigger, which should
be made so as to
m o v e readily
backward or for-
ward upon the
screw that fastens
it to the stock.

FIG. 135.—Pistol without a Plunger.

Fig. 135 shows how a pistol can be made to work without a
plunger. In this case the barrel is partly cut off from A to B.
The arrow should be made to fit in the groove, so that when the
elastic is loosened it will strike the arrow in the same manner

that the string of a cross-bow does. Both these pistols, if made with good, strong elastic, will shoot quite a distance, and if the arrows are armed with a tack or pin in the head they can be used in target practice. We now come to a gun in which the spring is the principal part.

The Spring Shot-Gun.

A certain old gentleman was at one time very much annoyed by fine bird-shot which at all times of the day came rattling against the window-panes of his study. Being somewhat of a philosopher, the old man at last became deeply interested in investigating the cause of his annoyance. From the window he could see a house separated from his study by a deep back yard, a vacant lot, and another yard. While peering out between the blinds of his window he saw a boy appear at one of the windows of the distant house ;

Spring Shot-gun.

the boy held something in his left hand which he pulled with his right; almost instantly there was a rattling of bird-shot against the old gentleman's window glass, and the boy disappeared. But so great was the distance that separated the two houses that it was impossible for the old man to distinguish what sort of an instrument the mischievous lad used to propel the fine shot so far and with such force. The youngster was at last waylaid, and the mystery solved. The machine used proved to be a spring shot-gun. No powder or explosive is used with one of these guns, neither does it possess stock, trigger, or sights, but simply consists of a stick of whalebone or any other elastic material, one end of which is armed with a large quill, corked at its lower end.

When the quill is filled with fine bird-shot and the end of the stick grasped by the left hand, the contents of the quill can be thrown an amazing distance by bending the quill end back and allowing it to suddenly fly forward, upon the principle of the whip bow. If instead of a small piece of whalebone a large and very elastic rod be used, with a tin tube in the place of the quill, an effective weapon will be produced useful for hunting and collecting purposes; although the shot cast from the tube will have sufficient force to stun a small bird, it will not injure the specimen by making ugly holes in the skin and staining the feathers with blood. All of the weapons described in this and other chapters should be used with care, for many of them are capable of inflicting severe wounds. Never aim a bended bow with arrow set at a companion or friend, for a little slip may cause irreparable harm. Even a blunt arrow propelled from a barrel-hoop bow has sufficient force to destroy an eye or make a severe bruise. A true sportsman has the greatest respect for his weapons and handles them with scrupulous care.

Autumn.

CHAPTER XXIII.

TRAPS AND TRAPPINGS.

SUMMER is over. Again the air becomes cooler. The straw hats are discarded, so also are the linen suits ; we begin to look up heavier clothing, for although the sun still shines brightly, the nights are growing chill. Even at midday we no longer seek the shady side of the streets or roadways.

In the woods all the little inhabitants are preparing for the approaching winter. Backward and forward, from the beech tree to his nest under the wood-pile, runs the nimble little brown-coated, striped-back chipmunk, each trip adding to the pile of beech nuts secreted in the storehouse of this provident little fellow. Scampering along the top rail of the fence the gray squirrel may be seen, also busily engaged in laying up a supply of winter stores. The birds are gathering in large flocks, with noisy twitterings and excited flutterings, preparatory to their yearly pilgrimage to the Sunny South. The bouncing hare is thinking of discarding its summer coat of brown and donning its white winter furs. The leaves of the ivy vines shine like red fire wreathed around the tree trunks. All nature seems busy going through a transformation scene—an air of preparation is visible everywhere.

The reports of the sportsmen's guns may be heard, and their dogs may be seen in the stubble-fields manœuvreing like well-drilled soldiers promptly obeying every command of their masters.

And far and wide—in the cold Northern regions, in the pine woods of Maine, in the Rocky Mountains of the West—the hardy trappers are busy collecting their traps and making preparations, or are already engaged in their annual campaign against all fur-bearing animals.

In order that my reader may not be behind the season, this chapter is devoted to the description of a few simple but effective traps and snares, such as may be made of the material always at hand, with the aid of a pocket-knife, hatchet, or other tools within the reach of boys.

Rats.

We have in North America more than fifty kinds of rats and mice, the largest of which is the muskrat. Next in size comes the great, ugly brown rat.

More than three hundred years ago the black rat found its way from Europe to this country, settled here with our ancestors, and, like them, increased and prospered. The black rat is rather a neater and prettier animal than the now omnipresent Norway brown rat. The latter is of Asiatic origin, and appears to have made its way to this country since the advent of the black rat, which it has supplanted and almost exterminated. The roof rat in the Southern States came originally from Egypt, and the little brown mouse that creates so much mischief in our closets is of Asiatic parentage. All rats may be caught in traps, and for an amateur trapper the house rat is a good subject to practice on. By no means a fool among animals, possessing a due regard for his own safety, and looking with suspicion upon most traps, the Norway brown rat is not so easily caught as one who has never baited a "figure four" might suppose. A very successful way to capture house rats is to carefully close all the doors of the kitchen, barn, or room infested with them, and after removing all small objects from the floor, bait each hole with crumbs of meal and cheese; over the holes place little doors made of tin or wire, hung on with strings or screw-eyes, these doors open but one way and are so arranged that the rat can easily push the door open from the inside, but as soon as the animal makes its appearance in the room the door falls back into place, thus cutting off all retreat. In a short time the room will be overrun with rats, and if allowed to remain undisturbed for a few hours they will all escape through new holes made by their sharp teeth; if a terrier dog or a few cats be let into the room, not many rats will live to tell the tale of the massacre.

The Paper Pitfall.

Over the top of an earthenware jar fasten a piece of writing

FIG. 136.—A Mouse Trap.

paper, tightly binding it with a string or elastic band. In the centre of the paper cut a cross as shown in the illustration (Fig. 136). Set the jar in the closet and suspend by a string a piece of toasted cheese over the centre of the jar. If there are any mice in the closet the bait will attract them, but just as soon as the first mouse reaches the centre of the paper he will drop into the jar, and the paper will fly back in place again ready for the next comer. A trap arranged in the same manner can be used for the capture of field mice, shrews, and harvest mice, some of which make odd and amusing pets. All of these pretty little animals may be found in the fields or under brush heaps in the clearings. A barrel covered with stiff brown paper can be used for common rats, but they will gnaw out unless the barrel be partly filled with water.

Jug Trap.

An old earthenware jug with a small hole knocked in the upper part may be utilized as a trap for small burrowing animals. Bury the jug in the earth (Fig. 137) near the haunts of the animal you are after; then arrange an artificial burrow extending from the surface of the ground to the hole in the broken jug;

FIG. 137.—Old Jug Trap.

strew appropriate bait along the passageway, and although the little creatures might hesitate to enter a broken jug above ground, they are said to have no fear of one beneath the sod, and either jump or fall inside, where they may be allowed to remain some time with no fear of their escaping.

The jug trap is only suitable for small animals.

The Mole and How to Trap Him.

Moles are, generally speaking, harmless creatures who render the farmer a great service by devouring immense quantities of grubs and larvæ; but when one of these little animals finds its way under the sod of the lawn it plays sad havoc with the looks of the grass, furrowing the surface with ridges, and marring the appearance by dirt hills.

From the fact that the mole travels under ground, I have spent considerable time in trying to find a trap to catch this subterranean animal. Among we boys that lived in the valley of the Ohio River, a mole skin was highly prized as a sort of fetich that, when used as a "knuckle dabster" to rest our hands on in a game of marbles, not only prevented our hands from becoming soiled —which was no great matter—but also insured good luck to the happy boy who possessed a knuckle

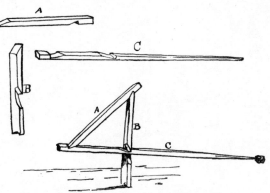

FIG. 138.—Construction of the Figure Four.

dabster made of a mole skin. There are but very few animals that can boast of fur as soft and fine as that which covers the back of the common mole.

A mole trap can be made in the old reliable figure four style, with which most of my readers are no doubt familiar.

The Figure Four

is made of three sticks ; a catch-stick, A, an upright, B, and a trigger, C (Fig. 138). When these sticks are set in the position shown by the diagram, and a weight allowed to rest on the top of the catch, A, the sticks will keep their positions and support the weight until the trigger, C, is touched.

At the slightest derangement of the trigger all the sticks fall, and the weight above, being left without a support, instantly drops to the ground. This trap has been ingeniously adapted to the purpose of a

Mole Trap.

A heavy weight is fastened on a piece of plank or board for a deadfall ; in the centre of the board some sharp-pointed spikes or nails are driven, so that the pointed ends extend sev-

FIG. 139.—Mole Trap.

eral inches below the deadfall (see Fig. 139). This trap should be set over a fresh mole-way, no bait need be used.

First press down the loose earth in a line across the ridge, then set the trap with a figure four, allowing the trigger-stick to rest in the place where you have pressed down the earth across the mole hill. The trap should be so arranged that the sharp spikes will be directly over the hill. The next time the mole makes his way through the underground passage he will sooner or later come to the place where the earth has been pressed down to make room for the trigger.

When the little animal reaches this point and proceeds to loosen the earth again, the movement will displace the trigger and bring the dead weight down, pinioning the mole to the ground with the sharp spikes, to which the loose earth of the mole hill offers but little resistance, if the weight be heavy enough. If the skin of the animal be desired, it is best to use as few spikes as practicable, for the fewer holes there are in a pelt the more valuable it is.

I object to deadfalls on principle, and it is not without some reluctance that I include them among the traps. As a boy, the only traps I ever used were made for capturing animals alive; but there are occasions when it is perfectly proper to use a deadfall. If the animal sought is a nuisance upon whose extermination you have settled for good reasons, then use a deadfall, or if you desire the animal for food and have no other means of capturing him, the deadfall is very convenient. Supposing your supply of fresh meat has run short at camp, or that you are on a canoe trip and are placed under similar circumstances, if there be a rabbit or squirrel in the neighborhood no one will find fault with you for trying to capture the game by any means in your power.

The Toll-gate Trap

is so called either from its resemblance to a toll-gate, or from the fact of its being set across the top of a rail fence, which has been called the " squirrel's highway." This trap can be made in a few minutes with the aid of a pocket-knife and a hatchet. The toll-gate is a deadfall, and the little traveller pays the toll with his life. With your hatchet cut a forked stick and drive· it in the ground a few feet from the fence; rest one end of a plank on this forked stick and allow the other end to protrude some distance beyond the opposite side of the fence. Select a heavy stick for the deadfall, and a very much smaller stick for the trigger; near the end of the trigger cut a notch for the catch-stick to rest in. Sharpen the ends of two small forked sticks and drive them into splits made near the ends of the board with the corner of the hatchet. Lay a cross piece from one forked stick to the other, and with a bit of string or vegetable fibre suspend the catch-stick from the centre of the cross stick. Tie the inside end of the trigger loosely to the deadfall, and adjust the trap so that when the end of the deadfall rests upon the catch-stick the latter will hold the trigger an inch or so

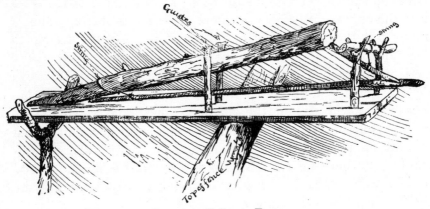

Fig. 140.—Toll-gate Trap.

above the plank. To prevent the trap from swaying and to guide the deadfall in the proper direction, two upright guide-sticks should be erected (Fig. 140). The weight of a squirrel's foot upon the bottom bar slips it from the catch-stick and down comes the deadfall upon the shoulders of the victim.

This same style of trap may be made upon a much larger

scale and set on logs or trees that have fallen across a water-course and are used as a bridge by minks, 'coons, or other animals. The forked sticks supporting the end of the plank must in this case be driven into the bed of the creek, and a plank twenty feet long substituted for the short one used in the trap designed for squirrels.

To be a successful trapper a boy must be a keen observer of the habits of the game ; by this means he will soon learn to take advantage of the very means designed by Nature as a protection for her creatures. For instance, the partridges are not good flyers, but their unobtrusive coats mingle and blend so closely with the stubble as to take a sharp eye to detect their presence ; hence we find that these birds are loth to take to the wing, but will run along any slight obstruction they meet, poking their heads about to find an outlet, apparently never once thinking of surmounting both the difficulty and the obstruction by using their wings. The '' down East '' Yankee boys are thoroughly acquainted with the habits of the partridge, and catch a great many of them by building little hedges like the one in the illustration entitled

The Partridge Snare.

The snare in this case consists of a slip-noose made of string. Make a bow-line knot (Fig. 58, diagram XIII., described on page 76) in one end of a piece of common string or fish line ; slip the other end of the string through the loop and make the free end fast to the top of an arch made of a bent stick (see Fig. 141). In a semi-circular form, around some feeding ground, build a low fence of sticks, brush or stones, leaving openings at intervals only large enough to fit in arched gateways. Make an arch for each opening and arrange a slip-noose in each archway ; spread the loops apart and keep them in this position by catching the strings slightly into notches made upon the outside of the arch (see Fig. 141). The birds, when they seek their accustomed feeding place, will walk into the semi-circle, and in searching for an outlet they will go poking their heads about until they come to an archway ; here they thrust their heads through the slip-noose, and as, instead of backing out, a part-

FIG. 141.—The Partridge Snare.

ridge will try to force its way through, the noose tightens and holds the bird a prisoner. Sometimes the youthful trapper will find the lifeless body of a rabbit with the fatal noose around its neck, and often he will miss one or two of his arches that have been uprooted and carried away by large game becoming entangled, and walking off, carrying arch, noose, and all with them. This partridge snare will also catch quail or prairie chickens.

Set-Line Snares.

Snares when used for catching birds alive should be closely watched ; which will not only prevent the captured wild birds from beating themselves to death, but will save them from suffering any more pain than is absolutely necessary.

Select a smooth piece of ground and drive two stakes ; to these attach a long cord, allowing it to stretch loosely upon the ground from one stake to the other. At intervals along the line fasten strong horse-hair nooses (Fig. 142). Sprinkle food

FIG. 142.—Set-Line Snares.

around and retire out of sight to watch. When the birds discover the food they will collect around it, and some one of them is almost certain to become entangled in one of the snares. As soon as a bird is snared it should be disentangled and put into a covered basket or a paper bag ; pin-holes may be made in the bag to allow the air to enter. In this way birds may be carried home without injury ; being in the dark they are not likely to hurt or disfigure themselves by struggling for their liberty. A cage is not only an awkward, unwieldy contrivance to carry in the field, but is objectionable from the fact that a wild bird caught and thrust into a cage will bruise its head and wings badly by striking against the bars in the efforts it makes to escape. Paper bags, pasteboard boxes, or covered baskets will do to carry home captured wild birds in.

The Spring Snare.

Make a low arch by pointing both ends of a stick and forcing them into the ground. Cut a switch and bend it into the form of a lawn tennis racket, and with a string fasten the small end of the switch to the part that answers to the handle of the bat or racket; just beyond the point where the small end terminates cut a notch in the large part or handle for the catch-stick to fit in. Make a short stick, with one end wedge-shaped, for a catch-stick. Drive a peg at such a distance in front of the arch that when the loop of the spreader is slipped over the peg the notch on the butt end will come just far enough to allow the catch-stick to hold it, as in Fig. 143. For a spring use an elastic young sapling. After stripping off the leaves

Fig 143. Fig 144.

and branches, attach a line to the top, tie the other end of the line to the catch-stick, and just above the cross stick fasten one end of a slip-noose to the line. To set the snare, bend the sapling until you can pass the catch-stick under the bender or arch, Figs. 143, 144. Raise the spreader from the ground about an inch; let the catch-stick hold it in this position, and spread the slip-noose over the loop-stick; your trap is now ready. To attract the birds, scatter some appropriate bait inside and very little outside. The birds will follow the trail of food up to the stretcher, and seeing the bait inside will hop upon the stretcher preparatory to going within. The stretcher, being only supported by friction where it bears against the catch and peg, will drop under the weight of a very small bird. The catch loosened slips out from under the bender, and the spring flying suddenly back draws the slip-noose around the wing, legs, or neck of the unfortunate bird. Unless speedily released by the trapper the bird will strangle or beat itself to death against the ground, or any objects within reach. *All snares should be watched if the birds are wanted alive.*

Hen-Coop Trap.

This rustic trap is sometimes set with an ordinary figure four (Fig. 138) by the colored people down South, and with it they catch a great many wild ducks and other water fowl.

The coop is made of sticks piled up after the manner of a log cabin (Fig. 145). To one of the bottom sticks a withe, made of a green wand,* is attached; the other end is then brought over the top of the trap and attached to the bottom

FIG. 145.—Hen-Coop.

stick upon the opposite side. The withe is tightened by forcing sticks under it at the top of the coop. When all is taut the sticks keep their positions, and unless very roughly used

---

* Withes may be made of ozier, willow, alder, hazel, white birch, white cherry, or even cedar branches.

Cut a branch or sapling, and after trimming the small branches off, place the small end under one foot, grasp the large end with both hands, and by a revolving motion twist the wand until the fibres become loosened and the stick looks like a rope. Indeed it will be a vegetable rope, which, if well made, will bear considerable strain, and be not only serviceable in making traps, but answer for binding logs together for a raft. Remarkably good and strong swings can be made of withes of wood.

will not slip out. Fig. 146 shows another manner of setting the hen-coop trap, by fastening a piece of willow or any other similar wood by two strings or withes to one end of the coop, so as to allow considerable freedom of motion to the semi-circular arch formed by the willow, which should be small enough

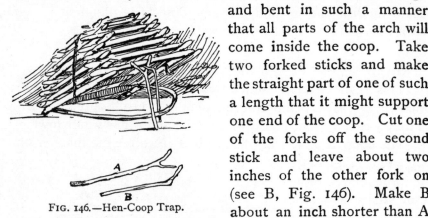

FIG. 146.—Hen-Coop Trap.

and bent in such a manner that all parts of the arch will come inside the coop. Take two forked sticks and make the straight part of one of such a length that it might support one end of the coop. Cut one of the forks off the second stick and leave about two inches of the other fork on (see B, Fig. 146). Make B about an inch shorter than A (Fig. 146). Raise the side of the coop, thrusting the crook on the end of B through the fork on the end of A, slip the crook under the edge of the coop, and push the bottom of B back inside of the willow, lifting the latter high enough to bear on the stick B and hold it in position. A will rest outside the coop, as in the illustration. A bird hopping upon the willow wand will cause it to slip down; this will displace the stick A, loosen the catch, and down comes the coop, enclosing the bird. A rustic trap of this description can be made without the aid of any other tools than a hatchet or a knife for cutting the sticks.

CHAPTER XXIV.

DOGS.

What They are Good For and How to Train Them.

IT is true that a boy *can* do without a canine companion and live to enjoy life, but he is almost incomplete; he lacks something; he has lost a gratification, a harmless, pleasant experience, and the loss leaves an empty space in his boyhood life that nothing can ever quite fill up. A boy without a dog is like an unfinished story. What your left hand is to your right,

a boy's dog is to the boy. More particularly is all this true of the lad who lives either in the country or within walking distance of forest and stream.

To be of any value either as a hunting dog, a watch dog or even a companion in one's rambles, it is absolutely necessary that the dog should be educated, and where there is a possibility of doing so, it is desirable to secure a young puppy. No matter what your choice in breed may be, whether it is a Newfoundland, bull, skye, greyhound, pointer, setter, or toy terrier, get the pup and *train it yourself.*

How to Choose a Dog.

"Blood will tell," whether it flows in the veins of a horse, man, or dog. The reader can readily understand that it would be not only absurd but absolutely cruel to keep a Newfoundland, deer-hound, water-spaniel, pointer, setter, or any other similar breed of dog confined within the narrow limits of that small bit of ground attached to the city house and dignified by the name of a yard. It would be equally as absurd and almost as cruel for a farmer boy to try and keep one of those expensive, diminutive, delicate, nervous, city dogs known under the general title of a "toy dog" or "fancy breed." The agile, bright-eyed "black-and-tan," and the delicate and graceful Italian greyhound, are full of fun, but as unreliable as beautiful. Thoughtless, rollicking, exquisites! Such dogs are scarcely the kind either city or country boy would choose for playmates or companions. What most boys want is a dog that combines the qualities of a boon companion and a good watch dog. By the latter is meant a dog whose intelligence is sufficient for it to discriminate between friend and foe, and whose courage will prompt it to attack the latter without hesitancy. It must also be a dog that may be taught to "fetch" and carry, to hunt for rat, squirrel, or rabbit, as well as to obey and trust in its master. It should be so cleanly in his habits as to be unobjectionable in-doors, and should possess judgment enough to know when its company is not agreeable, and at such times keep out of the way.

The poodle is perhaps the best trick dog, but is disliked by many on account of its thick woolly coat being so difficult to keep clean. The wirey-haired Scotch terrier is a comical, intelligent animal, and a first-rate comrade for a boy. The Newfoundland is faithful, companionable, and powerful enough to protect children, to whom, if there be any around the house, it will become very much attached and a self-constituted guardian. The spaniel is pretty, affectionate, and docile.

Almost all the sporting dogs make first-class watch-dogs, but are restless and troublesome if confined, and, as a rule, they are too large for the house. The shepherd is remarkably intelligent, and, when well trained, makes a trusty dog for general purposes.

The bull, although not necessarily as fierce and vicious as one would suppose from its looks and reputation, still is hardly the dog for a pet or companion, being of a dull and heavy nature, and not lively enough to suit the taste of the boy of the period. A little of the bull mixed in the blood of another more lively breed makes a good dog, of which a thorough-bred bull-terrier is an example. The Rev. J. G. Wood, in speaking of the latter, says :

" The skilful dog-fancier contrives a judicious. mixture of the two breeds, and engrafts the tenacity, endurance, and dauntless courage of the bull-dog upon the more agile and frivolous terrier. Thus he obtains a dog that can do almost anything, and though, perhaps, it may not surpass, it certainly rivals almost every other variety of dog in its accomplishments. In the capacity for learning tricks it scarcely yields, if it does yield at all, to the poodle. It can retrieve as well as the dog which is especially bred for that purpose. It can hunt the fox with the regular hounds, it can swim and dive as well as the New-foundland dog. In the house it is one of the wariest and most intelligent of dogs, permitting no unaccustomed footstep to enter ' the domains without giving warning.' " Although some may think the Rev. J. G. Wood to be a little too enthusiastic in his description of the bull-terrier's good qualities, still if they have ever owned a properly trained animal of this breed, they will undoubtedly agree with the great naturalist so far as to acknowledge this particular dog to be about the best for a boy's dog. With an ardor not excelled by his young master, the bull-terrier will chase any sort of game, and will attack and fight any foe at its master's bidding. Indeed the great fault of this kind of dog is that it is inclined to be too quarrelsome among other dogs, and careful attention should be paid to correcting this fault, which may be entirely eradicated by kind and firm treatment ; but should any canine bully attack your pet, woe be unto him, for, unless he comes from good fighting stock, he will rue the day he ever picked that quarrel.

How to Train Dogs.

First of all teach your dog that you mean *exactly what you say*, and that he *must* obey you. To do this you should never give a foolish command ; but if a thoughtless order be once given, even though you repent it as soon as it has escaped from your lips, do not hesitate, but insist upon your pupil instantly obeying—that is, if the dog, in your judgment, understands the order. Never, under any circumstances, allow him to shirk, and even a naturally stupid pup will learn to look upon your word as law and not think of disobeying.

Strict obedience to your word, whistle or slightest gesture once obtained, it is an easy task to finish the dog's education. Bear in mind that there is about as great a difference in the character and natural intelligence of dogs as there is in boys. Not only does this exist between the distinct varieties of dogs, but also between the different individuals of the same variety. All Newfoundlands possess similar characteristics, but each individual varies considerably in intelligence, amiability, and all those little traits that go to make up a dog's character. I mention this fact that you may not be disappointed, or make your poor dog suffer because it cannot learn as fast or as much as some one you may know of. And here let me say, and impress upon your mind, that to make your dog obey, or to teach it the most difficult trick or feat, it is seldom necessary to use the whip. If the dog, as he sometimes will do, knowingly and wilfully disobeys, the whip may be used sparingly ; one sharp blow is generally sufficient ; it should be accompanied with a reprimand in words. Never lose your patience and beat an animal in anger. To successfully train a dog it is necessary to place the greatest restraint upon your own feelings, for if you once give way to anger the dog will know it, and one-half your influence is gone. To be sure the special line of education depends upon the kind of a dog you have, and what you want him to do.

The pointer or setter you may commence to teach to " stand," at a very early age, using first a piece of meat, praising and petting him when he does well, and reprimanding when required. Do not tire your pup out, but if he does well once let him play and sleep before trying again. As he grows older, replace the meat with a dead bird. The best sportsmen of to-day do not allow their bird dogs to retrieve, saying that the " mouthing " of the dead and bloody birds affects the fineness of their noses. To bring in birds, the sportsman has following at his heels a cocker spaniel, large poodle, or almost any kind of dog, who is taught to follow patiently and obediently until game is killed and he receives the order to " fetch."

To Teach a Dog to Retrieve.

Commence with the young pup. Almost any dog will chase a ball and very soon learn to bring it to his master. When you have taught your dog to " fetch," he may be tried with game. It is very probable that the first bird he brings will be badly " mouthed ; " that is, bitten and mangled ; to break him of this, prepare a ball of yarn so wound over pins that the slightest pressure will cause the points to protrude and prick any object pressed against the ball. After the dog has pricked his mouth

once or twice with this ball he will learn to pick it up and carry
it in the most delicate manner ; he may then be tried again with
a bird.   This time he will probably bring it to you without so
much as ruffling a feather ; but if notwithstanding his experience with a ball of pins your dog still " mouths " the game, you
must skin a bird and arrange the ball and pins inside the bird
skin so as to prick sharply upon a light pressure ; make the dog
" fetch " the bird skin until he is completely broken of his bad
habit of biting or " mouthing " game.

Pointers and Setters.

At first you will have to give your commands by word of
mouth, but if you accompany each command by an appropriate
gesture, the pup will soon learn to understand and obey the
slightest motion of the hand or head.   The less noise there is
the greater is the chance of killing game.   Nothing is more un-
sportsmanlike than shouting in a loud voice to your dog while
in the field.

After teaching a dog to "heel," " down charge," and to
" hi on " at command, you may show him game and teach him
to " quarter " his ground by moving yourself in the direction
you wish the dog to go.   The dog will not be long in under-
standing and obeying.

When your pointer comes to a point teach him to be steady
by repeating softly, " steady, boy, steady," at the same time
holding up your hand.   In course of time the words may be
omitted ; the hand raised as a caution will keep the dog steady ;
but should he break point and flush the game, as a young
dog is more than liable to do, you may give him the whip and
at the same time use some appropriate words that the dog will
remember ; the next time the word without the whip will correct
him.   After your dog has been taught to obey, it is well to put
him in the field with an old, well-trained dog.

As every sportsman has a peculiar system of his own for breaking a dog, it is scarcely necessary for me to give more than these few hints ; only let me again caution you against using the whip too often.   Spare the lash and keep a good stock of patience on hand ; otherwise in breaking the dog you will also break his spirit and have a mean, treacherous animal that will slink and cringe at your slightest look, but seldom obey you when he thinks he is out of reach of the dreaded whip.

Pet Dogs.

All dogs, whether intended for the field, for pets, or for companions, should be taught to follow at their master's heels at the command of "heel," to run ahead at the command of "hi on," and to drop at the command of "charge" or "down charge."   When your dog learns to obey these simple commands, it will be found an easy matter to extricate and keep your canine friend out of scrapes.   Suppose you have a small but pugnacious dog and in your walk you meet a large, ugly-tempered brute much too powerful for your own dog to master in the fight that is certain to ensue unless by some command you can prevent it.   The strange dog will not obey you, but if you give the order to "heel" to your own dog he will follow with his nose at your heels, and the enemy will seldom if ever attack a dog while so near his master.

Study the characteristics of your dog, and by taking advantage of its peculiarities it may be taught many amusing tricks. I have a little dog called Monad, and whether his master walks, drives, sails or rows Monad always accompanies him, even sitting in front of the sliding seat of a single shell boat for hours at a time, perfectly happy and apparently conscious of the attention he attracts from all people on the shore or in the passing boats ; the latter he generally salutes with a bark.   Monad will, when requested to do so, close a door, sneeze, bark, or sit upon his haunches and rub his nose, besides numerous other amusing tricks.

One day Monad smelled of a lighted cigar ; the smoke inhaled caused him to sneeze ; this gave me an idea ; lighting a match I held it toward him, at the same time repeating, "sneeze ! sneeze, sir !" The smoke made him sneeze, and after repeating the operation several times I held out an unlighted match and commanded him to sneeze ; the dog sneezed at once. It was then an easy step to make him sneeze at the word without the match. Monad is now very proud of this accomplishment, and when desirous of "showing off" always commences by sneezing.

In much the same manner I taught him to rub his nose by blowing in his face and repeating the words, "rub your nose." The breath coming in contact with that sensitive organ apparently tickled it and he would rub it with his paws. After one or two trials he learned to rub his little black nose in a very comical manner whenever commanded to do so. By patting your leg with your hand and at the same time calling your dog, it will learn to come to you and place his fore paws against your leg. If you take advantage of this and pat the door the next time with your hand, the dog will stand on its hind legs and rest its fore paws against the door. Reward him with a bit of meat or a caress, and then opening the door a few inches go through with the same performance, giving the command to close the door ; by degrees, as the dog learns, open the door wider, and without moving from your chair or position in the room give the command, "close the door, sir." The dog will by this time understand your meaning, and resting his fore paws against the panels, follow the door until it closes with a bang. Perhaps there is no simple trick that excites more surprise than this. A friend comes in and leaves the door open ; you rise, greet your friend, ask him to be seated ; then, as if for the first

time noticing the fact of the door being open, speak to your dog ;
the latter closes the door and lies down again by the fireside in
a most methodical manner.   The friend is thoroughly convinced
that that particular dog has more sense than any other canine
in the world, and ever after, when dogs are the topic of conversation, he will tell the story of the dog that shut the door.

In the same manner innumerable odd, amusing, or useful
tricks may be taught, among the simplest of which are the ones
which excite the most applause from spectators.   If your dog
is fond of carrying a stick in his mouth, it will be an easy
matter to make him carry a basket.   Take advantage of every
peculiarity of your pet's character, encouraging and developing
the good points, but keeping the bad traits subdued, and you
will soon have an amusing and reasoning canine companion.

Never throw a dog into the water; it frightens him and
makes the poor animal dread a bath.   Let the dog wade at
first ; then by throwing sticks or other objects a little further
out each time, and commanding him to fetch, the dog will
not only learn to swim after the .object, but also learn to thoroughly enjoy the bath, and can even be taught to dive and jump
off of high places. ·There are dogs that will jump from an
elevation twelve feet above the water.   Always be firm but
kind ; teach your dog to have confidence in you, and you may
place implicit trust in your canine friend, and be sure whatever
misfortune befalls you, you will have a friend who, though he
be a four-footed one, will never forsake you, but live and die
for the master it has learned to love and trust.

CHAPTER XXV.

PRACTICAL TAXIDERMY FOR BOYS.

To the practical naturalist a knowledge of taxidermy is not only an interesting accomplishment from which to derive amusement, but is almost an absolute necessity, an indispensable adjunct to his profession. Probably there is no study the pursuit of which affords such opportunities for physical exercise and real healthy enjoyment as that of natural history. It is a study that, by broadening the horizon of thought, enlarges the capacity for pleasure. To the pride of the sportsman in exhibiting the results of his skill and success, the naturalist adds the intelligent pleasure of acquiring a more complete knowledge of the life and habits, nature and anatomy of his trophies, as well as the ability to detect at a glance any unknown genus or rare variety he may capture ; and here the practical knowledge of taxidermy enables him to properly preserve the other wise perishable specimen.

Captain Thomas Brown, F.L.S., says that *boys* ought to be instructed in the art of stuffing birds and mammals. So, boys, you have good authority for commencing young ; but do not suppose that after reading the following directions you can sit down, and, without any previous experience, set up a bird as neatly and perfectly as one of those you see in the museums or show windows. On the contrary, you must expect to make one or two dismal failures, but each failure will teach you what to avoid in the next attempt.

Let us suppose an owl has been lowering around suspiciously near the pigeon house or chicken coop, and that you have shot the rascal. Do not throw him away. What a splendid ornament he will make for the library! How appropriate that wise old face of his will be peering over the top of the book-case! (Fig. 147). He must be skinned and stuffed! With a damp sponge carefully remove any blood-stains there may be upon his plumage. Plug up the mouth and nostrils with cotton; also insert cotton in all the shot holes, to prevent any more blood oozing out and soiling the feathers. You may then lay him aside in some cool place until you are ready to begin the operation of skinning and stuffing the owl.

FIG. 147.—Stuffed and Mounted.

Measure the length of the bird, following the curves of the form, from root of tail to top of head, and its girth about the body; make a note of these figures.

Skinning.

Place the bird on its back upon the table, in such a position that the head will be toward your left hand; then, with the knife in your right hand you are ready to make the incision.

With your left hand separate the feathers, left and right, from the apex of the breast-bone to the tail (Fig. 148). Cut a straight slit through the skin between these points, using the utmost care to prevent the knife penetrating the flesh or the inner skin which encloses the intestines. With a bird as large as the owl, you will find that you can easily separate the skin from the flesh with your fingers, though it may be best to use a blunt instrument, such as a small ivory paper-cutter, to reach the back by passing it underneath the skin. In removing the skin you must try to shove in lieu of pulling, lest you stretch it out of shape. Press as lightly as possible upon the bird, stopping occasionally to take a view to see that all is right and that the feathers are not being soiled or broken. When you come to the head do not let the skin dangle from your hand or its own weight will stretch it. Bearing these things in mind, you can commence removing the skin in the following

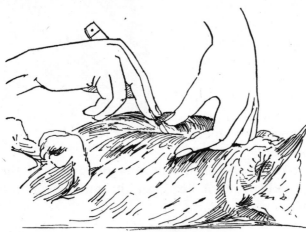

manner: Press the skin apart at the incision, and dust the exposed part with Indian meal to absorb any fluids that may escape; carefully lift the skin on one side and separate from muscles of the breast with the

FIG. 148.—The Incision.

point of your knife and a small ivory paper-folder alternately, as occasion may require, until the leg is reached and you have · approached as near as possible to the wings. Having accomplished this, and dusted again with the Indian meal, the thighs must be pressed inward and the skin turned back far enough to allow you to use your knife and disarticulate the hip-joint. Bend the tail toward the back; keep down the detached skin upon each side of the incision with the thumb and first finger of the left hand; then with your knife make a deep cut, exposing the backbone at a point near the oil gland, which you will find near the root of the tail; sever the backbone near this

point, but be careful to leave a large enough piece of it to support the tail feathers.

Take the part of the body which is now denuded of the skin
in the left hand and peel the skin upward to the wings ; during
this operation your knife or small scissors may be used to
cut any of the tendons which are met with. Separate the
wings from the body at the shoulder-joint. Next turn your
attention to the head and neck. Push the skin back toward
the head, after the manner of removing a kid glove from the
finger, until the back part of the skull is laid bare ; then with
your knife detach the vertebræ (neck bone) from the head.
This will sever all connection between the body and the skin.
The dismembered, denuded carcass may be thrown aside and
your attention turned to skinning the head, which member in
an owl is so large in proportion to the neck that care must be
used in drawing the skin of the neck over it, lest you stretch
the skin. A great deal depends upon the delicacy of your
touch, especially when you reach the eyes. Work slowly ; cut
the ears close to the skull ; do not cut either the eyelid or the
eyeball, but separate them carefully ; then remove the eyes,
which can be done by breaking the slender bones which separate the orbits (eye-holes) in the skull from the top of the
mouth. Cut away all flesh from the neck ; at the same time
remove a small portion of the base of the skull. Through the
opening thus made extract the brains with a small spoon or
some similar instrument, after which draw the tongue through
the same cavity. After removing all fleshy particles from the
head and neck, and scraping out the eye-holes, paint them
with arsenical soap and stuff them tightly with cotton. Be
careful not to detach the skin from the bill, as the skull must
be left in place. Coat the interior of the skull with arsenical
soap and fill it with tow.

The wings and legs still remain intact. Push back the wings

to the first joint ; lay the bones bare, removing all the meat. Paint with arsenical soap and return them to their places. Go through the same process with the legs and rump ; and after all flesh and fatty matter have been removed, paint the whole interior of the skin thoroughly with arsenical soap, and you are ready to begin the operation of

Stuffing.

Take a piece of straight wire (size 20) equal in length to the measurement you made from root of tail to top of head ; wind about it a bunch of excelsior (straw will answer as a substitute for excelsior shavings) ; secure this to the wire by repeated wrappings of stout thread, and mould the bundle into a shape resembling the bird's body ; regulate the girth by the measurement you noted down for that purpose before you commenced the skinning process. When you have completed the artificial body there will, of course, be a portion of the wire still bare, which represents the neck. File the extremity of this wire to a sharp point, then force it diagonally up through the skull to the top, where it must be clinched ; wrap the neck wire between the artificial body and the head with cotton batting (Fig. 149). Now draw the skin back so as to cover the artificial neck and body.

FIG. 149.—Owl-Skin and False Body.

The eyelids must be carefully pulled in place over the cotton in the eye-holes, or orbits ; pull the eyelids up nicely, to make the parts about the eye appear plump and natural. Push more cotton down the throat until it has a round, real look. For the legs use two pieces of wire, each sharpened at one end. The taxidermist must shove the wire through the ball of the foot and guide it with the other hand up along the side of the bones of the leg, the skin being turned back for that purpose (Fig. 150). This figure shows the leg with skin turned back, as it appears when the wire is pushed through.

Wind cotton around both wire and bone to the natural thickness of the thigh, and go through the same process with the other leg; then push the wires clear through the artificial body and bend the protruding ends into a hook form (Fig. 151). Taking hold at the part extending from the bottom of the foot, pull the wire of each leg down until the hooks fasten firmly into the

FIG. 150.—Wiring the Leg.

body. The ends of the wires protruding from the foot are left to fasten the bird to its perch, which is done either by wrapping the wires around the perch or by thrusting them through holes made for the purpose and clinching the ends. With a few stitches sew up the hole in the breast. For

FIG. 151.—Showing how Leg-Wire is attached to False Body.

small birds this is not necessary. After your owl is set up in this manner, gather the wings up close to the body and fasten them there by thrusting two wires, one from each side, diagonally through the skin of the second joint.

If you wish the tail to be spread you must push a wire across the body through each feather.

Eyes can be made of white marbles painted yellow with black centres, but glass eyes are better and cost very little. To fix the eyes, put a touch of glue upon the cotton in each orbit and insert the glass eyes, being careful to place them properly under the eyelids ; with a sharp needle pull the lids nicely in place.

The stuffing of the bird is now finished, and it may be placed upon the branch in some natural position (Fig. 147, page 233).

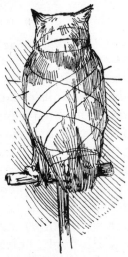

The attitude fixed, it only remains to put the feathers in their natural order as smoothly and regularly as possible, and to keep them in place by winding a thread over the body very loosely, beginning at the head and winding until all the feathers are secured (Fig. 152). The bird must be left in some dry place for several days. When it is perfectly dry the thread may be taken off and all protruding wires cut close to the body. The specimen is now ready for the parlor or library.

The above directions, with very little modification, will serve for any other bird.

FIG. 152. For practice, a chicken is the best subject, as it is easily obtained and large enough not to be readily damaged by the awkwardness of a beginner.

The more tools you have the better, but if my reader has carefully read the foregoing description he must have noticed that during the whole process of skinning and stuffing the owl the only tools used were such as are within the reach of every boy—a penknife, a paper-cutter, small spoon (a mustard-spoon will answer), and a thread and needle. Arsenical soap is the only material used not likely to be easily procured. This preparation is of course very poisonous and should be so labelled. It can be procured of any taxidermist or made by any drug, gist from the following recipe of Bécœur :

Arsenic in powder....................	2 pounds.
Camphor	5 ounces.
White soap..........................	2 pounds.
Salt of tartar........................	12 ounces.
Powdered lime.......................	4 ounces.

Mr. J. Wallace, the taxidermist, recommends the following recipe : ''Dissolve ten pounds of finely cut, best white soap in warm water ; add one pound of potash ; thicken with pipe-clay and a little lime to give the preparation body ; heat and stir well. When cooling add ten pounds of arsenic." Of course the young beginner will not need any such quantity as is represented in either of these recipes, but if he goes to the druggist that gentleman can make the soap in any quantity desired. The utmost care must be observed in handling this preparation and keeping it out of the reach of children and animals, although it is not very tempting in taste or looks and hence not as dangerous as other compounds might be.

A New Manner of Preserving Fish.

The boys at school used to say, '' You cannot eat your apple and keep it.'' Being not only fond of fishing and fish, but also taking an interest in the study of ichthyology, the question with me has been, How can I eat my fish and still preserve it for future reference ? A few experiments and several failures suggested a plan which has proved partially successful.

Having caught a very large bass or trout that you would like to preserve as a trophy, or some odd-looking fish that you want to keep as a specimen, the following is the plan to adopt :

Place your fish upon a piece of paper of any kind you may have, or a piece of birch bark ; spread out the fins and trace a careful and accurate outline ; then with your pocket-knife remove the tail at a point just beyond its junction with the body of the fish ; in the same manner cut off the fins, being careful not to injure them ; a small portion of flesh will be attached to

FIG. 153.—Portfolio of Fish.

each ; this must be removed with your knife. Put the fins in a safe place, and again taking your knife, insert the blade under the gill and cut up to the centre of the top of the head ; split the head down in a line exactly on the top to the upper jaw ; carefully cut through this and the lower jaw to where the gill commences underneath ; this will sever the whole side of the head. Cut away all the flesh from the inside and remove all the bony structures possible without injuring the outside. The eyes can be removed so as to leave the outside skin or covering unbroken. Wash the half of the head clean and put that with the fins in your note-book, taking care to leave a leaf of paper between each, to prevent their adhering together.

When you reach home you can have the fish cooked, and while it is cooking trace the outline of the fish upon a clean sheet of white paper ; take the fins, head and tail from your note-book, dampen them with a sponge or wet cloth, and with glue or mucilage fasten them in their proper places upon the outline drawing, distended by means of pins ; the latter may be removed after the glue or mucilage is dry ; write in one corner the weight of the fish, the date upon which it was caught, and the name of the place where it was captured. You can then frame it or number the sheet and place it in a port-folio (Fig. 153). In the course of a season's fishing quite an interesting and valuable portfolio of fishes can be made. The writer has often caught fish whose names were unknown to him, and in this manner preserved them, or enough of them to identify the fish at some future period when he had time to look it up.

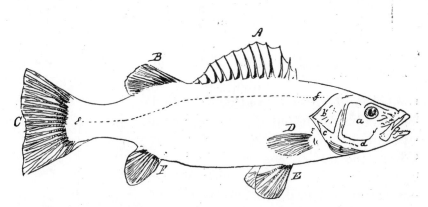

Diagram Showing the Parts of a Fish.—A, first dorsal fin ; B, second dorsal fin ; C, caudal fin ; D, pectoral fin ; E, ventral fin ; F, anal fin ; b, operculum or gill cover proper ; a, preoperculum or fore-gill cover ; d, interoperculum, or middle gill cover ; c, suboperculum, or under gill cover ; e, branchiostegous, or gill rays ; f, lateral line.

Design for a Sketching Aquarium.

If the reader desire to try his artistic skill and attempt a colored drawing of a fish, he should do it from life. To see the fish as it really appears, a very simple contrivance can be made in the form of an aquarium, with wooden ends and glass sides ; the wooden ends must have perpendicular grooves in them so

16

that an extra pane of glass can be used as a slide (Fig. 154).
Place the live fish in the aquarium, and when he is on one side

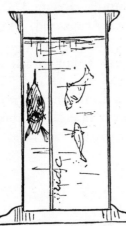

of it quickly slip the slide in so as to im-
prison the fish in such a narrow space
that he is unable to flop or turn around,
but must patient-
ly keep his broad-
side to the artist
until the picture
is finished.

Preserving Insects.

G r e a t   care
must be taken in
killing insects, in-

FIG. 154.—Cross Section of
a Sketching Aquarium.

tended for the cabinet, and death should
be produced without disfiguring them
or rubbing off the down or scales that
covers the bodies and wings of some
specimens.   A convenient and successful way to kill insects is to drop them
into a wide-mouthed bottle, the bottom
of which is lined with blotting-paper
that has been previously saturated with
ether, benzine, creosote or chloroform.
When a butterfly, bug, or beetle is put
into a bottle prepared in this manner,
and the bottle tightly corked, the insect
expires without a struggle, and hence
without injuring itself.   From the bottle

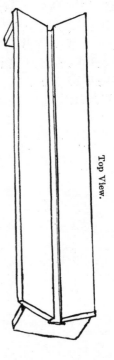

Top View.

End View.

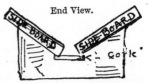

FIG. 155.—Mounting-Board.

the specimens may be taken and pinned upon a mounting-
board, consisting of two strips of wood resting upon supports at

each end, a space being left between the strips for the body of the insect. Under this space or crack a piece of cork is fastened (Fig. 155) in which to stick the point of the pin. After pinning the specimen to the mounting-board, spread the wings and

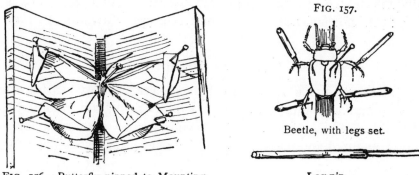

FIG. 157.

Beetle, with legs set.

Leg-pin.

FIG. 156.—Butterfly pinned to Mounting-Board.

legs out in a natural position, and if it be a butterfly or moth, fasten its wings in position with bits of paper and pins, as shown in Fig. 156. An ingenious and simple device for pinning the leg of an insect is illustrated by Fig. 157. It consists of two needles with their heads driven into a small pine stick.

Morse Insect Box.

Mr. E. S. Morse gives probably the best device for arranging an insect box for the cabinet. It consists of a light wooden frame with paper stretched upon the upper and under surface. Dampen the paper and glue it to the frame; when the

FIG. 158.—Cross Section of Morse Insect Box.

paper dries it will contract and become as tight as a drum-head. Inside the box upon two sides fasten cleats, and let their top edges be about one-quarter of an inch above the bottom. Rest the paper-covered frame upon these cleats and secure it in position. The bottom of the box should be lined with soft pine to receive the points of the pins. The space under the frame can be dusted with snuff and camphor to keep out such insects as delight to feed upon the prepared specimens of their relatives. Fig. 158 shows a cross section of a box upon Mr. Morse's plan.

The Lawrence Breeding Box.

The best moths and butterflies are obtained by rearing the caterpillars in cages made for the purpose. I am indebted to Mr. Albert Lawrence for the accompanying plan of a larvæ box, invented and used by himself for several seasons (see Fig.

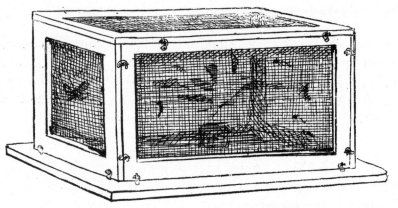

FIG. 159.—Mr. Albert Lawrence's Breeding Box.

159). The Lawrence box, as may be seen by the diagram, can be taken apart and packed away when not in use or during transportation.

The sides, ends, and top are wooden frames covered with wire netting; the bottom is a flat board. They are all joined by hooks and screw-eyes. To take them apart it is only necessary to unfasten the hooks.

Spiders

are very likely to lose their colors if placed in spirits, and if pinned and dried like beetles they will not only lose all color, but their bodies will shrivel up and change in form and proportion to such a degree as to make the specimens next to worthless. Mr. Ralph Hemingray, of Covington, Ky., sent the author some spider bottles manufactured under his direction of very thick, clear, white glass, three inches high by one and one-quarter inch broad, and three-quarters of an inch thick. These bottles are convenient in shape, and when a spider is put in one and the bottle filled with glycerine, the spider looks as if it might be imbedded in a solid block of crystal.

FIG. 160.—The Hemingray Bottle.

I have had some brightly colored garden spiders preserved in this manner for two years, and they have not only retained their original shape but color also. In the place of corks, pieces of elastic are stretched over the tops of the bottles; this allows the glycerine to expand or contract. Fig. 160 represents a drawing of one of these bottles with a spider in it. A case of specimens preserved in this manner makes not only an interesting cabinet, but a very pretty one. Although many persons have a horror of spiders, they lose all their nervousness when the insects are seen neatly labelled and enclosed in pretty glass bottles.

How to Make Beautiful or Comical Groups and Designs of Insects.

Many really beautiful, as well as some absurdly comical designs can be made of properly preserved insects by ingenious lads.

Butterflies may be made to have the appearance of hovering in mid-air by mounting them upon extremely fine wire.

Grasshoppers can be arranged in comical, human-like atti-tudes.

Beetles may be harnessed like horses to a tiny car made of the half of an English walnut-shell. A very pretty design can be made by seating a grasshopper in a delicate sea-shell of some kind, and glueing the shell to a bit of looking-glass; fine wires attached to the shell will answer the double purpose of a support and harness for a couple of flying beetles; a little moss glued around the sides so as to conceal the ragged edges of the glass will add greatly to the effect, and the whole will have the appearance of a fairy boat being drawn over the surface of the water by two flying beetles, guided by the long-legged imp in the shell.

Preserved insects are exceedingly brittle, the least touch will often break off a wing or leg or otherwise disfigure the speci-men, hence it is necessary not only to be very careful in hand-ling them, but to supply some sort of cover to protect them from accidents, dust, and injurious insects. Dome-shape glass-covers are best adapted for small groups or compositions, and these may be obtained from the dealers at moderate prices, or, if the young taxidermist has acquired sufficient skill to make his work valuable, he can readily trade off duplicate specimens for glass-covers, as many amateurs as well as some professionals do.

Marine Animals.

Starfish must be first placed in fresh water and allowed to remain there for several hours; they may then be removed and spread out upon a board, and held in position by pins or nails driven in the board alongside of the rays, but not into the creature. Put the board in a dry place out of the sun, and the air will absorb all the moisture in the specimens; the latter, as they dry, become hard and stiff.

I have several starfish preserved in this simple manner, and although no pickle or artificial preservative was used, they have kept in good condition for several years.

Small crabs may be dried in the same manner. The flesh must be extracted from the big pincers of the larger crabs and lobsters ; this may be done by breaking off the points of the pincers and removing the meat with a crooked wire. The points of the claws should be saved and glued in place after the animal is dry. The smaller claws may be allowed to dry ; small holes pierced in them will allow the air to enter and facilitate the drying process. The insides of both lobsters and large crabs must be removed from an opening made underneath. Wash them with cold water and inject carbolic acid and water into their extremities ; place them upon a board to dry, with their legs spread out ; after all moisture has evaporated, varnish them and fasten the bodies and legs of the specimens to a board with fine wires.

All soft-bodied animals, such as squids and slugs, can be preserved in spirits. Sea-urchins, such as are found upon our coast, may be dried like starfish, but it is best to remove the insides of the larger specimens.

With these suggestions, sufficient to help the young taxidermist, I will close this chapter. I have purposely avoided advising the use of expensive material or tools ; where it was possible, I have not suggested the use of poisonous preservatives, but have given the most simple and safe methods of mounting specimens for the cabinet or for decorations.

Egg Blow-pipe and Drill.

CHAPTER XXVI.

EVERY BOY A DECORATIVE ARTIST.

Shadow Pictures—Photographic Paper—How to Enlarge or Reduce a Picture, etc.

ONE day while the author was sketching, a piece of drawing-paper happened to fall upon the ground in the bright sunlight. As the paper rested on the sward the shadows of the grass and weeds were cast upon it. How beautiful and graceful they were! Stooping down the writer passed his brush over the shadows; the result was a sort of half silhouette, an excellent suggestion for a bit of foreground or a decoration. If the thousands of amateur decorators that are daily engaged in daubing pictures of all manner of unnatural-looking plants upon china would only confine themselves to tracing in one color the simple shadows cast by plants in the sunlight, what graceful and pleasing designs Mother Nature would furnish

FIG. 161.—Shadow cast by a Dandelion.

them ! How much more pleasant it would be to eat off dishes decorated in this manner than to be called upon to admire and eat from china covered with "finiky" little flowers or broad, meaningless daubs of color intended to represent something only known to the artist (?) who conceived the design. Any boy can make the most graceful designs by placing a piece of paper in such a position that the shadow of a flower or fern shall fall upon it. Then with a small paint brush and some ink he may carefully paint in the shadow just as it falls upon the paper. Fig. 161 shows a dandelion, a fac-simile of a sketch made in the manner just described. Fig. 162 is an anemone. Not only can beautiful designs be made, but valuable sets of botanical sketches can be obtained in this manner, as no skill is required with the brush ; all that is necessary is to follow the shadow on the paper.

FIG. 162.—Shadow cast by an Anemone.

A wooden frame or stretcher might be used with a candle or lamp at night. By tacking the paper over the stretcher, then placing a pot or vase containing plants in front of the light and the stretcher in front of the plants, the shadows of the plants will be thrown upon the paper and show through, so that they can be painted upon the opposite side of the paper without any danger of moving either the light or plants.

At most of the artists' material stores in New York there is to be found for sale a sensitive paper which changes color when exposed to the light. If a shadow be cast upon this paper by some object between it and the sunlight, the paper will grow lighter in color all around the shadow, and in a few moments the shadow is marked distinctly by the difference in tints. At this stage the paper, which is of a dark blue color, may be re-moved, and if it be held under a stream of water the parts that were covered by the shadow will become white and remain so. I have before me a photograph of a large dragon-fly, which shows all the beautiful network of veins in the wings of that in-sect traced in the most delicate white lines upon a background of dark blue. I allowed the dragon-fly to rest for a few mo-ments upon a piece of sensitive paper and then quickly placed the paper under a hydrant, with the result described.

Photographic paper is not expensive, quite a large sized sheet costing only fifty cents. Many pretty experiments can be tried with this material.

How to Enlarge or Reduce by Squares.

Suppose you have a picture of a horse and want to enlarge it. First draw a line under its feet, and at right angles with this line draw another line in front of the horse's head ; divide these lines into equal parts and then carefully rule lines across from these points so as to intersect each other at right angles, as illustrated by Fig. 163. When the horse is all enclosed in squares, take another piece of paper and make exactly the same number of large squares on the paper as there are smaller ones on the horse picture ; number the squares on both as in

the diagrams (Fig. 163). If you will look at the top diagram
you will see that the horse's head cuts off one corner of the
upper left hand corner square; with your pencil make a line
cutting off the same part of the corresponding large square;
curve the line like the copy. By again referring to the horse
picture you will notice that the line of the
neck continued strikes exactly at the intersection of the lines 1 and 2; draw it so.
The next point the line touches just above
is the intersection of the lines 2 and 3;
from this point the line of the back runs
almost straight to the
point on the tail at the
intersection of the lines
2 and 6; thus, by find-
ing and connecting the
points of intersection
you may reproduce the
whole horse as illustrat-
ed by the diagram. In
a s i m i l a r manner a
landscape, figure piece
or a plan can be accu-
rately enlarged by a
boy who may have little
or no talent for drawing,

FIG. 163.—Enlargement by Squares.

but who for some purpose wishes to reproduce a picture or plan.
By making the squares on your drawing-paper exactly the same
size as those upon the picture, you can draw a fac-simile of the
picture, and by making the squares smaller you may reduce a
picture. Remember these hints, for when I tell you how to
make a puppet show, although a pattern for each puppet is
drawn, there is not space in a book of this size to make all

the puppets large enough, and many or all may have to be
enlarged.

How to Make a Camera for Drawing.

This instrument necessitates an outlay of from fifty cents to
a dollar and a half for a lens ; unless the reader is fortunate
enough to already possess a double convex lens, or what is
known among boys as a "burning-glass." A small mirror or
piece of looking-glass, a small pane of common window glass,
and an old soap
or candle box,
or some pine
l u m b e r of
which to make
a box, is all the
m a t e r i a l re-
quired.

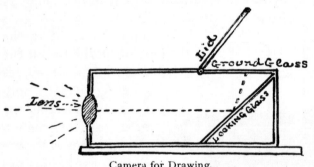

Camera for Drawing.

Let the box
be about eigh-
teen i n c h e s
long, nine inches deep, and twelve inches wide ; fasten the lens
in a hole cut for that purpose at one end of the box. A piece
of looking-glass must be fixed at an angle of forty-five degrees
at the opposite end of the box. The angle may be obtained
in this manner : if from where the top of the glass rests against
the end board, it measures nine inches to the bottom of the
box, then the bottom of the glass should be nine inches from
the end of the box.

Grind the surface of one side of the window-pane glass by
rubbing it upon a flat stone or sand-paper. Make a lid to the
top of the box, as shown in the illustration, and under the lid
fasten the ground glass. Paint or blacken the inside of the box,
and adjust the parts by experiment, so that when the lens is

turned toward any object, that object will be immediately reflected upon the piece of ground glass. No great difficulty need be anticipated by any one in the adjustment of the parts of a camera obscura, as it can be easily arrived at by trial.

If a piece of drawing-paper be placed over the ground glass, and the lens turned toward some object, that object will be reflected upon the glass and shown through the paper in all its natural colors, strong enough to be accurately traced and reproduced.

In this manner considerable amusement and instruction can be derived from a home-made camera obscura.

If one of these instruments be taken into a darkened room, and the lens allowed to point out through the window, everything that passes the house will be reflected upon the ground glass, making a sort of moving, colored, puppet show.

Winter.

FIG. 164.—Snow-Fort commenced.

CHAPTER XXVII.

SNOWBALL WARFARE.

How to Build Snow-Forts—How to Make Shields and Ammunition Sleds.

COLD gray clouds have long since usurped the heavens and driven away the white, fleecy summer cumulus ; the latter, like the birds, have gone to more congenial climes. For several weeks past heavy overcoats have been in demand.

The rowing season has closed ; the baseball bats and lawn tennis rackets are stowed away, and the college boys have settled down to study and in-door gymnasium practice.

In the cities the car and stage drivers swing their arms about and beat their muffled chests in a vain effort to start the blood to circulating in their benumbed fingers. Each passenger, as he reads the morning paper, exhales two streams of mist from his nostrils. The horses puff larger streams of steam and wear chest protectors. Everybody appears unhappy except the school-boy. The latter's cheeks glow with more than usual color and his eyes sparkle as if with inward merriment, for *he knows the signs,* and the dull, leaden sky to him is only a promise of a big snow storm and "lots of fun." The frost king has arrived and introduced jolly old Winter. Every boy knows that no season of the year can boast of more healthy out-door games, brimful of fun and excitement, than winter, and that there is no sport among winter games more exciting and amusing than snowball warfare. The interest and fun of the game is greatly enhanced if there be a fort to capture or defend.

How to Build the Fort.

All the boys must join in building the fort, selecting the highest point of the play-grounds, or, if the grounds be level, the corner of a wall or fence. Supposing the top of a mound has been selected as the place where the works are to be built, the first thing to do is to make out the plan of the foundation. The dimensions depend upon the number of boys. A circle twelve feet in diameter, or a square with sides of ten feet, will make a fort that will accommodate a company of ten boys. It is better to have the fort too small than too large. The chief engineer must set his men to rolling large snowballs; the smaller boys can commence them and the larger ones take the balls in hand when they have gained in size and become too heavy for the younger boys.

Make these balls of snow as large and dense as possible; then roll them in place upon the lines traced out for the foundation. We will suppose it to be a square. In this case, care must be taken to have the corners of the square opposite the most probable approach of the enemy. This will leave the smallest point possible exposed to the attack, and the inmates of the fort can, without crowding each other, take good aim at the foe. After the four sides of the square are covered by large snowballs, as in Fig. 164, all hands must pack the snow about the bottom and fill up each crack and crevice until a solid wall is formed. Then with spades and shovels the walls should be trimmed down to a perpendicular on the inside, but slanting upon the outside, as shown in Fig. 165. The top of the wall may be two feet broad and the base four feet. When

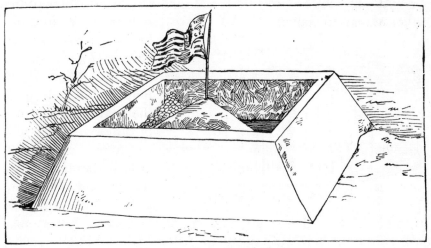

FIG. 165.—Snow Fort finished.

the wall is finished, prepare a mound of snow in the centre of the square for the flag-staff. This mound will be very useful as a reserve supply in case the ammunition gives out. A quantity of snowballs should next be piled up, inside the walls, at the four corners. This done, the fort is ready for its defenders, and it only remains to equip the attacking force.

The building of a fort generally uses up all the snow around it, making it necessary for the besieging party to carry their ammunition with them upon sleds made for that purpose.

The construction of these sleds is very simple, the materials and tools necessary consisting of a flour-barrel, a saw, a hat-chet, some shingle nails and an old pine board.

How to Make an Ammunition Sled.

To make the sled, begin by knocking the barrel apart, being careful not to split the head-boards, as they will be needed afterward. Pick out the four best staves, as nearly alike in breadth and curve as can be found, and saw two or three of the other staves in halves. Take two of the four staves first se-

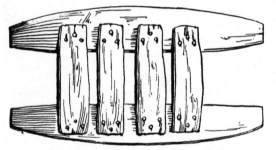

FIG. 166.—Top of Ammunition Sled.

lected and nail the half staves across, as shown in Fig. 166. These must be nailed upon the convex, or outside, of the staves; this will be found impossible unless there is something solid under the point where the nail is to be driven, otherwise the spring of the stave, when struck, will throw the nail out, and your fingers will probably receive the blow from the hammer. To avoid this, place a block, or anything that is firm, under the point where the nail is to be driven, and there will then be found no difficulty in driving the nails home. When this is done you will have the top of your sled as shown in Fig. 166; on this you will need a box or bed to hold the snowballs; this you can make of two pieces of pine board and two staves, thus: Take a board about the same width as, or a little wider than, a barrel-stave; saw off two pieces equal in length to the width of the sled; set them upon their edges, reversing the top of the sled; place it across the two boards and nail it on securely. Then take two staves

and nail them on for side boards, and you have the top portion
of your sled finished.

The two staves remaining of the four first selected are for
runners. Fit on first one and then the other to the staves of
the top. Nail-
holes will prob-
ably be found
near the ends of
the staves where
the nails were
that held the bar-
rel-head in;

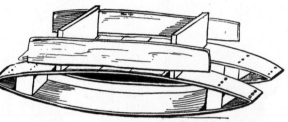

FIG. 167.—Ammunition Sled finished.

through these drive nails to fasten your runners; to do this
you must rest them upon some support, as was done before;
this will hold your sled together, but to make it stronger take
four wedge-shaped blocks of wood and slide them in between
the runners and the top, as shown in Fig. 167, and nail these
firmly in place from above and below.

If all this has been properly done, you now have made a
sled which it will be almost impossible to break; and, with a
rope to pull by, one boy can haul snowballs enough for a
dozen companions.

How to Make the Shield.

The shield is made from the head of a barrel. Lay the
barrel-head upon some level surface, so that nails can be driven
in without trouble.

From a strip of board half inch thick and two and one-half
inches wide saw off two pieces long enough to fasten the parts
of the barrel-head together, as you see them in Fig. 168.
Fasten these strips on firmly with shingle nails.

Lay your left arm upon the shield, as shown, mark a place
for the arm-strap just in front of elbow, and another for the

strap for the hand. From an old trunk-strap, or suitable piece
of leather, cut two strips and nail them on your shield at points
marked, being careful that the **arm-strap** is not too tight, as it
should be loose
enough for the arm
to slip in and out
with ease. This
done, you have a
shield behind which
you may defy an
army of unprotected
boys.

FIG. 168.

Rules of the Game.

The rules of war-
fare governing a
snowball battle are
as follows :

Two command-
ers, or captains, must be elected. If the forces engaged be
very large, each captain may appoint one or two assistants, or
lieutenants. These officers, after being elected and appointed,
are to give all orders, and should be promptly obeyed by their
respective commands. The captains decide, by lot, the choice
of position.

In choosing sides, the captain who is commander of the fort
has first choice, then the two captains name a boy, alternately,
until two-thirds of the boys have been chosen. The defenders
of the fort then retire to their stronghold, leaving the boys un-
chosen to join the attacking army, it being supposed that one-
third behind fortifications are equal to two-thirds outside.

Only the attacking party is allowed shields and ammunition sleds.

At least thirty yards from the fort a camp must be established by the outsiders or attacking army, and stakes driven at the four corners to locate the camp. Imaginary lines from stake to stake mark its limits.

Each party will have its national colors, in addition to which the attacking party has a battle-flag which it carries with it in the assault.

The defenders of the fort must see to it that all damages to the fortifications are promptly repaired.

Any soldier from the fort who shall be carried off within the limits of the camp becomes a prisoner of war, and cannot leave the camp until rescued by his own comrades.

Any one of the attacking force pulled into the fort becomes a prisoner of war, and must remain in the fort until it is captured.

Prisoners of war cannot be made to fight against their own side, but they may be employed in making snowballs or repairing damages to fortifications.

Any deserter recaptured must suffer the penalty of having his face washed with snow, and being made to work with the prisoners of war.

When the outsiders, or attacking army, can replace the enemy's colors with their battle-flag, the fort is captured and the battle is won by the attacking party; all fighting must then immediately cease.

But if, in a sally, or, by any means, the soldiers of the fort can take the colors of the opposite party from the camp and bring them inside their fortifications, they have not only successfully defended their fort, but have defeated the attacking army; and this ends the battle, with double honors to the brave defenders.

No water-soaked or icy snow-balls are allowed. No honorable boy uses them, and any one caught in the ungentlemanly

act of throwing such " soakers " should be forever ruled out of
the game.

No blows are allowed to be struck by the hand, or by anything but the regulation snowball, and, of course, no kicking
is permitted.

The following sketch of a snow battle in which the author
took part when a boy, will give an idea of the excitement and
interest of the game :

A Snow Battle.

It was a year when the Indian summer had been prolonged
into the winter. Christmas had come and gone and a new
year begun, but not one flake of snow had fallen on the river
bank or neighboring hills.

Such was the condition of things one January morning in
a Kentucky town upon the banks of the Ohio River, where
myself and some sixty other boys were gathered in a little
frame school-house.

We had about made up our minds that old Jack Frost was
a humbug, and winter a myth ; but when the bell tapped for
recess, the first boy out gave a shout which passed from mouth
to mouth until it became a universal cheer as we reached the
play-grounds, for floating airily down from a dull, leaden, gray
sky came hundreds of white snow-flakes !

Winter had come ! Jack Frost was no longer a humbug !
Before the bell again recalled us to our study the ground was
whitened with snow, and the school divided into two opposing
armies. That night was a busy one—all hands set to work
manufacturing ammunition sleds and shields for the coming
battle. It was my fortune to be chosen as one of the garrison
of the fort. There was not a boy late next morning—in fact,
when the teachers arrived to open the school, they found all the
scholars upon the play-grounds, rolling huge snowballs. All

night the snow had continued to fall, and it was now quite deep. When we went out at noon a beautifully modelled fort of snowy whiteness stood ready for us, and from a mound in the centre floated the battle-flag.

Our company took their places inside the fortifications.

We could see the enemy gathered around their captain at their camp some two hundred yards distant, their ammunition sleds loaded with well-made snowballs. The lieutenant bore their battle-flag.

Our teachers showed their interest by standing shivering with wet feet in the deep snow to watch the battle. At a blast from a tin horn on rushed the foe ! They separated and came in two divisions, approaching us from the left and right.

" Now, boys," cried our captain, " be careful not to throw a ball until they are within range."

Then, calling the pluckiest among us, a flaxen-haired country boy, to his side, he whispered a word or two and pointed to the flag in the enemy's camp. The boy, who had been nicknamed " Daddy " on account of his old-looking face, slipped quietly over the rear wall of the fort, dodged behind a snow-drift and then behind a fence, and was lost to sight. Forward marched the enemy, their battle-flag borne in advance of the party to the right. Their captain was at the head of the division to the left.

Having engaged our attention on the two flanks, where we stood ready to receive them, as they neared us, by a quick and well-executed manœuvre, rushing obliquely toward each other, the two divisions unexpectedly joined, and advanced, shield to shield, with the ammunition sleds in the rear. It was in vain we pelted them with snowballs ; on they came, encouraged by a cheer from the teachers and some spectators who by this time had gathered near the school-house.

Three times had our noble captain been tumbled from his

perch upon the mound in the centre of the fort, when another burst of applause from the spectators announced some new development, and as we looked, we could see "Daddy" with the colors of the enemy's camp in his arms, his tow hair flying in the wind as he ran for dear life.

In an instant the line of the enemy was all in confusion; some ran to head off "Daddy," while others in their excitement stood and shouted. It was our turn now, and we pelted their broken ranks with snow until they looked like animated snow-men. Another shout, and we looked around to find our captain down and the hands of one of the besieging party almost upon our flag. It was the work of a second to pitch the intruder upon his back outside the fort. Then came the tug of war. A rush was made to capture our standard, several of our boys were pulled out of the fort and taken prisoners, and the capture of the fort seemed inevitable. Again and again a number of the enemy, among whom was their color-bearer, gained the top of our breastworks, and again and again were they tumbled off amid a shower of snowballs that forced them to retire to gain breath and clear their eyes from the snow. Once their lieutenant, with the red-bordered battle-flag, had actually succeeded in reaching the mound upon which stood our colors, when a combined attack that nearly resulted in his being made prisoner drove him from the fort to gather strength for another rush. "Daddy" was now a prisoner, and the recaptured flag again floated over the enemy's camp, when the school-bell called us, fresh and glowing with exercise and healthful excitement, to our lessons. The battle was left undecided, but our fort was soon captured by a force stronger than any our companions were able to bring against it, for a warm south wind sprang up from the lowlands down the river, and our fortification quickly yielded to its insidious attack, and the snow campaign was over.

How to Bind a Prisoner Without a Cord.

A gentleman who was much interested in the foregoing description of snowball warfare sends a sketch of the manner he and his playmates used to bind their prisoners taken in snow battles. The captive was taken to a post or smooth-trunked sapling and compelled to put his arms and legs around it as if he were about to climb. The right leg crossed the left leg, and the toe of the right shoe was pushed behind the post or tree trunk in the position shown by the illustration. After taking this position the prisoner was gently pushed down into a sitting position. It is next to impossible for a person so fixed to arise without help. The toe of the left shoe binds the right leg; the toe of the right shoe binds the post, and the arms can be only used to hold on by.

A Prisoner of War.

When a friend reaches the captive he takes him by the arms and lifts him up. As soon as the prisoner assumes an upright position he can free himself without difficulty.

Company Rest.

The same gentleman who sent the above ingenious device also tells of some funny manœuvres the boys used to go through. For instance, during a lull in the battle, the commander would call out " Company rest ! " One man then assumed a stooping position; the next man sat on the right knee of the first man ; a third man would sit upon the right knee of the second man and so on until a circle was formed, each fellow sitting in some other fellow's lap and yet no one sitting upon anything else. "Thus," says the correspondent, "we all were enabled to sit down without using the damp snow for a camp stool."

"Advance under Fire."

CHAPTER XXVIII.

SNOW-HOUSES AND STATUARY.

IN "the land of the midnight sun," the far arctic regions where Jack Frost rules supreme, where the glistening ice and thickly packed snow covers the landscape almost the whole year round, the hardy inhabitants live in huts built of frozen

FIG. 169.—Showing the construction of a Snow-House.

blocks of snow. The interior of these icy dwellings are not, as might be supposed, uncomfortably cold, but, on the contrary, are quite warm and cosey. Boys who are inclined to doubt this may make the experiment for themselves. After the first good old-fashioned snow storm has covered the play-ground, roads, and house-tops, and while the merry jingle of the sleigh-bells tinkles through the wintry air let them busy themselves rolling huge balls of snow after the manner described in the chapter on " Snowball Warfare," making the foundation of

FIG. 170.—A Snow-House Finished.

the house exactly in the same way as that described for the snow-fort (page 258).

The roof is made of boards or planks covered with snow. A barrel placed over a hole in the roof, and surrounded by packed snow properly shaped, will make a very good chimney. A pane of glass can be set in the square hole made for a window ; a heavy piece of carpet can be hung from the ceiling over the doorway, so as to act as a curtain ; or if the young work-people choose to take trouble enough, they can put up a framework inside of the door-way and hang a wooden door to it by leather or canvas hinges. An old stove, or a fire-place made near the wall under the chimney, adds a finish to the house that will be found quite snug and comfortable as long as the snow lasts. The fire inside, if the weather be cold, will not melt the walls. The pictures of the house (Figs. 169 and 170) show so well how it is constructed, and how it looks when it is done, that very little explanation is necessary.

The walls are made of large snow-balls properly placed, with snow packed between them to make the surfaces tolerably even, and then the whole shaved down with a spade, outside and inside. It will be found impossible to put one tier of balls upon the top of the others by lifting them in place, but this difficulty may be overcome by sliding the balls up an inclined plane made of a strong plank, one end of which must be placed upon the ground and the other allowed to rest upon the top of the first or foundation row of snowballs.

FIG. 171.—Making the Pig.

Snow Statuary.

The statuary may be of various kinds.   It is very seldom

FIG. 172.—A Snow Pig.

that pigs are sculptured in marble or cast in bronze, and it

FIG. 173.—Making "Frenchy."

would be well to make some of snow, so as to have statues not likely to be found elsewhere. An oblong mass of snow forms the body (Fig. 171); the legs, nose, and ears are made of sticks surrounded by snow, and a bit of rope nicely curled will make a very good tail. The various parts can be shaped and carved according to the skill of the young artist. A number of pigs, of different sizes, will give a lively and social air to the yard of a snow-house. Fig. 172 shows a finished pig.

A statue of a Frenchman in an ulster is also rather uncommon, and is not hard to make. The foundation of the body, head, and legs consists of several large snowballs, as seen in Fig. 173, and the arms are made of smaller balls stuck on two sticks, which are inserted in the body at proper angles. When the whole figure has been "blocked out," as the artists say, it must be carved, with broad wooden knives or shingles,

FIG. 174.—Frenchy in his Ulster.

into the proper shape, as shown in Fig. 174. The moustache should be made of icicles, which may be stuck in the face.

FIG. 175.—Carving the Owl.

Arctic owls, which are very large and white, can also be made of snow, in the manner shown in the adjoining picture.   These figures can be placed on snow pedestals if they are small, but if they are monster owls, like those in the illustrations (Figs. 175 and 176), they must be placed upon the ground.

In either position, if they are fashioned properly, they will look very wise and respectable.

When the snow is too dry to make a snowball it cannot be used to make statuary, but after a slight thaw or a fresh fall of snow it readily adheres upon a slight pressure, and can be formed or fashioned in almost any shape.

Many curious objects and figures may be carved out of solidly packed balls of snow.   A lawn covered with a number of large snow figures presents a most grotesque appearance, and is sure to attract the attention of all passers-by.   With practice not a little skill may be acquired by the young sculptor, and if the statuary be made of large proportions, they will sometimes last for weeks after the snow has disappeared from the ground and house-tops.

FIG. 176.—An Arctic Owl.

CHAPTER XXIX.

SLEDS, CHAIR-SLEIGHS, AND SNOW-SHOES.

THE construction of one of the simplest sleds is shown by Fig. 177 ; it consists of nothing more nor less than three pieces of board nailed upon two barrel-staves.   The barrel-stave sled possesses the advantage of being so simple in design that a child might make one, and although this primitive sled can

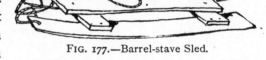

FIG. 177.—Barrel-stave Sled.

lay claim to neither grace nor beauty, it will be found useful in a variety of ways ; it may be used for coasting, or for transporting loads of snow when building snow houses, forts or figures.

If, instead of the long top board, a kitchen chair be fitted on, as shown in Fig. 178,

FIG. 178.—A Chair-Sleigh.

A Chair-Sleigh

will be had. It is necessary to nail on four L-shaped blocks at a proper distance apart on the cross board to hold the chair in place (Fig. 178). Any boy who is fortunate enough to have a mother or sister who takes sufficient interest, and has the time to accompany him on his skating trips, will find a chair-sleigh quite a handy thing to possess, and when he moves from one part of

the ice to a distant portion of the pond or river he can skate
behind the sleigh with his hands upon the back of the chair,
and push his lady friend rapidly over the ice, adding much to
her enjoyment as well as his own.

The cumbersome wooden kitchen chair is heavy to carry if
the skating pond be far from home, but a

Folding Chair-Sleigh

may be made from a few sticks and pieces of leather for hinges.
This chair is made upon the same principle as the one described

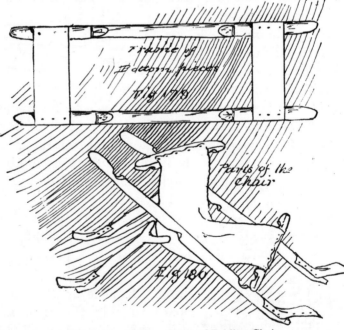

FIGS. 179 and 180.—Parts of Folding Chair.

in the chapter devoted to, "How to Camp Out." Figs. 179 and
180 show all the parts in detail as they would look before being
joined together. The seat may be made of a piece of carpet,
canvas, or any strong material, the hinges of leather. Fig.

181 shows the chair after it has been put together. The runners consist of skates, which may be strapped on or taken off at pleasure, without injuring the skates in the least. If the chair

is to be carried it can be folded up. When the chair frame is lifted the forked sticks that support it will slip from the notches in the side bars and fall on to the runner bars ; the chair

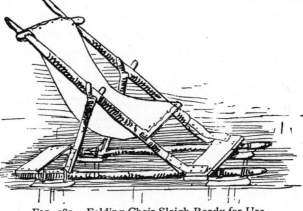

FIG. 181.—Folding Chair-Sleigh Ready for Use.

frame can then be let down and the whole frame-work will form a flat, compact mass (Fig. 182), that can be easily carried by quite a small boy. By using light sticks, regular metal hinges, and a prettily worked cloth for the seat, a very light and beautiful chair-sleigh can be made that, with the skates removed, will make an ornamental parlor chair for summer, and when the ice again covers the surface of the water, it will be only necessary to strap on the skates, and the easy chair becomes trans-

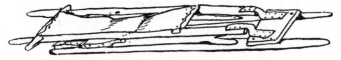

FIG. 182.—Folded Up.

formed into a chair-sleigh, to be pushed about over the glittering ice wherever its occupant may direct or the whim of the boy who forms the motive power may take him.

The Toboggan.

This sled, familiar to all who visit Canada or the Provinces during the winter months, is more like a mammoth snow-shoe than the ordinary sled, sleigh or jumper that we are accustomed to see. It is suitable for the deep snow and heavy drifts of the northern countries, where the runners of a common sleigh

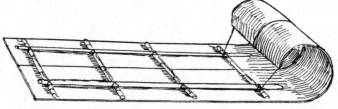

FIG. 183.—The Toboggan.

would be liable to break through the crust and bury themselves, thus impeding, if not altogether stopping, the vehicle. The toboggan presents a broad, smooth bottom to the snow, and glides over the crust.

To make one of these sleds you must procure two pieces of quarter-inch pine lumber eight or ten feet long and one foot wide. Place the two boards side by side and join them together by the means of round cross sticks; the latter are bound to the bottom board by thongs; the thongs pass through holes in the bottom boards on each side of the cross stick, and are made fast by a series of "hammock hitches" (see page 80, and Fig. 159, E). Where the thongs pass underneath the bottom board grooves are cut deep enough to prevent the cord from projecting; the grooves are quite necessary, for if the cords were allowed to project beyond the surface of the boards they would not only impede the progress of the toboggan, but the friction would soon wear out the thongs and the sled would come apart. On top of the cross sticks two side bars are lashed;

the front ends of the board are then curled over and held in position by two thongs made fast to the ends. Fig. 183 shows a finished toboggan drawn from one manufactured by the Indians in Canada.

Snow-Shoes or Skates.

The Norwegian ski is a snow-shoe, or rather a snow-skate, nine feet long, used by the Norwegians to glide down the mountains or hillsides when the latter are covered with snow.

Great fun can be had with a pair of snow-shoes made on the same principle as the Norwegian skate shoe, and it is little trouble to manufacture a pair from two barrel staves.

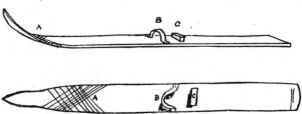

After selecting a couple of straight-grained staves, score

FIG. 184.—Top and Side View of Barrel-stave Skate.

one end of each stave with grooves cut in the wood either with your knife or a small gouge, as shown by the lines at A, Fig. 184. Smear the end thickly with grease and hold it near a hot fire until you find that it can be bent into the form shown by the diagram (Fig. 184); bind it in position by a cord and let it remain so until the wood retains the curve imparted. Make two blocks, each one inch broad and high enough to fit under the heels of your shoes; fasten the blocks on to the snow-skates by screws (C, Fig. 184); at a proper distance in front of the block fasten two straps securely (B, Fig. 184). By slipping the toes of your shoes through the straps and allowing the hollow of the foot to rest over the blocks C, C, so that the heels of your shoes bear against the blocks, you can keep the shoes on your feet, and, with the aid of a stick to steer by, go sliding down the coasting hill among the sleds and jumpers, creating as much fun for the others in your first attempts as you do for yourself; but with practice skill can be acquired in the use of snow-skates.

CHAPTER XXX.

HOW TO MAKE THE TOM THUMB ICE-BOAT AND LARGER CRAFT.

ALTHOUGH a full-rigged, delicately balanced ice-yacht looks like a very complicated piece of mechanism, when it is carefully examined the framework will be found to consist of two pieces crossing each other at right angles. The top of the cross is the bowsprit, the bottom of the cross the stern, and the sides the runners. At the intersection of the cross pieces the mast is stepped. The principle is simple enough, and with some sticks, two small pieces of inch lumber, three old skates, and two boards, a real little "Tom Thumb ice-yacht" can be built to hold a crew of one, and to be rigged like a catboat or with a jib and mainsail. The cross board may be made about 3 feet long and 6 inches wide. Make two runner blocks of inch lumber, and let them be each 6 inches long and 3 inches wide. With a bit and brace or a red-hot poker bore holes at proper distances apart for the straps of old-fashioned skates to pass through. One inch from each end of the cross board, fasten on the runner blocks securely with nails or screws (Fig. 185). For the centre plank use a board about 6 inches wide and 5 feet long. Nail the cross plank on to the centre plank in such a manner that a line drawn through the centre of the latter will intersect the cross board exactly at its middle. The planks must be at right angles to each other, forming a cross, the cen-

FIG. 185. — End of Cross-board, showing Runner - block and Skate.

tre piece extending about one foot beyond the cross piece ; this end will be the bow of the ice-boat and the opposite end the

stern. Bore a large hole in the stern for the rudder-post to pass through. The rudder-post may be made in a variety of forms ; a simple and convenient one is shown by Fig. 186. Another hole must be made through the point where the centres of the cross and centre planks intersect for the mast. Fig. 187 shows a leg-of-mutton sail, but the young yachtsman

FIG. 186.—Rudder with Tiller-ropes.

may make a sail of any description that may suit his taste. By referring back to the chapter on " How to Rig and Sail Small Boats," he can find several simple kinds of sails illustrated. Fig. 188 shows the top view of an ice-boat a trifle larger than the one just described ; the braces shown in the diagram are unnecessary on very small craft. To hold the mast more securely in larger yachts, a bench is made after the plan of Fig. 189 ; this will prevent the mast from being carried away under any ordinary circumstances, and also prevent it from swaying with every puff of wind. Where a seat is made as in Fig.

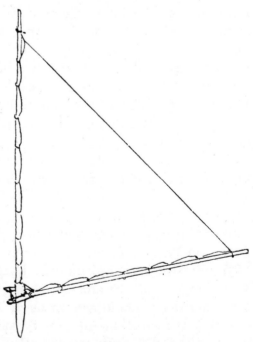

FIG. 187.—Leg-of-mutton Sail.

188, a wooden handle can be substituted for the tiller-ropes (Fig. 190).

The rudder is made of a skate; the latter is fastened by the screw at the heel and then strapped on a board nailed on to a

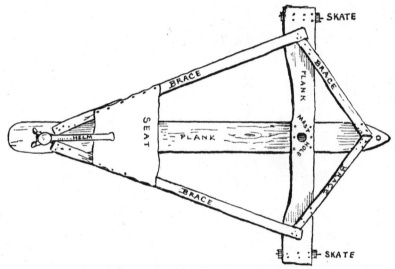

FIG. 188.—Top View of Ice-Boat.

club, shaped like a potato-masher; the small part of the club runs through a hole in the stern of the centre-board. A forked stick can be used for a tiller and must be fastened on to the rudder-post by running a pin or large wire through holes bored for the purpose in the rudder-post and the prongs of the forked stick. If the top of the rudder-post be squared, a tiller may be made of a stick with a square hole to fit over the end of the rudder-post, as shown in the illus- tration at the end of this chapter.

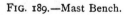

FIG. 189.—Mast Bench.

Perhaps some of my readers will invent more ingenious and simple steering apparatus than the ones given here; if

not, and the rudder-post and tiller seem to be a little too difficult, they may be omitted, and a stationary runner block substituted in their place. The boat must then be steered by the
feet of the crew. To do this he should have on skates. If a

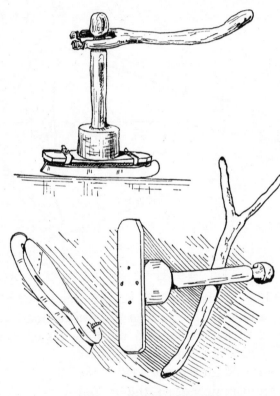

FIG. 190.—Steering Apparatus.

long handle be attached to the stern like the back to a sleigh-
chair, the steersman with skates on can guide the boat with
his feet by standing behind and holding on to the handle at
the stern. With this rig, the boat can accommodate a passenger aboard, as the steersman does not occupy the boat itself but
tends the sheets and steers while being towed behind. A

common sled may be fixed with holes in it so that a cross board can be attached by movable pegs, and with a mast stepped in the bow it will make tolerable speed and may be steered by a boy on skates.

A Tom Thumb and Crew.

CHAPTER XXXI.

THE WINGED SKATERS, AND HOW TO MAKE THE WINGS.

SKIMMING over the glassy surface of an ice-bound river or pond, propelled by the wintry blast blowing against artificial wings of cloth, is but a degree removed from flying. The friction of your skate runners upon the ice is so slight that it is not difficult to imagine that you have left the earth and are soaring in mid-air.

Every boy who has had any skating experience knows what hard work it is to skate against a stiff wind, and almost all who ever fastened skates to their feet must have enjoyed the luxury of sailing over the ice before the wind with a spread coat or open umbrella doing duty as a sail.

For some time back people in widely separated parts of the world have made more or less successful attempts at transforming themselves into animated ice-yachts, and in Canada, Norway, and other cold countries, men with sails rigged on their backs or shoulders have "tacked," "come about," and "luffed" themselves in a novel and highly entertaining style, but lately, for some reason or other, this sport has been allowed to almost die out, and we are now indebted to two or three writers for reintroducing skate-sailing to the public with original suggestions and improvements. Mr. Charles L. Norton, editor of *The American Canoeist*, was, I believe, the first to call the attention of the public in general, and the boys particularly, to this delightful sport. In an article published in the *St. Nicholas Magazine*, entitled " Every Boy his Own Ice-Boat," Mr. Norton describes a new and original device, consisting of a double sail, which is so simple in construction, and yet so strong, light, and easy to manage, that it is sure to become a favorite rig with the boys, both large and small.

In another article entitled " White Wings," which appeared in *Harper's Weekly*, the same author describes a number of queer sails used by different people. Following in the footsteps of Mr. Norton, and adding to our information on this subject, comes T. F. Hammer with an interesting article published in the *Century Magazine*, in which this gentleman gives some personal experience as a winged skater and a detailed description of the Danish skate-sail.

Among the many reasons given by skate-sailors why this new and highly exhilarating pastime should come into general favor are these : skate-sailing can be practised and enjoyed on ice too rough for ordinary skating, and a light fall of snow that ruins the ice for the common skater improves it for the winged yachtsman.

Salt-water ice that is too soft for one to enjoy a skate upon affords a better foothold than smooth, hard, fresh-water ice, and is preferable on that account. Wherever you can skate there you may sail, and when the skating proper is ruined, it often happens that the qualities of the ice are improved for sailing. There is no record of a serious accident happening to any skate-sailor, although one may attain, literally, the speed of the wind, the higher the rate of speed the less danger there appears to be, for in falling a person will strike the ice at such an angle that he is merely sent sliding over the surface, and little or no damage is done.

Bat Wings.

After procuring a suitable piece of cloth, spread it out upon the floor and tack it there, then spread yourself out on the cloth with your arms extended at right angles to your body, and your feet spread apart. While in that position, have some one mark on the cloth the points where the crown of your head, your wrists, and ankles come. With a chalk or pencil connect these points by lines, and, allowing for the hem, cut the sail out according to the pattern made.

Turn the edges over and make a strong broad hem all around the sail, sew in straps or bands at the ankle, waist, wrists, and head. When the sail is to be used, adjust the head-band around the forehead, fasten the waist, wrist, and ankle straps, and the ship is rigged. By spreading the arms, the sail is set; when the arms are folded the sail is furled. It would become exceedingly tiresome to hold the arms outstretched from the sides for any length of time without support; to obviate this, a stick may be carried, which, when thrust behind the back, will make a support for the hands as they grasp it near the ends. The man-bat steers with his feet, using his legs and arms for sheet-lines. Skaters rigged up in this novel style present a most grotesque appearance as they flap their wings about in going through various evolutions.

The Norton Rig

is a double sail, and might be called a schooner rig. It is in many respects superior to the somewhat cumbersome single sails, the chief advantage being the fact that the crew can see in every direction, and thus avoid running foul of any other craft or skater. Another improvement is the double main spar which, without increasing the weight, affords a stronger support for the cross pieces, or fore and main masts. The main spar may be made of spruce pine or bamboo. Cane fishing-poles are inexpensive, and can probably be readily obtained by most boys. Select two pieces, each about ten feet long, and bind the butt or large end of one to the small end of the other; lash the other ends firmly together in like manner, so that the two poles will lay side by side firmly bound at each end.

For the fore and main masts or cross yards, Mr. Norton recommends bamboo, five-eighths of an inch in diameter, but American cane will also answer for that purpose. Pick out two pieces five-eighths of an inch in diameter at the smallest ends,

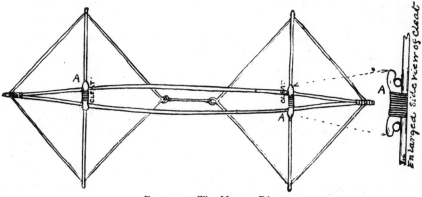

FIG. 191.—The Norton Rig.

and let each be four feet six inches long. Near the ends of the cross yards fasten metal buttons or knobs, and fasten similar knobs near the ends of the main spar. Make a small cleat for the middle of each cross spar (A, A, A, Fig. 191) and lash it firmly on.

Make the sails of the heaviest cotton sheeting, if it can be procured; if not, take ordinary sheeting and double it, or what cloth you can procure. Mark out the sails, making allowance for the hem, and let them measure four feet across the diagonal after the hem has been turned down; bind the sails with strong tape, and see that the corners particularly are made very strong.

Sew to the " clews " or corners small metal rings, or loops of strong cord, to fasten on the buttons at the ends of the spars.

Attach the sails to the cross spars by slipping the rings at the clews over the buttons at each end of the spars. Spring the main spar apart and slip the cleats of the cross spar between the two pieces, so that they fit as shown by Fig. 191. Fasten the outside clews to the buttons on the ends of the main spar and bind the two inside clews tightly together with a cord as shown in the diagram, and you are all ready to give the novel device a trial. Go to the nearest sheet of ice, put on your skates, and after seeing that they are securely fastened, take up the sails and let yourself go before the wind, steering with your feet. After practising awhile you can learn to tack, and go through all the manœuvres of a regular sail-boat.

A most beautiful " rig " is described by Mr. Norton, in which the main spar consists of four pieces of bamboo joined at the middle by brass fishing-rod ferrules. Brass tips are used for holding the small ends of the bamboo together at the ends of the main spar. This rig can be taken apart like a jointed fishing-rod, and, like it, put in a comparatively small case, occupying not much more space when the sails are rolled up than an old-fashioned cotton umbrella. Sails may be made of fancy striped cloth and brilliantly colored penants rigged to their corners ; combine this with a suitable uniform, and the winged skater will present a most striking and dashing appearance as he goes flying over the ice.

The Norwegian Rig.

This is a very simple sail to make, as may be seen by referring to Fig. 192. The spars can be made of the same material as the ones described for the Norton rig. The Norwegian rig requires a crew of two, and in this particular differs from all the rest. The man at the bow grasps the main spar with one hand

just behind the fore cross yard, and with the other hand takes
hold of the main spar behind him ; the helmsman must stand at

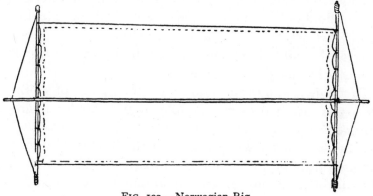

FIG. 192.—Norwegian Rig.

the stern or "aft" end of the sail, so that he can see to steer.
The man in front must hold on and trust to Providence and the
steersman.   This is rather an awkward rig, but it has the advantage of carrying two instead of one, and is consequently in
favor with people who like
sociability.

The Danish Rig
consists of a mainmast and
topmast.   The latter can be
let down when required.   The
diagram (Fig. 193) is made of
dimensions suitable for a good-
sized boy.   The straps near
the bottom of the topmast are
for the purpose of binding the
sail to the back of the crew,

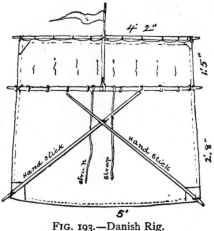

FIG. 193.—Danish Rig.

like a knapsack.   The hand-sticks are only attached to the lower
corners of the sails, the other ends are held by the crew, crossed

and used as sheet-lines are in an ordinary sail-boat. The spars may all be made of spruce, pine, cedar, bamboo, or Southern cane, and the sail of heavy cotton sheeting or strong cotton duck, of double thickness at the clews. In experimenting with this rig, it is best to choose a day when there is only a moderate wind, for the sail being bound to your body cannot be cast aside by simply letting go.

The mainsail and topsail are all of one piece of cloth. The topmast is fastened to the middle of the shoulder yard by a leather strap passing around the yard. The topmast is held in place by the wind blowing it against the head of the crew. By running a little into the wind the topsail will fall back and leave only the mainsail up, or if you loosen the cross knot at the upper part of the topmast you can roll the topsail down to the reefing points and lash it there. The steering is done with the feet of the crew. To learn to sail this or any other craft practice is needed. You might as well try to learn to swim from reading a book as to expect to become an expert sailor without going to sea.

FIG. 194.—English Rig.

The English Rig

consists of a mast and two spars (Fig. 194); the bottom of the mast rests in straps fastened to one leg of the crew, who supports the sail by placing one arm around the mast, holding on to the top spar with the other hand. This makes quite a pretty craft, though, like the Danish rig, the sail must be bound to the crew, which always appears objectionable from the fact that in case of accident there must be more danger of breaking the spars or tearing the sail than there is where the whole thing can be dropped in an instant. The English rig is on something of the same principle as

The Cape Vincent Rig,

which consists of a long spar and a sprit, the spar being in some cases twelve or fifteen feet in length ; one seven feet long will make a sail large enough for a boy. The sprit is fastened at the bottom securely to the sail, and fits on to the main spar with a crotch, fork, or jaw. The sail being cut in the right shape

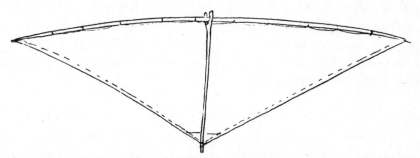

FIG. 195.—Cape Vincent Rig.

and proper proportions, and made fast to the long spar and to the end of the sprit, as soon as the latter is forced into place it will stretch the sail out flat, as in Fig. 195. A boy with one of these rigs on his shoulder makes a very rakish-looking craft. The spar is carried "as a soldier carries his rifle"—on the shoulder ; the sprit, or small cross spar, is allowed to rest against the crew's back. According to one writer, who is supposed to have had experience, this rakish craft will not in the least belie its looks. In speaking of it he says : " I should say that on good, smooth ice, with a twenty-five or thirty-mile wind, they went at the rate of eighty or *one hundred miles an hour.*" This sounds like an exaggeration, but when we remember that a good ice-yacht, well handled, can make a mile a minute or more, travelling much faster than the wind itself, the statement of the enthusiastic advocate of the Cape Vincent rig does not appear so improbable. In speaking of the speed attained by regular ice-yachts, Mr. Norton says :

" There is no apparent reason why a skate-sailor should not attain a like speed. Other things being equal, he has certain advantages over the ice-yacht. His steering gear is absolutely perfect, assuming, of course, that he is a thoroughly confident skater, and it is in intimate sympathy with the trim of his sail. This nice adjustment between rudder and sails is an important point. Again, there is no rigidity about the rig. Everything sways and gives under changing conditions of wind, and experience soon endows the skater with an instinct which teaches him to trim his sail so as to make every ounce of air-pressure tell to the best advantage."

A Country Rig.

The two forked sticks from which the framework of this sail is made must necessarily be nearly of the same dimensions. After their ends have been firmly lashed together, as shown by Fig. 196, a sail made of an old piece of carpet, awning, hay - cover, or any cloth that is strong enough or

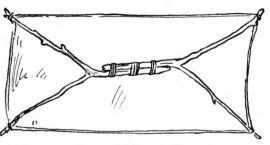

FIG. 196.—Country Rig.

can be made strong enough by doubling, may be lashed on at the four prongs of the forks. This rig will convey a crew of two over the ice with as much speed as the more elaborate Norwegian sail (Fig. 192). The country sail may not be handsome, but it possesses the advantage of being easily constructed and costing little or nothing, except the work of cutting and trimming the spars and sail.

CHAPTER XXXII.

WINTER FISHING—SPEARING AND SNARING— FISHERMEN'S MOVABLE SHANTIES, ETC.

The pleasures of fishing are naturally and almost invariably connected in our minds with warm weather, particularly with Spring or the first coming of Summer, the bright freshness of

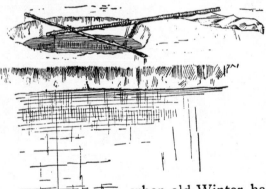

bursting bud and new-opening wild blossom, and with those latter days in the Autumn over which the Summer King sheds his brightest glories. But in our northern and easterly States, when old Winter has spread his mantle of frost and snow over the face of Nature, and hermetically sealed all the lakes and ponds under covers of ice, as an agreeable addition to the fun of skating, hardy, red-cheeked boys cut round holes in the thick ice, and through them rig their lines for pickerel-

FIG. 197.—Flip-Up Set. fishing. A very simple but ingenious contrivance enables a single fisherman to attend to quite a number of lines if the holes be all made within sight of the fisherman, the fish itself will give the signal for the particular line that requires attention.

The construction of this automatic fishing-tackle is so simple that it may be made in a few moments by any one. The preceding illustration shows how it is arranged (Fig. 197). At the end of a light rod a foot or two in length is fastened a small signal flag; a piece of any bright-colored cloth answers the purpose. This rod is bound with strong string at right angles to a second stick, which is placed across the hole, lying some inches upon the ice at either side; the flag also rests on the ice, leaving a short piece of the flag-rod pro-

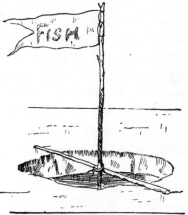

FIG. 198.—The Signal Flying.

jecting over the cross stick; to this short end the line and hook are fastened. The hook is baited with a live minnow or other suitable bait and lowered through the hole. The tackle is then in readiness for the capture of a pickerel. When the fish is hooked his struggles keep the flag flying (Fig. 198).

Smelt Fishing and the Smelt Fisher's House.

From about December 20th until the middle or latter part of February the smelt fishing season is in its height along the coast of Maine. The fish are caught through holes in the ice. In the vicinity of Belfast clam worms are used for bait; the worms are found in the clam flats.

Notwithstanding the reputation for original inventions possessed by the inhabitants of the Eastern States, the "Down East" smelt fishermen of Maine have for years, while fishing through the ice, exposed themselves to the piercing winter winds, apparently without once thinking of providing any other shelter than their heavy overcoats and perhaps a rude barricade of ice blocks and evergreen boughs. There is no telling how long this state of things might have continued, but during the winter of 1877–78* a single fisherman, more enterprising than his comrades, appeared upon the fishing grounds with a small canvas tent, inside of which he at once proceeded to make himself comfortable, and at the same time excite the envy of the unprotected, shivering fishermen scattered over the ice. The latter were not long in taking the hint, and the next season found the ice dotted all over with the little canvas houses of the fishermen. During the best of the season the smelt fishing grounds now have the appearance of Indian villages ; the blue smoke curls up from the peaked roofed lodges and floats away on the frosty air, while the figures of men and boys passing to and fro on different errands might at a distance be easily mistaken for the aboriginal red Americans at their winter camp.

The framework of a smelt fisher's house consists of a light wooden frame about six feet square, with a sharp roof. After the frame is firmly fastened together it is put upon runners, furnished with a bench for the fisherman to sit upon, a stove to keep him warm, and a covering of light canvas to keep out the cold. The canvas is a better protection against sleet and frost if it has been covered with a coat of paint. Sometimes the houses are made large enough to accommodate more than one fisherman. Snugly ensconced beside a warm stove, with pipe in mouth, the old veterans spin their yarns, and, oblivious to the raging northwest winds, watch their lines, which are attached to a rack overhead and hang down, passing through a hole in the ice. The bait dangles about eight or ten feet under the water. When a fish bites, the motion of the line apprizes the fisherman of the fact, and he pulls it out, unhooks the fish and again drops

* According to the Belfast (Me.) Journal.

his line. In this manner one man will succeed in catching from
ten to fifteen pounds in a day.

A gentleman who seems to be posted upon the subject of
smelt fishing sends me the following device, which ought to
have been included in the chapter on odd modes of fishing.
My correspondent
says : " During the fall
months the smelt run
in large schools up the
creeks and streams
emptying into the
ocean, and are caught
with seines or nets by
professional fishermen
for market. To be

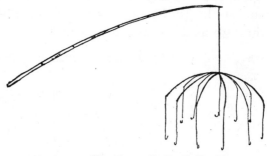

FIG. 199.—The Umbrella Smelt Tackle.

sure, no true sportsman could make use of such means for capturing game ; still, as it is necessary to take these small fish in
large numbers to make a respectable mess, some ingenious
sportsman has evolved a fishing-tackle with which one can
legitimately do wholesale fishing. To a line on an ordinary
pole is attached an apparatus resembling an umbrella-frame
without the handle ; from the point of each bow hangs a line
and hook (Fig. 199) ; in this way six or eight smelt may be taken
in the time it would require to catch one with a single line."

For boys who live inland where smelt fishing is out of
the question, there are other fish whose gamy nature will im-
part more fun and excitement to their capture. Long rods
would be out of place within the narrow limits of a little cloth-
covered fishing box ; but hand lines or short rod and reel may
be used. When a short rod is used it is only for the purpose of facilitating the use of the reel, and the rod should not
be over two and one-half feet long. Fish may also be snared
or speared through holes in the ice by boys concealed in little

wooden shanties built for the purpose. This sport is much in vogue on some of the small lakes in the Northwest.

The Spearsman's Shanty.

The great drawback to spearing fish through holes in the ice, is the inability of the spearsman to see objects under water, and to keep the cold winds from chilling him through and through as he stands almost motionless watching for his game ;

FIG. 200.—Framework for Spearman's Shanty.

but if the sportsman will supply himself with one of the little wooden shanties used by the fish spearers in the Northwest, he will overcome both these difficulties. The shanty, when the door is closed, is perfectly dark inside, having no other opening except a round hole, about a foot and a half in diameter, in the floor just over the hole in the ice. The only light seen by the fisherman is the bright, shining water, which glows like a full moon underneath him. As his eyes become accustomed to the peculiar condition of things, the nebulous objects first discernible in the luminous water resolve themselves into floating grasses and reeds ; the bottom, even where the water is quite deep, becomes plainly visible, and every passing fish is distinctly seen by the spearsman, while he, being in total darkness, is invisible to the creatures below. This effect can be readily understood when one remembers that the ice, unless it be covered with snow, is transparent, and that the light shining through illuminates the water. It is as if you were standing outside of a house on a very dark night looking through a window into a brilliantly lighted room.

The fishermen's shanties are provided with small sheet-iron stoves, which require but very little fire to make the house warm enough for one to sit with his coat off. The stoves are provided with small pipes, which issue through the roof or side of the house. A bench, camp-stool, or chair complete the furniture.

Snaring Fish.

Catfish may be chummed for ; that is, attracted by bait cut up and dropped through the hole in the ice. The bait will attract many other fish, which can be snared with a slip-noose made of fine copper or brass wire and attached to the end of a line. There is nothing alarming in the looks of this instrument, and a fish will not notice the snare until it finds the fatal noose tightly drawn about its body. It requires a little practice to snare fish successfully. I well remember my first attempt. A large " mud sucker " was discovered under an overhanging bank. Cautiously I crept to the edge of the stream, and with trembling, yet careful hand, I let the snare glide gently into the water. The fish did not move ; by degrees I slipped the noose over the comical slippery head of the creature, and with a mighty jerk landed—not the fish, but my snare in the boughs of a tree that overhung the water. I was thunderstruck when I discovered that the fine wire of the snare had cut the fish completely in halves, and as the muddy water, stirred up by the commotion beneath, rolled away down stream, I beheld one-half of the "mud sucker" with the puckering mouth still moving, and the other half with its tail flapping in the water beneath.

It requires experience to learn just how hard to pull on a snare to catch a fish and hold it without breaking the line or cutting the game.

Spearing Fish

is far more exciting and sportsmanlike than snaring them. The fish may be attracted by dead bait dropped through the hole in the ice, after the manner before described, or if it be pickerel you are after, a trolling spoon can be danced up and down, and round and round, until it attracts the attention of the fish. Some fishermen use a wooden minnow weighted at the bottom with lead and provided with fins and tail made of tin. Such a decoy, to be effective, should be decorated with a brilliant red stripe on each side, a white belly, and a bright green back. By means of a line fastened to the wooden fish it can be made to swim around under water in a most frisky and life-like manner, completely deceiving the unwary pickerel. The decoy must be kept out of reach when the fish dart at it, and at the same time the spear must be poised, ready to cast at the first opportunity. Often the unsuspicious pickerel will stop and remain for some moments motionless directly under the hole in the ice, apparently considering the best mode of capturing the lively and gaudy minnow that dances so temptingly near his hungry jaws. This is a golden opportunity for the young fisherman, and waiting only such time as it may require to take aim, the lance should be launched. A good fish spear is described on page 188 and illustrated by Fig. 121. As soon as a fish is speared it should be thrown upon

the ice outside the shanty and allowed to freeze. In this manner the meat is kept much sweeter and fresher than it is possible
to preserve fish in warm weather, even for so short a time as it
requires to carry the game home from the fishing grounds.

How to Build a Fishing House.

Fig. 200 shows the framework for a small fishing house ;
the posts and cross pieces are made of such sticks as can be
found along the bank of any stream or lake. Fig. 201 shows

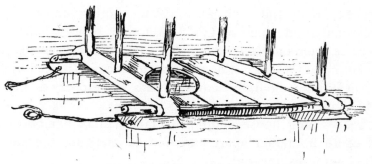

FIG. 201.—Floor and Runners of Spearsman's Shanty.

how the floor is made of planks, with a hole in the forward part
to fish through. The whole frame may be covered with pieces
of an old hay-cover, canvas, or what is better still, pieces of old
oil-cloth, such as is used for dining-room or hall floors. If the
framework be covered with any light cloth, the cloth should be
tacked on and thickly coated with paint so as to admit no light.
A frame like the one illustrated by Figs. 200 and 201 may be
made, fitted up, and kept stored away until wanted for use.
After hauling it out on the fishing grounds and cutting a hole
through the ice, the frame can be covered with thick blankets,
and without injuring the material the covering can be fastened
by pins and strings over the framework and removed when the
day's sport is finished. If, instead of rough forked sticks, regu-

lar square posts be used, the whole can be covered with quarter-inch pine lumber, thus making a light but serviceable
shanty. If the light come in under the house, pack snow
around it. If the snow cover the ice to such a thickness as to
darken the water beneath, sweep a place clean around your
shanty, and the light admitted through the clear ice will illumi-
nate the water beneath your hut or tent. Fig. 202 shows another form of fisherman's hut, made upon the same principle as
the cabin of the Crusoe raft (Figs. 70 and 71, pages 99 and 100).
Select hickory or any other elastic saplings, taking care to have
them all about the same size. After boring holes with an
auger in the side bars of the floor frame, bend saplings over
and force their ends into the holes as shown in the diagram.
The floor can be laid in the same manner as illustrated by Fig.
201, and the whole frame covered with some opaque fabric, or
cloth made opaque by a coating of paint. A very beautiful
and light fishing house might be made with a bamboo frame
that could be taken apart and packed away for the summer
like a jointed fishing-rod.

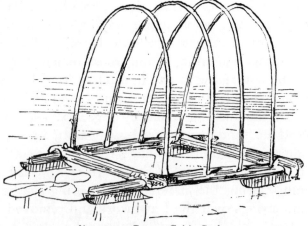

FIG. 202.—Crusoe Cabin Style.

CHAPTER XXXIII.

IN-DOOR AMUSEMENTS.

THERE will frequently occur gaps, in the long winter evenings, that are hard to fill up satisfactorily, hours when, tired of reading or study, a boy does not know what to do. Again, occasionally through the winter one's companions and friends are likely to drop in and spend an evening. The most accomplished host is at times at a loss to know how to entertain his company, after the old, worn, threadbare games have been repeated until they have become monotonous and tiresome.

To the filling of these gaps, and for the relief of the worried host, I propose to devote a limited space and chapter in explaining and suggesting some novelties in the way of in-door amusements.

Bric-à-brac, or the Tourist's Curiosities,

is a comparatively new game, which, in the hands of a smart boy or a fluent speaker, can be rendered entertaining, startling, or boisterously funny. The company, seated at a long table in a very dimly lighted room, must be particularly requested to keep their hands under the table, pay strict attention to the tourist, and maintain a solemn silence. The tourist, from the head of the table, commences his narrative something as follows :

"In the year 1867 I was travelling in Egypt, having been commissioned by a certain scientific association to procure for them as perfect a specimen of a mummy as I could find. I

2Q

made it my particular business to associate as much as possible
with the native Arabs, whose ostensible business of guides and
donkey masters is but a disguise, and, at the same time, a help
to their real trade of grave robbers.　Through my interpreter, I
let it be known that I was willing to pay a good price for the
mummy of some king or noble person—such mummies, being
more carefully and skilfully embalmed, are in a much more
perfect state of preservation.　For some months I was fooled
and fretted by these Arab swindlers and cheats, who would
take me long distances to show some very common broken
specimen.　Finally, finding I would not be imposed upon, I received a call one night from a most villainous-looking native,
who said for so much money he would introduce me to a certain Amed al Hamu, who could procure me what I wanted.　To
shorten a long story, I met Amed al Hamu, and after a week's
dickering and bargaining made an appointment to meet him
alone at his home—one could scarcely say house, for he lived in
a sort of tomb cut out of the solid rock some twenty feet up a
precipitous rock on the edge of the desert.　At the appointed
time he met me at the foot of the rock, and after cautiously
looking to see if we were watched, led me to his cave.　Passing
through this, with light in hand we entered a narrow passage
cut in the rock ; through this we stooped and crawled for about
a hundred yards ; here the passage ended abruptly, as though
unfinished.　On one side, near the end, was a large crack or
fissure, through which I squeezed myself after my guide, and
stood upon the brink of a bottomless pit.　From its hiding-
place Amed al Hamu produced a rude specimen of rope-ladder,
by the means of which we descended some ten feet into the
pit ; getting off on a ledge of rock I was ushered into a small
cavern and found a really valuable mummy in an unusually fine
mummy case, after showing which Amed offered to deliver it
to me at some *fifty per cent. above* the price originally agreed

upon. We finally settled the bargain and started to return. As but one at a time could use the rope-ladder, I sent the Arab on first, thinking while he was ascending I might look around, for I felt certain that all those excavations were never made for a single mummy. In the hasty glance I took of the chamber nothing new could be seen, but remembering that the ladder was a very long one, when it came my turn I went down instead of up. Passing a ledge similar to the one just left, I continued down and discovered a narrow landing on the opposite side of the pit. By swinging the rope I reached it and got off. Stepping through a small doorway I stood in a large, spacious chamber; pieces of broken mummy cases and fragments of linen bandages strewed the floor; boxes filled with porcelain statuettes, precious vases of alabaster, jars of bronze and terra-cotta were piled against the walls. Standing upright and laid at length upon the floor were huge sarcophagi of painted wood. Mummy cases fashioned after the human form crowded the room. Evidently I was amidst the kings and rulers of Pharaonic Egypt. Examining one of the richest sarcophagi I discovered that it had been lately opened, and upon trial lifted the cover off easily; the mummy case inside was broken and half open. There was no doubt, from the fineness of the linen, that the occupant had been royal. It would be hard to say what my emotions were when I opened this mummy case; surprise and astonishment certainly predominated, for there, with bandages and wrappings half torn and cut off, was the most wonderfully preserved specimen ever seen or heard of. It was, or had been a thousand years ago, a princess of great beauty, and so perfectly was the form preserved that but for the color I should have said she slept !

" It was evident at a glance that the grave-robbing ghouls had here found a prize which they meant to keep a secret until they discovered the most advantageous way of disposing of it.

Upon closer examination I was shocked to discover that one hand of the beautiful mummy had been severed at the wrist, probably for the purpose of more easily obtaining the bracelet that had once encircled the arm. Pulling aside some of the bundled bandages, I discovered the little delicate, shapely hand. A terrific yell from the Arab above startled me so that I dropped the light, which was instantly extinguished, leaving me in total darkness. Thrusting the mummy hand into an inside pocket I groped my way out to the ledge, shouting help! murder! fire! at the top of my voice; in fact, so loud did I yell that the swarthy son of the desert ceased his shouting, and as he reached the ledge upon which I stood held his light aloft, and discovering me, with no light, standing upon the brink of the dark abyss, his villainous features relaxed into a smile, and, motioning me to proceed, he followed me up the ladder. After I had returned to my stopping-place and taken counsel with some friends, in spite of their advice I dispatched a messenger to Amed al Hamu, proposing to purchase some of the treasures that I knew were hidden in the but half-explored cave. The only answer I received was a message from the sheik, or chief of the village, stating that I had in some way 'incurred the ill will and animosity of the populace,' and had better therefore absent myself immediately, as he, the sheik, 'was powerless to protect.' It is hardly necessary for me to state that I acted upon this hint and left; I am free to acknowledge that I think more of my own body than any mummy that was ever embalmed. The beautifully shaped hand I still have as evidence of my adventure, and if you will kindly pass it to one another under the table each may feel its peculiar texture."

The tourist then takes from a basket at his side a kid glove, previously prepared by stuffing it with damp sand and allowing it to rest on ice for an hour or so. The guests should be repeatedly cautioned about dropping the specimen, otherwise the peculiar cold, damp feeling of what seems to be the hand of a mummy will cause the nervous ones to throw it from them in a hurry. After this has made the circuit of the table, the tourist places it upon a waiter in front of him and proceeds to explain the capture of a very curious sea-urchin, which turns out to be a pincushion with the points of pins sticking out all over it. Next comes a piece of the Japanese weeping crystal from a cave in the centre of Simoda—simply a piece of ice ; and so the game continues with as many queer specimens as the ingenuity of the tourist can invent. A glib talker can so excite the imagination of his hearers as to often make them believe for the time that the object they are handling under the table is genuine. When, after the game is over, the contents of the tourist's basket are exposed for the audience to examine by sight as well as touch, there is always a great laugh as each one recognizes some familiar object, which, with the help of a dark room and a vivid imagination, sent the chills down his back.

Mind-Reading.

This is more in the nature of a trick than a game, but as anything that creates surprise or approaches the wonderful always proves attractive and entertaining, I introduce this plan of reading the contents of a folded paper by laying it across the forehead. The mind-reader seats himself at a table at one end of the room ; the audience must not approach nearer than five feet, and should be seated in a semicircle in front of him. Slips of paper, all the same size and shape, are then distributed among the audience, with the request that each one write thereon a short sentence, plainly and in English. While they are busy writing, the mind-reader, or medium, is preparing for the trial by first making sundry passes across his forehead, rubbing each arm slowly from shoulder to wrist, and then sitting calm and silent, staring at the wall. Each person folds his piece of paper carefully, and they are all collected by some one, who, standing alongside the medium, presses the first paper folded on the medium's forehead, who with closed eyes immediately reads the contents out loud, and then verifies it by taking, opening, and re-reading it with his eyes open, and requests the writer to acknowledge it, after which the second paper is treated in a similar manner, thus continuing until every paper has been read and acknowledged. All this appears very wonderful and inexplicable to the uninitiated, but perfectly simple when explained. The party who collects the papers is the medium's confederate, and should be selected from among the guests some time before the game is proposed, and in another room be thoroughly drilled so as to make no mistakes. The confederate's part is very easy. It is simply to let the medium know what is to be written on his piece of paper, and be careful to leave that particular message for the last one to be read. On these two points depend the success of the experiment, for it makes no difference what the first message is. The medium reads out whatever the confederate was to write, and while pretending to verify it by re-reading with his eyes open, he really is fixing in his memory the lines in the first paper, which he reads out as the contents of the second message. The second is read as the third, and so on through them all. The confederate's message, which was read out as coming first, being the last, brings them out even.

A Literary Sketch Club

is a new idea, which has been tried and has proved very successful, the original club having prospered through three winters, and still boasts of some thirty enthusiastic members. The idea of the club is that each member illustrate the same subject (previously selected) in any way he thinks fit—the artists, if there be any present, by a drawing or painting on the subject ;

a member who sings may select, adapt, or originate a song that will express his idea of the subject. Instrumental music may be made to tell the story; short sketches, in prose or poetry, original essays, or selections carefully made from good authors; in fact, there is scarcely any one who cannot illustrate the subject in some way that will add to the entertainment of the evening. I annex the Constitution of the original club, which I know from practical experience works well:

CONSTITUTION.

I. Name.

The name of this society shall be the —— Literary Sketch Club.

II. Officers.

The officers of this club shall consist of a president, a secretary, an editor, and an associate editor.

The duties of president and secretary shall be such as usually pertain to such offices.

The editor shall have entire control of a paper to be issued by the club.

The duties of the associate editor shall be to assist the editor in the work of publishing the paper, and to take control of the paper in case of the illness or absence of the editor.

The election of officers shall take place at the first meeting held each season, their term of office to expire upon the next election day.

III. Meetings.

The regular meetings of the —— Literary Sketch Club shall be held once in every two weeks.

IV. Subjects for Illustration.

The subject to be illustrated must be selected by the member who is to next entertain the club, and announced by him at the meeting preceding the one to be held at his house.

V. Sketches.

A sketch illustrating the subject selected will be expected from each member present.

The said sketches may be essays, poems, songs, music, pictures, or any other method of illustration that may suggest itself. Original sketches are not absolutely required.

Contributions for the club paper must be sent to the editor ; they may be anonymous.

VI. Election of New Members.

Candidates for membership may be proposed at any meeting and the election proceeded with, two black balls excluding the candidate from membership.

VII. Absence.

Absence from three consecutive regular meetings, without an acceptable excuse, will be considered equivalent to a resignation, and the absentee's name may be acted on accordingly.

VIII. Order of Business.
1. Roll call.
2. Reading of the minutes of the previous meeting
3. Presentation of sketches.
4. Reading of the club paper.
5. Reports of committees.
6. Miscellaneous business.
7. Proposals and election of members.
8. Adjournment.

IX. Amendments to Constitution.

This Constitution can be amended only at a regular meeting by a two-thirds vote, due notice of intended amendment having been given at the previous regular meeting.

Printing Presses.

Little printing presses may be had at such reasonable prices that some member might have one ; in that case the club paper, printed in due form, would prove a souvenir which would be prized and carefully kept by each member, especially should it contain an article by himself. In the original club the paper was carefully and neatly written in a blank-book, and in some instances illustrated by an artistic member.

CHAPTER XXXIV.

THE BOY'S OWN PHUNNYGRAPH,

TO BE EXHIBITED

By Prof. Edd and Son.

IN winter-time, when a great part of a boy's fun must be found in-doors, it is a good thing to know how to get up amateur exhibitions of various kinds. In this way boys can have a good time while preparing the shows, and may also afford a great deal of pleasure to their companions and friends who make up the audiences.

One of the most entertaining parlor exhibitions which can be given at a moderate expense by a party of bright boys, accustomed to the use of carpenters' tools, is '' The Boy's Own Phunnygraph,'' invented by the author, who once exhibited one at an amateur performance before an audience of five hundred people.

The first thing necessary in the construction of this very peculiar machine is a dry-goods box, large enough for a boy to sit inside of it without discomfort. The top must be firmly nailed on and the two sides taken off, thus leaving nothing but the top, bottom, and two ends of the box. The sides, each of which probably consists of two or three pieces of board, are to serve as doors, and therefore must be firmly fastened together by means of cleats or narrow strips of board nailed across them. One side of the box, which we shall call side A, must be

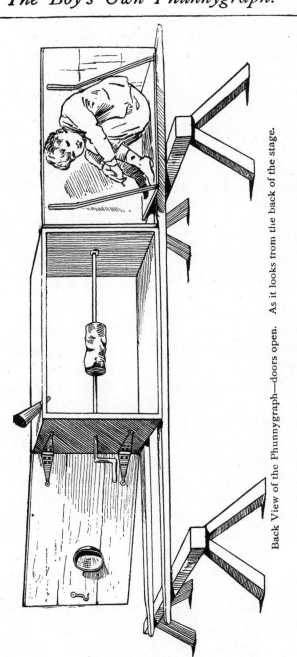

Back View of the Phunnygraph—doors open. As it looks from the back of the stage.

very strong, and will probably require three cleats. The other side, B, which is in front when the apparatus is in use, must now be fastened to the box by a pair of hinges strong enough to sustain its weight. There should be a hook on it, to keep it shut when necessary.

A shelf wide enough for a small-sized boy to sit upon must be attached to side A, and should be supported by iron braces. Strong leather straps will do if a blacksmith is not handy, but they must be very firmly fastened to the shelf and to the back door of the box, as we shall now call side A. As a small boy with a strong voice is to sit on this shelf, it would ruin the exhibition if the shelf were to break down, not to speak of the damage which might be done to the boy. Hence this back door must be fastened to the box by heavy gate or barn-door hinges.

Two strong wooden bars or handles must now be secured to the bottom of the box, and should project far enough at the ends of the box to allow a boy to stand between them, at each end, when the box is to be lifted or carried.

The rest of the necessary work is very easy. A crank, or turning handle (which will turn nothing), is to be fastened to one end of the box ; and two holes—about two inches in diameter—are to be made, one in the front door and one in the top of the box. In each of these a tin or pasteboard horn is to be fastened—the one on top to be smaller than the other.

Then on the inside of the box a round stick—a broom-stick will answer—is to be placed on two notched blocks fastened to the ends of the box, so that it can be easily taken out of its place by the small boy, and put back again, when occasion requires. A tomato-can may be stuck on the broom-handle, so that it will look like a tin cylinder containing something or other of importance. This round stick, with its cylinder, is only for show, but it should not be omitted.

Nothing more is now necessary but a pair of wooden trestles, or horses, such as carpenters use, on which the box is to stand during the exhibition.

Having explained how to make this novel phonograph, I have only to tell you how it is to be used. It is evident, from what I have said, that there is to be a small boy in that box, and the fact is that he is the most important part of the whole machine ; for this is only a piece of fun, intended to excite curiosity and amusement in the audience, who may, perhaps, imagine that there is a small boy somewhere about the apparatus, but who cannot see where he is.

The phunnygraph, which should stand in a room opening into that in which the audience is to assemble, or it may be behind a curtain, must be arranged in working order some minutes before the time fixed for the exhibition to commence.

The way to arrange it is as follows : The back door of the box must be opened and the small boy seated on the shelf. The door is closed, the boy going into the box as it shuts. The front door is also shut. If the broom-handle and tomato-can are in the boy's way, he can take them down and put them on one side.

The Professor—who is to exhibit the workings of the machine, and who should be a boy able to speak fluently and freely before an audience—must now come out and announce that the exhibition is about to begin. He should see that the wooden horses are so placed that the box will rest properly upon them, and should make all the little preparations which may be necessary. Then, after a few words of introduction, he may call for his phunnygraph, and the box will be borne in by two boys.

After the bearers have walked around the stage, so that both sides of the box may be seen by the audience, it must be

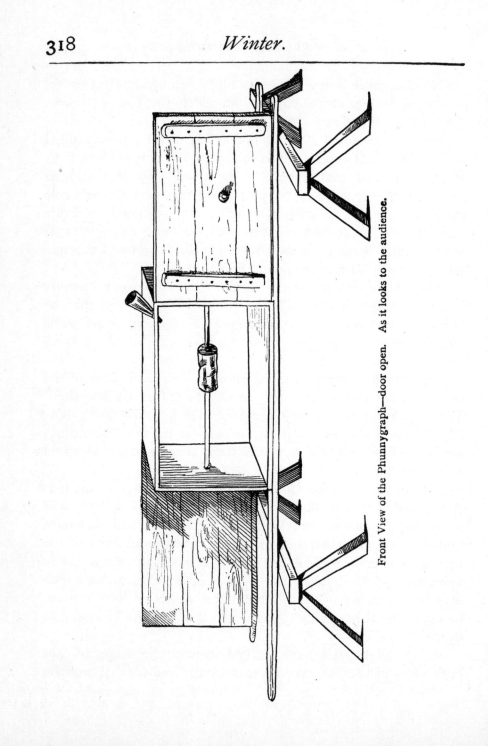

Front View of the Phunnygraph—door open.   As it looks to the audience.

placed on its trestles, or stands, with the front door toward the company.

The Professor will then call attention to the fact that the persons present have seen each side of the box, and can see under and all around it, thus assuring themselves that it has no connection with anything outside of it, except the stands on which it rests. He will then proceed to open it, taking care to open the back door first. The small boy swings back with the door, which conceals him from the audience as it stands open. As soon as the Professor announces that he is about to open the box, the small boy must put the broom-stick in its place if he has taken it down. Then the Professor throws open the front door and shows that there is nothing in the box but the rod and cylinder, which seem to be attached to the crank. What machinery may be concealed in that little tin cylinder, he does not feel called upon to say.

After a few minutes for a general observation of the inside of the box, he closes it, being very careful to shut the front door first. Then the small boy takes down the broom-stick, puts it out of his way, and proceeds to make himself comfortable and ready for business.

The Professor now begins to exhibit the phunnygraph by speaking into the horn at the top of the box. He generally commences with a short sentence, pronouncing each word loudly and clearly, so that every one can hear it. He gives the crank a few turns and calls upon the audience to be very quiet and listen, and then, in a very few moments, the same words that he used are repeated from the horn in the front of the box, the small boy within imitating, as nearly as possible, the voice and tone of the Professor.

The exhibition may go on as long as the audience continues to be interested and amused. All sorts of things may be spoken into the box, which, after a few turns of the crank, will be repeated from the mouth-piece or horn in the front door. Various sounds may be reproduced by means of this machine, and an ingenious Professor and a smart small boy can make a deal of fun.

A startling final effect may be produced if, after the Professor has crowed into the upper horn, the boy inside can manage, unperceived—say by means of a small sliding-panel—to throw out a live, strong-voiced rooster.

But it must not be supposed that an exhibition of this kind will be successful without a good deal of careful preparation and several rehearsals. Every one should be perfectly familiar with his duty before a performance in front of an audience is attempted. The box-doors should work perfectly, the small boy should be able to sit on his shelf in such a way that his head will never stick up when the back door is open, and he should practice putting up the broom-stick when the Professor announces that the box is to be opened. By the way, if the box is opened several times during the performance to oil the rod, or to do some little thing to the cylinder, it will help to excite the curiosity of some of the audience ; but the Professor must not forget that the front door must never be open when the back door is shut. The boys who carry the box should also carefully practice their business, so as to set the box down properly on its supports, and to see that it is firmly placed. It may be necessary for one or both of them to sit on the front handles when the back door, with the boy on it, is swung back, so as to balance his weight and prevent an upset. But experiment will show whether this is necessary or not.

As to the business of the Professor and the small boy, that, of course, must be carefully studied. It will not do to rely on inspiration for the funny things which must be said by the Professor, and imitated by the boy in the box. The Professor may bark like a dog, crow like a cock, or make any curious sound he pleases, provided he knows, from practise at rehearsal, that the small boy can imitate him.

The cost of the box, hinges, braces, etc., will probably be between two and three dollars. If the box is painted, or covered with cheap muslin, it will look much more mysterious and scientific.

21

CHAPTER XXXV.

HOW TO MAKE PUPPETS AND A PUPPET-SHOW.

THE puppet-show is certainly an old institution; and, for aught I know, the shadow-pantomime may be equally ancient. But the puppet-show here described originated, so far as I am aware, within our family circle, having gradually evolved itself from a simple sheet of paper hung on the back of a chair, with a light placed on the seat of the chair behind the paper.

The puppets (not the most graceful and artistic) originally were impaled upon broom-straws, and by this means their shadows were made to jump and dance around in the most lively manner, to the intense delight of a juvenile audience. As these juveniles advanced in years and knowledge, they developed a certain facility with pencil and scissors; the rudimentary paper animals and fairies gradually assumed more possible forms; the chair-back was replaced by a wooden soap or candle-box with the bottom knocked out; and the sheet of paper gave way to a piece of white muslin. Thus, step by step, grew up the puppet-show, from which so much pleasure and amusement have been derived by the writer and his young friends that he now considers it not only a pleasure, but his duty, to tell his readers how to make one like it for themselves.

The construction of properties and actors, and the manipulation of the puppets at an exhibition, are by no means the least of the fun. To start the readers fairly in their career of stage-managers, this chapter tells how to build the theatre, make the actors, and the next chapter gives an original adapta-tion of an old story, prepared especially for a puppet-show.

How to Make the Stage.

Among the rubbish of the lumber-room, or attic, you can hardly fail to find an old frame of some kind—one formerly used for a picture or old-fashioned mirror would be just the thing. Should your attic contain no frames, very little skill with carpenters' tools is required to manufacture a strong wooden stretcher. It need not be orna-mental, but should be neat and tidy in appearance, and about two feet long by eighteen inches high.

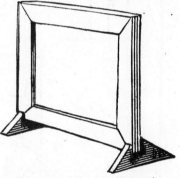

On the back of this tack a piece of white muslin, being careful to have it stretched perfectly tight, like a drum - head. The cloth should have no seams nor holes in it to mar the plain surface.

FIG. 203.—Wooden Frame for Puppet-Show.

A simple way to support the frame in an upright position is to make a pair of "shoes," of triangular pieces of wood. In the top of each shoe a rectangular notch should be cut, deep enough to hold the frame firmly. Fig. 203 shows a wooden frame, and the manner in which the shoes should be made.

The Scenery

can be cut out of card-board. Very natural-looking trees may be made of sticks with bunches of pressed moss pasted upon the ends. Pressed maiden-hair fern makes splendid tropical foliage, and tissue or any other thin paper may be used for still water. Thin paper allows the light to pass partially through, and the shadow that the spectator sees is lighter than the silhouette scenery around, and hence has a sort of translucent, watery look. Scenery of all kinds should be placed flat against the cloth when in use.

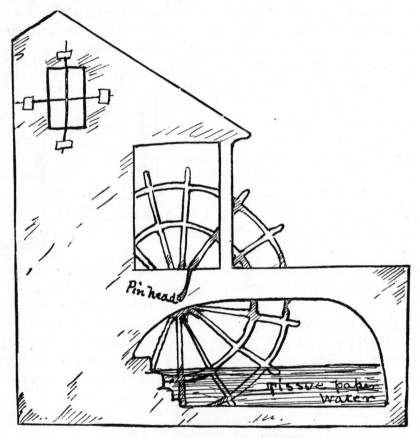

FIG. 204.—Diagram of the Old Mill.

And now that you have a general idea how the show is worked, I will confine my remarks for the present to the play in hand. It is a version of the old story of "Puss-in-Boots," and there will be given here patterns for all the puppets necessary, although in the court scene you can introduce as many more as you like.

The first scene is

THE OLD MILL.

This scene should be made of such a length that, with the bridge, it will just fit in the frame. Take the measurement of the inside of the frame. Then take a stiff piece of card-board of the requisite length, and with a pencil carefully copy the illustration (Fig. 204), omitting the wheel. Lay the card-board flat upon a pine board or old kitchen table, and with a sharp knife (the file-blade is the best) follow the lines you have drawn. Cut out the spaces where the water is marked, and paste tissue-paper in their place. Take another piece of card-board and cut out a wheel; in the centre of this cut a small square hole,

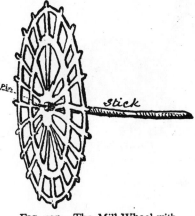

FIG. 205.—The Mill Wheel with handle attached.

through which push the end of a stick, as in Fig. 205. Drive a pin into the end of the stick, allowing it to protrude far enough to fit easily into a slot cut for that purpose in the bridge where it comes under the mill (see Fig. 204). The wheel can then be made to turn at pleasure by twirling between the fingers the stick to which the wheel is attached.

PUSS.

To make puss, take a piece of tracing-paper and carefully trace with a soft pencil the outlines of the cat, from the illustration here given. Tack the four corners of the tracing reversed (that is, with the tracing under) on a piece of card-board. Any business card will answer for this purpose. Now, by going over the lines (which will show through the tracing-paper) with a hard pencil, you will find it will leave a sufficiently strong impression on the card to guide you in cutting out the puppet.

Puss as he first appears.

The Bag and Puss-in-Boots.

Live Rabbit.

Dead Rabbit.

Almost all puppets can be made in the same way. Puss as he first appears, the rabbit, rat, and bag, should be impaled upon the end of a broom-straw; but the remaining puppets should each have a stick or straw attached to one leg, or some other suitable place, just as the stick is pasted to the donkey's leg as represented in Fig. 206.

CORSANDO AND THE DONKEY

are made of two separate pieces, as indicated in Fig. 206. The dotted line shows the continuation of the outline of the forward piece. Cut out the two pieces in accordance with the diagram, and then place the tail-piece over the head-piece, and at the point marked "knot," make a pin-hole through both pieces of the puppet. Tie one end of a piece of heavy thread into a good hard knot; put the other end of the thread through the holes just made, draw the knotted end close up against the puppet, and then

FIG. 206.—Corsando on his Donkey.

tie another knot upon the opposite side, snug against the cardboard; cut off the remaining end of the thread. Having done this, tie a piece of fine thread to the point near the knee of Corsando, and fasten a stick to the foreleg of the donkey, as shown in Fig. 206. Paste a straw in one of Corsando's hands for a whip, and two pieces of string in the other hand for a halter or bridle. By holding in one hand the stick attached to the leg of the donkey, and gently pulling the thread, marked "string" in the diagram, the donkey can be made to kick up in a most natural and mirth-provoking manner.

THE ROYAL COACH.

When you make the king and princess in their coach, by

FIG. 207.—King and Princess in the Royal Coach.

cutting out the king separately and fastening the lower end of his body to the coach in the manner described for joining the two parts of the donkey, the king can in this manner be made to sit upright, or to fall forward and look out in the attitude shown by Fig. 207, which explains the construction perfectly, A and B being two small blocks pasted on to the card-board

FIG. 208.—Leader, or First Horse, of Royal Coach.

for the king's arm or body to rest on. Fig. 208 shows the first horse of the royal coach; the second horse is a duplicate of the first, minus the rider. Fasten the horses and coach together by pasting a long flat stick extending across from horse to horse, and to the coach, where the traces would be.

CARABAS.

Fig. 209 shows Carabas in a *bathing suit*.
Fig. 210 shows the same gentleman in court dress.

FIG. 209.—Carabas in *Bathing Suit.*   FIG. 210.—Carabas in Court Dress.

How to Work the Puppets.

To make puss carry the bag, the operator will have to use
both hands, holding in one hand the stick attached to puss, and
in the other the straw attached to the bag. Then, by keeping
the bag close against pussy's paws, it will appear to the
audience as if he were holding the bag. In the same manner
he is made to carry the dead rabbit to the king. When the
rabbit seems to hop into the bag, he in reality hops behind it,
and then drops below the stage.

The operator must remember never to allow his hands

to pass between the light and the cloth, as the shadow of an immense hand upon the cloth would ruin the whole effect. All the puppets for each scene should be carefully selected before the curtain rises, and so placed that the operator can at once lay his hand upon the one wanted. There must be no talking behind the scenes, and the puppets should be kept moving in as life-like a manner as possible while their speeches are being read for them. Several rehearsals are necessary to make the show pass off successfully.

Stage Effects.

One would naturally suppose that with only a candle and a cloth screen for a stage, and some puppets cut out of card or pasteboard for actors, that the stage effects would be very limited, and consequently the plays stiff and uninteresting ; this is, however, not true ; any of the familiar old fairy tales may, with a little alteration, be arranged for a puppet-show and put upon the stage in such a manner as to amuse and interest an audience of young and old people. Jointed puppets, by the aid of movable lights, sticks, and strings, may be made to go through the most surprising contortions and manœuvres.

Boys that have a talent for drawing will find an unlimited amount of amusement in drawing and cutting out the puppets ; but for those boys who have neither a talent nor a taste for the use of the pencil, original puppets are necessarily out of the question. All the characters of any play can be made by selecting appropriate figures of animals and men from illustrated books and papers, and enlarging or reducing them after the manner described in Chapter XXVI., page 250. In this manner the puppets given in this chapter may be enlarged to almost any required proportions.

At a Sunday-school entertainment, given in Brooklyn last winter, the following play of " Puss-in-Boots " was produced by pasteboard actors a foot high, to the great delight of a large and enthusiastic audience of mixed young and old folks.

How to Make a Magical Dance.

Have one or two jointed figures appear and commence to dance, and while they are capering around, let another light be brought in ; immediately there will be two figures for every one that first appeared upon the scene. Each light casts a shadow, and the shadows are all that is visible to the audience, so to them the puppets appear to fall into doubles in the most unaccountable manner. If the puppets are kept stationary, and the two lights moved backward and forward, the puppets will appear to move around, pass and repass each other ; thus, with two or three lights moving behind the screen, two or three puppets can be transformed into a crowd that will be in constant motion.

How to Make a Sea Scene.

Cut two duplicate pieces of pasteboard in the form of waves (see Fig. 211). Let each piece be a little longer than the

FIG. 211.—Pasteboard Waves.

frame of the puppet-show stage. When the light throws the shadow of one of these pieces of pasteboard upon the muslin screen, it looks like a simple row of scallops ; but when the two pieces are moved backward and forward, it gives motion to the shadows, and they have the appearance of rolling waves; a pasteboard ship rocking upon the waves will add to the effect. A lighthouse can be cut out of pasteboard and placed upon a pasteboard rock at one side ; thunder may be imitated by rolling croquet balls over the top of a wooden table, and lightning represented by small flashes of gunpowder.

If the puppet ship be held at first some distance from the screen the shadow will be large, and if the puppet slowly approach the screen it will decrease in size and have the appearance of gradually sailing away. In this manner the hero and heroine may be made to escape aboard a vessel from the irate and stern parents. Many other scenes can be produced with very simple means that will suggest themselves to the young showmen after a few experiments with the puppet-show. Colored lights used very sparingly often come in with telling effect. A phantom ship can be made to follow the real one by having another light some distance off; one light will cast a heavy shadow and the other a faint one, which will move as the light moves; move the light up and down, and the ship and waves follow and keep time with the light. Many other effects I used to produce in my puppet-shows that at present escape my memory, but no doubt the reader will think of them himself if he becomes interested enough to make a puppet-show for the entertainment of himself and friends, Christmas or New Year's eve; in which case Old St. Nicholas, with his sleigh drawn by deer and loaded with toys, must form part of the show.

Miller.   Carabas (not yet a Marquis).

CHAPTER XXXVI.

PUSS-IN-BOOTS.

Dramatized and Adapted for a Puppet-Show.

PUSS-IN-BOOTS.

PUPPETS: CARABAS, afterward the MARQUIS; his oldest brother, the MILLER; CORSANDO, his next older brother; PUSS-IN-BOOTS; WOLFGANG, the Ogre; KING; PRINCESS; KING'S SERVANTS; DONKEY; RABBIT; BAG; RAT. Also, if desired, COURTIERS.

Act I.   Scene 1.

SCENE: Landscape with tree, bridge, and mill at one side.   CORSANDO discovered riding the DONKEY backward and forward over the bridge.   MILLER and CARABAS emerge from the mill and stop under tree.

MILLER: Come, come, brother Carabas, don't be downcast!
You know, as the youngest, you must be the last.

Our father, of course, left to me the old mill,
And the ass to Corsando, for so reads the will ;
And he had nothing else but our big pussy-cat,
Which is all he could give you.   A fool can see that !
Yet Dick Whittington once the Lord Mayor became,
And his start and yours are precisely the same.
But see ! I am wasting my time from the mill,
For while I am talking the wheels are all still.
I have nothing to give you—be that understood.
So farewell, my brother !   May your fortune be good.

[Exit MILLER into mill, when wheel begins to turn.   CORSANDO approaches,
and stopping the DONKEY in front of CARABAS, addresses him.]

CORSANDO :   Now, dear brother Carabas, take my advice :
Go hire out your cat to catch other men's mice.

[CORSANDO turns to leave ; PUSS comes out and gives the DONKEY a scratch, caus-
ing him to kick wildly as he goes off.]

CARABAS : O Fortune, befriend me ! what now shall I do ?
Come, Pussy, stay by me—I depend upon you.
You are all that I have, but can do me no good,
Unless I should kill you and cook you for food.

PUSS : Meow ! Meow !   Kill me not, my good master, I pray—
Have mercy upon me !   Now list what I say :
I'm no common cat,
I assure you of that !
In the top of the mill, where the solemn owl hoots,
You will find, if you look, an old pair of top-boots.
Bring them to me,
With the bag you will see
Under the mill, by the roots of yon tree.

CARABAS : Well, Puss, what you ask for I will not refuse,
Since I have all to gain and have nothing to lose.

[Exit into the mill.

[PUSS stands a moment as if to think, then capers up and down the stage and speaks.]

PUSS :   A rat ? Bah ! what's that ?
           Sir Whittington's cat
           Would have grown very fat
      Had she lived upon such prey
      All the time, day after day,
   Till she made a Lord Mayor of her master !
        But mine shall gain a name
        Through much sweeter game,
   And not only climb higher but faster !

                                  [Exit.
[Shift the scene by removing the light and, while the stage is dark, removing the
mill and in its place setting up some trees.]

Act I. Scene II.

SCENE : Woods. Enter PUSS-IN-BOOTS, carrying BAG.

PUSS : Mey-o-w ! m-e-y-o-w !
  Were it not for these boots I should sure have pegged out ;
  But if I'm not mistaken, there's game hereabout,
        For I scent in the air
        A squirrel or hare.
  I wonder now whether he's lean, lank, or stout ?
        But I know a habit
        Of the shy little rabbit :
  He'll enter this bag, and then, my ! won't I grab it ?

[Arranges BAG and hides ; RABBIT comes out, and after running away several times,
enters the BAG, when PUSS pounces upon it.]

PUSS : To the King in a moment I'll take you, my dear,
  For he's e'en over-fond of fat rabbits, I hear.
        An' I once gain his ear
        I see my way clear ;
  For I'll tell him a story both wondrous and queer.
  And then my poor master'll have nothing to fear—
  If he acts as I bid him, good fortune is near !

                                  [Curtain.]

Act II.   Scene I.

SCENE : King's Palace. KING discovered standing behind a throne. PRINCESS and attendants standing around. A loud "meow !" heard without. KING and COURT start. Enter PUSS, with RABBIT in his paws.

PUSS : Meow ! My great liege, may your Majesty please
　To smile on a slave who thus here, on his knees,
　　　A humble offering
　　　From Carabas doth bring.
And, Sire, my master further bade me say,
If it please his gracious King, he will gladly send each day
The choicest game that in his coverts he can find ;
And your kind acceptance of it still closelier will bind
A hand and a heart as loyal and true
As e'er swore allegiance, O King, unto you !

KING : Your master has a happy way
　　　Of sending gifts.   Thus to him say,
　　　That we accept his offer kind,
　　　And some good day, perhaps, may find
　　　A way to thank him which will prove
　　　We value most our subjects' love.
　　　Carabas, is your master's name ?
　　　What rank or title doth he claim ?
　　　Shall we among the high or low
　　　Look for your lord, who loves us so ?

PUSS : A marquis is my master, Sire ;
　　　In wealth and honor none are higher.

The King : " Your master has a happy way of sending gifts."

22

[Aside.

(Cats must have a conscience callous
Who work their way into a palace!)
     Now, if it please your Majesty,
     I will return, and eagerly
     To my marquis-master bring
     This kind message from his King.

[Exit, bowing.   Curtain.]

Act II.   Scene II.

SCENE: High-road; one or two trees.   CARABAS and PUSS-IN-BOOTS discovered.

PUSS: Meow! my good master, have pa-
     tience, I pray.

CARABAS: Patience to doctors! I'm hungry,
     I say!

PUSS: All will go well if you mind me to-day,
     And while the sun shines we must surely
     make hay.

CARABAS: Carry your hay to Jericho!
     Who can *eat hay*, I'd like to know!

PUSS: Meow! my good master, your help I
     implore,
     And while I help fortune, you open the
     door.

CARABAS: No house do I own, so where is
     the door?—
     Ah! Pussy, forgive me, I'll grumble no
     more,
     But help all I can in your nice little plan;

The Princess.

For I know you have brains, Puss, as well as a man.

PUSS: Meow! my good master, e'en though you froze,
     You must bathe in yon river!

[Exit CARABAS.]

And now for his clothes!
The King's coach is coming, and I've laid a scheme—
Though of that, I am sure, the King doesn't dream.
The coach is in sight! Now, may I be blessed
If I don't wish my master was wholly undressed!

[Loud cries without.]

There! now hear him screaming—the water is cold;
I'll go bury his clothes, for they need it! they're old.

[Exit PUSS, who soon returns. As he re-enters, the KING'S coach appears.]

PUSS : Meow! my good master! Alas for him!
  Help! fire! murder! My master can't swim.

[Runs to coach.]

Servant with boat-hook. "Ho, slaves! to the rescue!"

Help! help! gracious King, or Lord Carabas drowns!
KING : Ho, slaves! To the rescue! A hundred gold crowns

Will we give to the man who saves Carabas' life !

[SERVANTS rush across the stage. KING continues, aside :]

My daughter shall soon make the marquis a wife.
PUSS (aside) : Mighty keen are a cat's ears !
        Who knows all that Pussy hears !
This is better than I hoped for, by a heap.
        What a very lucky thing
        The blessed, kind old King
Doesn't know this shallow river isn't deep !

[Exit PUSS, running after SERVANTS. PUSS immediately returns, crying :]

        O King ! what a combobbery !
        There's been an awful robbery,
And no clothing for the marquis can we find.
KING :   That is no great disaster,
        For tell your worthy master
We always pack an extra suit behind.
        If we can trust our eyes,
        He's just about our size.
So, while in yonder grove we take a rest,
        Your master'll not encroach ;
        Tell him to use our coach,
And not to haste, but drive up when he's dressed.

[Exit coach, backing out, the DRIVER crying :]

        Whoa ! Back ! Back ! No room to turn here !
        Whoa ! Back ! Back !

[Enter CARABAS, in bathing suit. PUSS runs after him.]

PUSS :   Meow ! my good master !
        I couldn't do it faster.
But I've now a costly suit, and just your size.
        In the King's coach you're to ride,
        With the Princess by your side ;

Make love to her, and praise her beauteous eyes.
And, master, list to me !
Whate'er you hear or see,
Be very sure you never show surprise.

[Curtain.]

Act III. Scene I.

SCENE : Interior of Ogre's castle. PUSS-IN-BOOTS discovered.

Wolfgang : " Blood and thunder !! "

PUSS : I'm here at last !
Much danger's past ;
But such long tramps my liking
hardly suits ;
'Twas wisdom when I guessed
That it was surely best
To secure these blessed, helpful
old top-boots.
I was made to understand
That all this beauteous land
Belonged to this man-eating old
Wolfgang ;
But as down the road I sped,
To each laborer I said :
Your life upon your answer now
doth hang.
When the sovereign comes
this way,
When he questions, you,
straightway,
" This land belongs to Carabas," must say.

[Awful growling and noise heard, and WOLFGANG enters.]

WOLFGANG : Blood and thunder !
Who, I wonder,

Sent me such a tempting pussy-cat for dinner?
  I can't under-
  Stand the blunder;
But I'm glad, my pussy-cat, that you're no thinner.

PUSS: M-e-o-w! My brother Wolfgang (ah, how rich!)
  I wouldn't have believed
  You so easily deceived.
Know that I am Catoscratch, the witch.

WOLFGANG: Rattledy bang!
  Snake and fang!
So you're a witch, all skilled in herbs and roots!
  My power is no less,
  But I must confess
That I ne'er before this saw a cat in boots!

PUSS: Meow! my brother, speak not of my skill:
  'Tis true I can change to a cat, but no more,
  While fame says that you can assume at your will
  Any form that you please, be it higher or lower.
  Many a league,
  With much fatigue,
From a country of ice and snow,
  On my broomstick steed
  Have I come, with speed,
These great wonders to see and know.

WOLFGANG: Cuts and slashes!
  Blood in splashes!
Who dares doubt what I can do?
  Now tell me, old witch,
  Of the many forms, which
Shall I take to prove this to you?

PUSS: Meow! my great Wolfgang, it seems to me that
  Of all 'twould be hardest to turn to a rat!

[WOLFGANG must be drawn backward toward the light. This will cause his shadow to grow to immense proportions. After slowly lifting him over the candle, take up the RAT and just as slowly put it over the light, and move the puppet up until it touches the cloth. The audience will see WOLFGANG swell up to a shapeless mass, and then, apparently, reduce himself to a tiny rat. PUSS must then be made to pounce upon the RAT, and by passing the RAT behind PUSS, and then letting it drop, it will look to the audience as if PUSS swallowed the RAT whole.]

PUSS: Bah! Ugh! Spat!
　　　What a horrid rat!

[Struts up and down the stage.]

　　Well, I think for a cat I'm pretty plucky!
　　　Now I'll go and bring
　　　The Princes and the King
　　To the castle of Lord Carabas, The Lucky!

[PUSS, dancing frantically, laughing and purring, nearly tumbles against the KING, CARABAS, and the PRINCESS, as they enter.]

PUSS: Pardon, most gracious Sire, pardon, great King!
　　That your humble servant should do such a thing;
　　　It's because I'm delighted,
　　　More than if I had been knighted,
　　That the marquis, my master, should entertain the King.

KING: A truly faithful servant you must be, Pussy.
　　When the marquis can spare you, come to me, Pussy.
　　　We'll see that you're not slighted;
　　　Even now you shall be knighted—
　　Sir Thomas Cat de Boots your name shall be, Pussy.

KING (continuing to CARABAS):
　　This castle, marquis brave,
　　Beats the very best we have.

CARABAS: Most gracious Sire, there's not a thing
　　Belongs to me ——

[PUSS rushes frantically to CARABAS, and whispers in his ear; then returns.]

CARABAS : But to my King.
    For my life and all I have to thee I owe.
KING : My Carabas, we're pleased ;
      Our mind is cheered and eased,
    For we feared that this great castle held a foe.
      'Tis a princely home, 'tis true,
      And we'll make a prince of you.
You shall wed my charming daughter, ere we go.
PUSS : M-e-o-w ! M-e-o-w ! M-e-o-w !
    What would say his brothers now,
  If they saw Lord Marquis Carabas the Great ?
      And until the last horn toots
      (With Sir Thomas Cat de Boots),
He shall occupy his present high estate !

                  [All dance. Curtain.]

"A rat ? Bah ! what's that ?"

CHAPTER XXXVII.

HOW TO MAKE A MAGIC LANTERN—A KALEIDOSCOPE—A FORTUNE-TELLER'S BOX, ETC.

UPON opening his eyes late one summer morning the author was very much startled and astonished at an apparition he beheld upon the wall. He saw at one side of the room, in a waving circle of light, a horrible, gaping monster that was about to make a mouthful of a wriggling, big-headed creature, as large as a cat. Upon turning over in bed and facing the window, the cause of this strange phenomenon was seen. The "gaping monster" proved to be a tiny gar, and the wriggler nothing more nor less than a tadpole. The curtains of the window had fallen down upon each side of a glass globe in which some aquarium pets were quarrelling. A ray of the morning sun had found its way into the darkened room through the fish globe, and by some unaccountable means transformed the globe into a sort of magic lantern lens and slide, throwing the magnified reflections of the inmates of the aquarium upon the wall. The gradual change in the position of the sun caused the vision to fade away in a few moments, and the writer has never since been able to arrange the light so as to reproduce the same effect. Fortunately, however, some one else has discovered the principle, and from it evolved a simple magic lantern, which any boy can make for himself; an account of this invention lately appeared in the *Scientific American*, and the editors of that paper have kindly consented to allow the description to be used for the benefit of the "American Boys."

All that is required for this apparatus is an ordinary wooden packing-box, A (Fig. 212), a kerosene hand-lamp, B, with an Argand burner, a small fish globe, C, and a burning-glass or magnifying-glass (a common double or plano-convex lens), D. In one end of the box, A, cut a round hole, E, large enough to admit a portion of the globe, C, suspended within the box, A, with the lamp, B, close to it. The globe is filled with water, from which the air has been expelled by boiling.

Now moisten the surface of a piece of common window-glass with a strong solution of common table salt, dissolved in

FIG. 212.—A Magic Lantern.

water, and place it vertically in a little stand made of wire, as shown at F, so that the light from the lamp, B, will be focused on it by the globe, which in this case answers as the condenser. The image of the glass will then be projected on the wall or screen of white cloth, G, providing the lens, D, is so placed in the path of the rays of light as to focus on the wall or screen. In a few minutes the salt solution on the surface of the glass, F, will begin to crystallize, and as each group of crystals takes beautiful forms, its image will be projected on the wall or screen, G, and will grow, as if by magic, into a beautiful forest of fern-like trees; it will continue to grow as long as there is any solution on the glass to crystallize. Then by adding a few drops of any transparent color to the water in the globe, the image on the screen will be illumined by shades of colored light. If the room in which the experiment is performed be very cold, frost crystals can be made by breathing on the glass, F. Many other experiments will suggest themselves, and when tried will be found both entertaining and instructive.

A Home-made Kaleidoscope.

At all glaziers' shops there are heaps of broken glass, composed of fragments of what were once long strips, cut with the diamond from pieces of window-pane, when fitting them for the sash. If you secure three of these strips of the same size, and tie them together in the form shown by Fig. 213, the

FIG. 213.—Kaleidoscope.

strings will keep the glass in position. Cut a piece of semi-transparent writing-paper in the form shown by Fig. 214, so that it will fit on one end of the prism. With mucilage or paste fasten the overlapping edges to the glass; then with dark or opaque paper make another piece to fit upon the opposite end of the kaleidoscope; the opaque end-piece should have a round hole in its centre about the size of a silver twenty-cent piece —this is for the observer's eye. All that now remains to be done is to cover the sides of the apparatus with the same paper used for the eye-piece, and the kaleidoscope is finished.

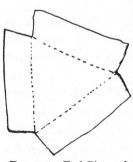

FIG. 214.—End Piece of Kaleidoscope.

Drop a few bits of colored glass, beads or transparent pebbles in and turn the writing-paper end to the light; place your eye at the hole cut for that purpose in the opaque paper end, and as you look keep the prism slowly turning ; the reflection in the glass will make the objects within take all manner of ever-changing, odd, and beautiful forms. A kaleidoscope made in the manner described is as serviceable and produces as good results as one for which you would have to pay several dollars at a store. One of the home-made ones can be manufactured in ten minutes if the pieces of glass be of the same length, and need no trimming to make them even.

The Fortune-Teller's Box.

There exists in all countries a class of people who make their living out of the proceeds derived from tricks and deceptions practised upon the ignorant, credulous, or superstitious portion of the population.

In the by-streets of almost any large city may be seen signs posted up on dingy-looking houses, which, if they were to be believed, would lead us to think that the gifted race that live in these dwellings can, by the aid of spirits, fairies, or by the signs in the heavens, give accurate information of all past or future events.

Some of these so-called mediums make such bungling attempts at magic and necromancy that it is a wonder that they are able to deceive any one. Others, however, perform some really wonderful tricks.

With a little trouble and no expense any boy may fit himself out as a fortune-teller, and have an unlimited amount of fun with his friends, who may be mystified and puzzled by simple contrivances, which, if explained to them, would be immediately understood. The professional fortune-teller will take persons into a dimly lighted room and ask if they wish to see their future wives or husbands, as the case may be ; of course they do. The witch then leads them up to a table, which has an apparatus on top arranged so as to allow the dupes to peer in for a sight of their lover. When they really see what appear to be live, moving figures inside the tube, they go their ways rejoicing, fully convinced that there is truth in magic.

One of these fortune-teller boxes can be made of any old wooden box. Such as is used for soap or candles is generally about the proper dimensions.

Knock one end of the box out, and cut a square hole in the lid in which to fit an inverted L-shaped apparatus. The L should be open at both ends, but tightly closed upon the four sides. A small mirror must be fitted in the L at the angle (see B, Fig. 215), and the L fitted in the square hole in the top of the wooden box in

FIG. 215.—Construction of Fortune-Teller's Box.

such a manner that any image cast upon the large looking-glass, A, in the wooden box, will be again reflected in the smaller mirror, B, at the angle in the L, and from thence to the observer's eye when placed at the open end of the L. This can best be arranged by experiment. The open end of the wooden box must fit closely in a square hole cut in the partition or curtain that separates the young magician's apartment from a room or closet occupied by an accomplice. Cover the box with a cloth which has a square hole in it, and fits snugly around the bottom of the L, covering and concealing the suspicious-looking, large box beneath. If the work has been neatly done, the machine will look like an ordinary table or stand with an innocent-looking peep-box on top of it.

Secure some friend for an accomplice, whom you know to possess a ready wit and a knack for "making himself up," with the aid of burnt cork and a few old clothes, so as to take any comic character that the occasion may require, with only a few moments' notice.

Supply him with what wardrobe he may require, burnt corks, flour, etc., and then fix up the programme between you, so that the boy behind the screen will know just what to do, from listening to what is going on in front, at the fortune-teller's box.

When all is arranged, the fortune-teller may announce to what friends or visitors he may have, that, owing to the conjunction of certain planets, he is enabled to entertain them by showing to all who have any desire or curiosity to see such wonders, glimpses of the past and future, and to prove it, if any of the company would like to behold a life-like, moving image of a future wife or husband, he (the fortune-teller) can bring up the image in a magic telescope, which was obtained from a direct descendant of Aladdin. The young magician must, by preconcerted arrangement, bring a man or boy out for a first peep. At a private signal of a word or exclamation, the accomplice steps in front of the open end of the wooden box behind the partition, dressed as an old colored lady. The image is at once reflected upon the mirror at A, and from that to B, thence to the observer's eye. After the latter has had a good look, the rest of the company may be asked to take a peep and see their fortunate (?) friend's choice for a wife. When they see the old colored lady there will be a great laugh, in which the boy upon whom the joke has been played will join with all the greater zest, because he knows he will soon have a chance to laugh at some one else. The fortune-teller must guard with zealous care the secret of the box, and must discourage any too curious persons from handling or examining the apparatus. A little mystery is necessary to keep up the fun.

The Magic Cask.

After the fortune-teller has amused his friends sufficiently with his magic telescope, he may end the *séance* by inviting the company to another room and bidding them remain at the door while he examines something at the other end of the apartment—the something is covered with a cloth. Upon reaching the object, the magician must turn suddenly and face the guests in the doorway, and, in vehement language, accuse them of doubting the reality of the visions he has conjured up for them, stating that he overheard some among them say that it was nothing but a trick. Rather than be ac-

Fig. 216.—The Magic Cask.

cused of such deception, he, the great wizard, prefers to perish! At this part the conjurer must quickly remove the cloth concealing the object in the corner, and disclose a barrel, marked in large letters, Gunpowder! Striking a match, the seemingly desperate wizard applies it to a fuse that hangs from the bung of the barrel, and, assuming a tragic attitude, awaits

the result. The guests will be uncertain what to do, and, half
in doubt whether to laugh or run, they will probably stand their
ground, but anxiously watch the fuse as the light creeps up
toward the bung of the terrible cask of gunpowder. When the
fire reaches the barrel there is an instant of suspense ; then
some one in the secret lets an extension-table leaf fall upon the
floor in the hall or adjoining room, startling the guests and
making a loud noise ; instantly the staves of the barrel fly apart
and fall upon all sides of the head, radiating out like the petals
of a sunflower, from the centre of which the fortune-teller's accomplice steps forth and greets the company.

How the Barrel is Made.

Any cask or barrel large enough to hold a boy in a crouch-
ing position will do to manufacture a magic barrel from. To
make one of these trick-boxes requires no particular skill. It is
necessary to remove one head for the top, and, after joining the
parts of the other head firmly together by cleats nailed upon
the inside (see Fig. 168.—Snow-ball Warfare), burn a hole with
a red-hot poker through each stave near the bottom, then burn
corresponding holes through the bottom head ; make the staves
fast to the bottom by tying them with pieces of heavy twine.
Around the top of the staves of the barrel tie another piece of
twine ; remove all the hoops, and all that will hold the staves
together will be the twine at the top (see Fig. 216) ; as soon as that
is severed, the staves will fall asunder. Inside the barrel the
accomplice crouches with open pen-knife in hand, and at the
proper time he cuts the string by passing the blade of his knife
between two staves. Left without support the barrel staves fall,
exposing the gentleman within to the frightened spectators, who,
when they discover that there really was no gunpowder in the
cask, will welcome the new-comer most heartily.

In amateur theatricals the magic cask can be brought in very effectively with the aid of a red light and appropriate ceremony. The audience may be led to expect a most terrible explosion, and with bated breath watch the fuse as the light slowly creeps up nearer and nearer to the bung of the cask. When the time comes as much noise must be made as possible ; then, as the staves fall on all sides and spread out like a sunflower, a red light suddenly thrown upon a boy dressed like a scarlet imp, makes a pretty as well as a mirth-provoking transformation scene.

Before exhibiting it, the barrel should be tried to see that it works properly, and the boy in the barrel should rehearse his part, and not forget to have a sharp-bladed knife ready to cut the cord at the given signal, otherwise the whole scene will fall very flat.

23

CHAPTER XXXVIII.

HOW TO MAKE THE DANCING FAIRIES, THE BATHER, AND THE ORATOR.

THE guests are led to a room, which is discovered to be dimly lighted and apparently unoccupied; they are then told that it is the fairies' night, and that although the little people are incapable of appearing in their natural form so as to be discernible, yet on certain nights of the year the fairies are willing to enter into and animate artificial figures made for their use. While talking in this style, the performer must borrow three or four pocket-handkerchiefs from the guests, and, after bidding the latter be seated, proceed to make the handkerchiefs up into little figures.

How to Make a Handkerchief Doll.

Roll up both edges of the handkerchief, as shown by Fig. 217. Fold the end A over toward the end B, as shown by Fig. 218. Next draw the end B up between the corners of A until the handkerchief takes the form illustrated by Fig. 219. Bring the ends of B under C, and tie them in a simple knot, allowing the ends to project as in Fig. 221, which shows the back. The handkerchief now has the appearance of a little white man (Fig. 220—front view).

After the handkerchief men are finished, the company must be requested to stand or sit where they are, near the door, and on no account to move for fear of frightening the little people. Carrying the handkerchief dolls to the middle of the room, under the chandelier, and making some passes over them, the magician leaves the figures sitting upright upon the floor. One of the company may be then asked to play upon the piano. No sooner does the first note struck upon the instrument sound through the room, than signs of life become noticeable among the handkerchief figures ; they move, and, one by one, rise and stand. As the music becomes lively the handkerchiefs lose

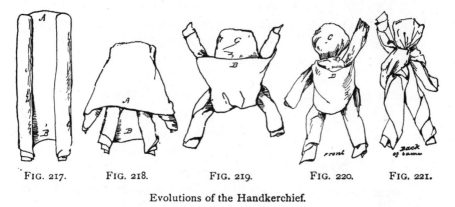

FIG. 217.   FIG. 218.   FIG. 219.   FIG. 220.   FIG. 221.

Evolutions of the Handkerchief.

their diffidence and dance about in a very active manner. After the dance is over the handkerchiefs are returned to the owners and the room vacated, to give the *fairies* an opportunity to rest, and the *children*, that have, during the performance, been hiding behind the furniture, an opportunity to make their escape unobserved. The children are as necessary as the handkerchief dolls, for it is by means of silken threads in the hands of the little folks that the fairies are made to dance and move about. For each handkerchief there is a piece of thread long enough to reach over the chandelier down to the floor. Each piece of thread terminates in a hook made of a crooked pin. While the magician is making the customary passes, he deftly hooks the figures on to the pins. Old and worldly wise people have been completely mystified by this simple little trick.

In any attempt at magic or fortune-telling, the success of the experiment depends more upon the manner in which the deceptions are performed than upon the tricks themselves. The magician or fortune-teller must be a person not liable to become flustered and confused at any little mishap. A boy with a cool head and ready invention can smooth over the most palpable mistakes and make his audience believe them all in the programme.

FIG. 222.—First position of Handkerchief.

The Bather

is sure to produce a laugh whenever exhibited by a clever person. The preparations must be made in an apparently careless manner, so as not to attract attention. Tie a simple knot in the end of a handkerchief and let it rest against the knuckles of the left hand, while the rest of the handkerchief dangles below, as in Fig. 222; do this as if you were only absent-mindedly playing with your pocket-handkerchief. Wrap the handkerchief around your two first fingers, as in Fig. 223; then, as if you had just thought of it, ask the company if they ever noticed how becoming the bathing costumes are to most people, adding, that to you a bather running down the beach always looks like this—here you

FIG. 223.—The Bather.

make the little figure run rapidly along your lap or the table-top toward the company (Fig. 223). The ends of the fingers protruding from below the white handkerchief look exceedingly comical, while the knot on top will be at once recognized as the bather's head, done up in a handkerchief or towel to keep the salt water out of the hair.   If among the company there be any

who are familiar with the scenes at seaside summer resorts, they will be convulsed with laughter.   Some people can entertain a company for a whole hour with nothing but a glib tongue and a pocket-handkerchief.

The Orator.

This comical little toy can be made by a boy who has really no knowledge of drawing.

From some colored chromo or illustrated paper cut out an appropriate face

FIG. 224.—The Orator.

and paste it on a piece of card-board, as in the accompanying illustration (Fig. 224).   Where the arms are to be, cut two holes large enough to admit two fingers of your hand.   From a piece of dark cloth cut two pieces shaped like the front of a coat and paste them on in the proper place (Fig. 224).   Cut another triangular piece of cloth for the vest; let it be red or some bright color.   Paste the vest on as shown by the diagram;

make a collar by drawing the outlines as in the illustration and leaving it white between them ; any bit of bright ribbon will do for the necktie. Draw a couple of straight lines beneath the figure to represent the top to a speaker's stand. From the same

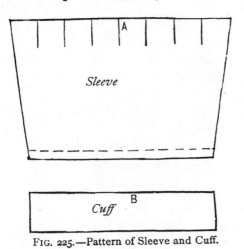

material that is used for the coat cut two pieces of cloth, of the shape shown by Fig. 225, A, for the sleeves. Let them be of such length that when the top edge is folded back the distance of the vertical cuts shown on the diagram, and the sleeve wrapped around the forefinger, the end of the finger will protrude the length of the nail. Sew or paste the edges of the sleeves together

FIG. 225.—Pattern of Sleeve and Cuff.

and put the slit ends (A, Fig. 225) through the arm-holes cut in the card-board ; bend back the slits and paste them upon the back of the card-board. Make the cuffs of white paper (Fig. 225, B), and fasten them inside the sleeves by a few stitches of thread.

The orator is now finished and ready to deliver his oration. Hold the card up in front of you and thrust your first two fingers through the sleeves. The flesh-colored tips of your fingers peeping from beneath the white cuff look like little fists, and when the fingers are moved around in mimic gestures, the effect is comical beyond measure and will create a laugh wherever exhibited. If the picture-head of some well-known public man can be procured, it will add greatly to the effect produced upon the audience. A comical speech should be prepared and recited with accompanying movements of the arms (fingers). The little man can be made to scratch his nose, roll up his sleeves, and go through many other movements in a most natural and life-like manner.

CHAPTER XXXIX.

HOW TO MAKE VARIOUS AND DIVERS WHIRLIGIGS.

WHO can watch machinery of any kind in motion, without experiencing an indefinable sort of pleasure? No matter how simple the contrivance may be, if it move it immediately interests us. This instinct, if I may so call it, that prompts us to watch and play with machinery is implanted in the brain of the lower animals as well as of man. I think no one can doubt that a kitten or a dog enjoys chasing a ball, and enters into the sport with as much zest as a college-boy does his game of football. It is this same indefinable desire for observing and experimenting with moving objects that prompts us to throw stones for the purpose of seeing them skip over the surface of the water, and to this instinct must be attributed the pleasure experienced by the school-boy with his

The Potato Mill.

Potato Mill,

which consists of simply a stick, a potato, a buckeye, or a horse-chestnut, and a string. The stick is whittled into the form shown in the illustration; a string is fastened to the stick about one-half inch below the knob on the top. The buckeye has a large hole bored through the middle, and a small hole bored through one side, to the middle hole ; the string from the stick passes through the hole in the side of the buckeye ; the end of the stick is sharpened and thrust into a potato.

If the string be wound around the stick, and the buckeye held between the thumb and forefinger, the stick and potato may be made to spin rapidly by alternately pulling the string and allowing it to slacken ; the motion imparted by the first pull continues long enough to wind the string in the opposite direction, and thus, for an indefinite time, or until the string wears out by friction, the potato mill may be kept buzzing at a great rate.

Another machine the boys used to be very fond of was called

A Saw-Mill ;

it was generally made out of the top of a tin blacking-box, with the rim knocked off and the edge cut into notches like a saw. Two strings passing through two holes near the centre gave a revolving motion to the "buzzer" (Fig. 226 shows a saw-mill).

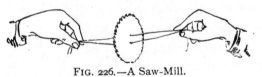

FIG. 226.—A Saw-Mill.

By holding the strings so that the wheel hangs loosely in the middle, and swinging the wheel or "buzzer" around and around until the string becomes tightly twisted, the machine is wound up. As with the potato mill, the revolving motion is imparted by alternately pulling and allowing the string to slacken, only in this case you must hold one end of the string in each hand (Fig. 226). When the boys can make a buzzer actually saw into a piece of board or shingle by allowing the edge of the wheel to strike the wood, the saw-mill is pronounced a success, and its value increased.

Very pretty and amusing toys may be made on the same principle as the saw or potato mills described. One of these little machines, a very fascinating one, is sold upon the streets of New York by the novelty peddlers. As the writer was passing along Broadway the other day, he saw an old acquaintance, known to almost all New Yorkers by the name of " Little Charlie." Little Charlie is not a small man, as his name might imply, but a large, good-natured, red-faced peddler, who stands all day long at the street corners. During the winter he sells small india-rubber dolls, crying out to the passers-by : "Well! well! well! Little Charlie! double him up! double him up!" He doubles the little india-rubber dolls up in a comical manner to attract customers. The torrid summer heat is too much for the india-rubber dolls, and makes them sticky, so that they are laid aside during the hot weather, and Little Charlie, with the perspiration streaming from his face, no longer calls out in his accustomed manner, but stands silently twirling his summer novelty, trusting to the ever-changing colors of the toy to attract purchasers. One was bought that it might be introduced among the other whirligigs in this chapter.

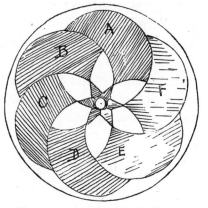

FIG. 227.—A disk of the Rainbow Whirligig.

The Rainbow Whirligig.

If you have a pair of dividers, make a circle upon a piece of card-board about two inches in diameter; inside this circle make six other circles (Fig. 227). A pair of scissors can be made to do the duty of a pair of dividers by spreading them apart the required distance and thrusting the points through a card to hold them in position (Fig.

228). Make a duplicate figure or disk and paint the parts of the inside circles, shaded in the diagram, different colors; for

instance, A and D may be made blue, B and E green, C and F red. The points of the star in the centre made by the intersection of the circumference of the circles should be painted the same color as the parts of the circle adjoining. Upon the second disk paint A and D blue, B and E yellow, C and F red.

Cut a piece of one-quarter inch pine into a square, with sides of about **two** and one-quarter inches in length; cut off

FIG. 228.—A Pair of Dividers.

the corners as shown by I, Fig. 229. In a hole in the centre of I fasten tightly the round stick J. Whittle out another piece for a handle K, and bore a hole through the top for the stick J

to fit in loosely; bore another hole through one side for the string to pass through. In the illustration, as in the original from which the drawing was made, there is a large hole bored through two sides; but this is unnecessary, and only put in the diagram to better show the position of the string inside. Upon the wooden plate I, describe a circle about one and three-quarter inches in diameter. In the centre of the two paper disks make holes large enough to fit with shoe-eyelets; then with tacks (L, Fig. 229) fasten

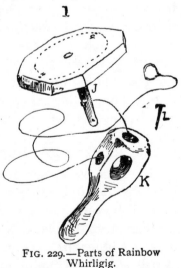

FIG. 229.—Parts of Rainbow Whirligig.

the two paper disks on to the wooden plate at the points G and H, in such a manner that the tack passing through the eyelets

will allow the disks to revolve freely. Attach a string to the
stick J at a point that will come opposite the string-hole in the
side of the handle, when the stick J is slid into the hole at the
top of the handle K. The wooden disk is made to spin exactly
in the same manner that motion is imparted to the potato mill
already described. When in motion the colors on the paper
disks will blend and produce, with
each change of position, a number
of beautiful variations. The two
paper disks blend together, making
a large circle three and one-half
inches in diameter, composed of
concentric rings of the most lovely
hues—red, pink, purple, green, and
all the different shades and combi-
nations imaginable are portrayed
with ever-changing variety by the
spinning rainbow whirligig.

A Paradoxical Whirligig

is a very ingenious toy, consisting
of a circle of white card-board, upon the surface of which any number of black rings are painted, one

FIG. 230.—Paradoxical Whirligig.

within the other, until it resembles an archery butt or target.
The disk is tacked or glued securely to a stick or handle
(Fig. 230) so that it is impossible for it to really revolve, yet if
you grasp the toy by the handle and give your arm a motion
similar to that of the shaft of an engine, the disk upon the stick
will appear to revolve like a wheel, and so closely does the opti-
cal delusion resemble actual motion that it will deceive almost
any one who is not familiar with the experiment.

A picture of a wagon, with wheels made like the disks of the paradoxical whirligig, may be made, and the wheels will have all the appearance of revolving when a wabbling motion is imparted to the picture. There are many curious experiments that can be tried in this line—spirals may be made to twist around ; pictured machinery may be given the appearance of actual moving wheels, etc. The philosophy of all this is best explained in the description of the next whirligig.

The Phantasmoscope, or Magic Wheel.

The phantasmoscope, or magic wheel, is comparatively simple, consisting, as may be seen by the accompanying illustration, of a disk of any diameter revolving upon a pin in the centre. Figures in different poses of arrested action are painted or pasted upon the one side ; under each figure is an oblong opening or slot. Much amusement can be derived from this old and simple toy. We herewith give one with the correct positions of a horse trotting a 2:40 gait, drawn in silhouette upon the outer margin of the wheel.

Make a careful tracing of the illustration (Fig. 231) with a lead-pencil upon tracing-paper ; reverse the tracing-paper upon a piece of card-board so that the side with the pencil-markings on it will be next to the card-board ; after which fasten both card-board and paper to a drawing-board or table-top with tacks, so that neither tracing nor card-board can slip. With the point of a hard pencil, a slate-pencil or any similar instrument, go carefully over each line of the tracing as seen through the tracing-paper ; be careful not to omit a single mark ; it is very provoking to discover, after removing the tracing-paper, that part of the drawing is wanting ; but if you have been careful, when the tacks are removed you will find the picture neatly transferred on the card-board. Go carefully over each line on the card-board with a pen and black ink, and fill in the outlines of each picture with ink, making a silhouette of the figures.

Cut the phantasmoscope, or magic disk, out, following the

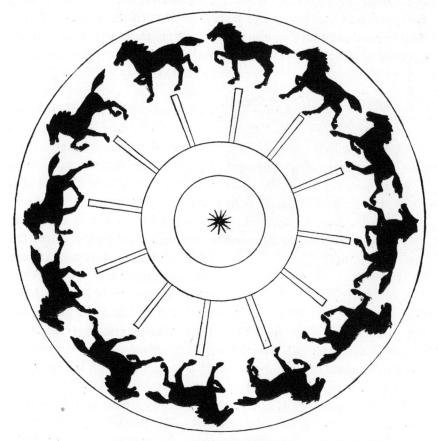

FIG. 231.—The Magic Wheel.

outer circle with the scissors, and under each figure, where the oblong places are drawn, cut a corresponding opening through the pasteboard. Fasten the wheel to a stick or handle by means of a pin at its centre, on which it can freely turn.

If a larger machine be wanted, the illustration here given may be enlarged by the process described on page 250. To use the magic wheel, stand in front of a mirror, as shown in the small illustration; hold the disk before the eyes; look through the slots under the figures, and turn the wheel rapidly. The horses' legs will commence to move as in life, and as each successive position drawn upon the phantasmoscope is the exact one taken by a trotting horse, the horses in the mirror will all appear to be in actual motion, on a fast trot. If the eye is directed over the margin of the paste-board disk, an indistinct blur is all that is seen. The principle is generally well known and easily explained. It pertains to the phenomenon known as the persistence of vision. When the eye is directed through the

Making the Horses Trot.

slot, the figure of a horse is seen for an instant as the opening passes the eye, and the impression is retained after the object is shut off by the intervening portion of the board between the slots until another horse appears through the succeeding opening, when an additional impression is made, the same as the preceding impression, except a slight change in the position of the legs. These impressions follow each other so rapidly that they produce upon the retina of the eye the effect of a continuous image of the horses, in which the limbs, replaced by a succession of positions, present the appearance of a file of horses in actual motion.

The instantaneous photographs taken nowadays of people, horses, and other animals in motion, opens a new field for investigation, and one which, with the aid of the simple toy described, will be found very entertaining as well as instructive.

Mr. Muybridge's celebrated photographs of animals in motion can all be adapted by smart boys to home-made phantasmoscopes, and it will probably not be long before the wonderful photographs of birds and bats on the wing, taken by E. J. Marcy with his revolving photographic gun, will be within reach of the public. Then with the magic disk the reader can make birds fly, horses trot, men ride bicycles, and reproduce every movement as correct as in nature.

For young scientists these beautiful experiments will be found very entertaining.

CHAPTER XL.

THE UNIVERSE IN A CARD-BOX.

Smoke-Rings.

A JOVIAL-LOOKING commercial traveller once won a wager from the landlord of a certain Detroit hotel by making over a hundred rings with one mouthful of smoke. The writer was sitting in the hotel office at the time, and becoming interested in the conversation, watched to see how the trick was done. Taking some cards from his card-case, the young man proceeded to bend up the edges in such a manner that the centre part of each formed a perfect square. Six cards he folded in this manner; then, after fishing in his pockets for some time, he produced a dime and a lead-pencil. Placing the ten-cent piece upon the centre of one card, he made a ring with the lead-pencil by following the edges of the coin. Opening a pocket-knife at the file blade, with the point he cut a round hole in the card, following the circle made by the pencil. He then put the cards together, in the form of a light but strong box (Figs. 232, 233, 234, and 235), and taking a long pull at a cigar which was between his lips, he filled his cheeks, and blew the smoke into the paper box. By this time all the idlers in the office had collected around the smoker, who, with a triumphant smile upon his face, commenced to tap the sides of the box with his lead-pencil. At each tap a tiny but perfect and beautiful ring of smoke shot into the air—one hundred and ten were counted before the smoke was exhausted. Fig. 236 shows how similar rings can be made with a lamp-chimney in which a card disk with a hole in it has been placed ; a piece of paper or membrane fastened over the other end serves for a vibrating surface, which, when struck with the thumb, forces out the little rings of smoke.

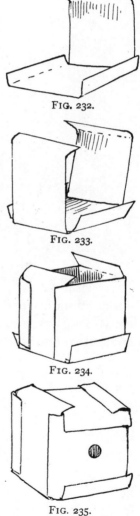

FIG. 232.

FIG. 233.

FIG. 234.

FIG. 235.

How to make a Card-box.

The reader must not for a moment suppose that it is necessary to use tobacco smoke to perform this beautiful experiment ; any other smoke will answer just as well to make the " vortex rings," as they are scientifically called. If after dipping a paint-brush into india ink, or any water-color paint, you gently insert the tip of the brush into a glass of clear water, you will see the pigment fall from the end of the brush, and, gradually sinking to the bottom, form rings exactly similar to the circles of smoke described.

The rings made by skipping a flat stone over the water are but another example of the vortex, and the jolly commercial traveller, when he was exhibiting the little paper box and

24

smoke-rings to the laughing crowd of fellow-travellers in the hotel office, was standing upon the threshold of a mighty mystery, experimenting with laws, and showing the action of the

FIG. 236.—Lamp-Chimney
Smoke-Box.

same forces that are supposed to have produced the wonderful rings around Saturn! Indeed, it is asserted that the broad, misty band of light which we see at night stretched across the heavens, and known to every boy as the milky-way, is nothing more nor less than a gigantic vortex ring, composed of millions of heavenly atoms. Some very learned men think that the secret of the whole universe, the origin of gravitation and electricity, are all locked up in the mystery which controls the formation and motion of a simple smoke-ring.

As Adrien Guebhard wisely remarks, in an interesting article upon this same subject, " Nothing is vulgar to one who knows how to see, and nothing indifferent to one who knows how to observe."

CHAPTER XLI.

LIFE INSTILLED INTO PAPER PUPPETS, AND MATCHES MADE OF HUMAN FINGERS.

MANY strange and unaccountable occurrences are attributed by ignorant people to "animal magnetism," some even going to such an extreme as to refuse to shake hands with other persons for fear of parting with some of their precious magnetic properties. Where there is much smoke there must be some fire, as the old adage goes, and although the marvellous stories current in a certain class of literature are wholly untrue, animal electricity undoubtedly exists. All boys who use a comb to smooth out their tangled locks upon a cold winter morning, no doubt hear and wonder at the crackling of the electricity as the comb passes through their hair. Many of my readers have probably tormented poor puss by holding her in a dark closet, and watching the sparks fly from her fur as, with a pitiless hand, it was briskly rubbed the wrong way until a severe scratch or bite from the cat warned them that she took no interest in such scientific experiments. A less cruel and more entertaining experiment is to cut out a lot of little paper figures, and the next cold day, when your hair begins to snap and stand on end in its effort to follow the electrified comb, hold the comb over the figures; the little puppets will immediately appear to be endowed with life and commence to jump and dance, or stick to each other and to the comb (Fig. 237), as if fastened by glue.

Often one little figure will stand on his head, and another, fixing himself by one hand, hold his tiny form upright in a most comical manner ; sometimes they will form themselves into long strings and go through all manner of queer and seemingly intelligent movements. The same result can be produced by rubbing a piece of gutta-percha smartly upon a piece of woollen cloth, and then holding it over the paper puppets. When one of those intensely cold waves from the North strikes the country and frightens the mercury in the thermometers, until it retreats down to the very bottom of its glass tube, electricity is often so easily generated that I have known persons to light a gas-jet by simply applying the ends of their fingers to the burners.

FIG. 237.

A certain professor, well known to the public, was so startled at seeing the gas blaze up upon touching the burner with his finger, that he dropped into a sitting posture upon the floor, and there, with his feet spread apart, and his eyes and mouth open, he presented a perfect picture of astonishment and wonder.

To Light the Gas with your Finger,

turn it on without applying a light, walk around the room, sliding your feet over the carpet, until you again reach the burner, touch the tip of the burner and instantly the light will blaze up as if by magic.

From what has been already said, the reader will understand that the gas-jet experiment is only successful under peculiar conditions of the atmosphere. Do not try to turn on the gas with one hand and light it with the other, for as soon as the first hand touches the metal key the electricity is expended, and there is none left in the other hand to ignite the gas. Turn the gas on first, walk around the room in the manner described, and touch nothing with your hand before it is applied to the burner.

There are many other experiments that may be tried by boys interested in this subject, but as they necessitate more or less complicated and expensive instruments they are omitted, it being the object of this book to describe only such things as can be manufactured by the boys themselves.

CHAPTER XLII.

HOME-MADE MASQUERADE AND THEATRICAL COSTUMES.

The White Man of the Desert.

IN 1876 quite a large party were returning from New Orleans to St. Louis on board the largest of Mississippi steamers. Every night was devoted to merriment, in which all joined, passengers and officers. One morning, large posters, made with colored chalk on brown paper, and hung at both ends of the cabin, announced a grand masquerade as the programme for the evening.

As a rule, masquerade costumes are not to be found aboard Mississippi River steamers, yet, that evening, when the band struck up a march, every stateroom door opened, and from each doorway issued some queer or fantastic figure. One costume in particular was so simple, and yet so complete, as to be noteworthy. A boy had taken two sheets from his berth, and, by wrapping one around each leg, fastening them at the ankles with strings and at the waist with a shawl-strap, made quite a presentable pair of Turkish pants. The shawl-strap, worn with the handle in front, had the appearance of an odd-looking double belt; a pair of white stockings, drawn over a pair of slippers and the bottom of the pants, answered for white boots; his shirt served as a white waist. A sheet hanging from his shoulders, after the manner of a cape or shawl, combined, with a turban made of a towel, to give a decided Arab look. The boy's face and hair had been made snowy white by an application of flour.

The disguise was complete, and the costume pronounced by all to be the very best in the cabin. In a similar manner many characters may be personated, and the costume made up of such material as can be found about home.

Many proposed tableaux, masquerade, or parlor play is abandoned because the costumes necessary are either unattainable or altogether too expensive.

There is "lots of fun" to be had at entertainments of this kind and for fear that my reader might miss some such opportunity to have a "good time," this chapter is devoted to describing two or three costumes, and showing how first-class character dresses can be made without an expenditure of money.

"The Fourteenth Century Young Man"

can be clothed with modern garments altered to suit the occasion. Tights are necessary, and may be made of an ordinary suit of knit underclothes (Fig. 238) by the addition of a little trimming and a pair of trunks to cover the top part of the drawers. But let us commence at the top of the man and work down, describing each article of dress in the order in which it comes.

The Fourteenth Century Young Man.

The Mediæval Hat.

Soak an old felt hat thorough-ly in hot water; put it over the top of some blunt-ended object, a bed-post, for instance, and,

FIG. 238.—Fourteenth Century Costume, Untrimmed

FIG. 239.—Stretching the Hat.

FIG. 240.—The Mediæval Hat.

grasping the brim with both hands, pull down steadily and firm-ly until the crown becomes elongated to the proportions of the ones belonging to the hats worn by the clowns in the circuses (Fig. 239). In stretching the hat be very careful not to tear the felt. Turn the brim up in the back and pull it down in front.

Fasten a long feather of any kind, a chicken or turkey feather will answer, to the back of the hat, and let the plume droop over the front, as shown by Fig. 240.

The Wig.

To make this you will probably have to ask your mother's or sister's assistance. Induce one of them to make a cloth skull-cap of the shape shown by Fig. 241. Cover, and sew to

FIG. 241.—Skull-Cap.   FIG. 242.—Spanish Moss Wig.   FIG. 243.—Excelsior Wig.   FIG. 244.—White Cotton Wig.

this cap Spanish moss or " curled horse-hair," such as is used by upholsterers (Fig. 242). Cotton or excelsior will make very respectable wigs when nicely arranged and sewed on to neatly fitting skull-caps (Figs. 243 and 244).

Eyebrows, Moustache, and Beard

can be made of white or black cotton, fastened to the face with a little mucilage.

The Doublet,

to be in keeping with the mediæval hat, must fit quite closely, and an ordinary knit undershirt is just the thing, especially if

it be a bright-colored garment.   At the neck fasten a broad
white collar, a piece of lace or a ruff, borrowed for the occa-

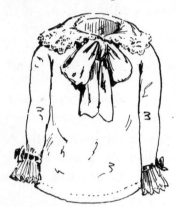

sion from some lady friend.   From
the same source procure a large bow
of ribbons to fasten at the throat and
conceal the band and button on the
front of the shirt.   If ruffs or lace
cuffs be added to the sleeves, the
doublet will be complete, and the
shirt so disguised that no one will sus-
pect its true character (see Fig. 245).

FIG. 245.—The Doublet.

Trunks.

Take any pair of old pants and
cut them off at the knees ; if they are a trifle too large for you,
they will make all the better trunks.

Let the same lady friend that made the skull-cap, hem the
bottom of the pants.   The hem should be strong enough to
hold strings within for drawing the bottoms tightly around the
limbs (Fig. 246).

If you do not wish to impose too much upon the good na-

FIG. 246.—Trunks.   FIG. 247.—Slashed Trunks.

ture of your lady friends, you may put the strings in the pants
yourself after the manner shown by Fig. 247.

Half a dozen slashes cut in the trunks through which some bright-colored cloth is allowed to show, adds greatly to the general appearance.

Tights.

A pair of knit drawers arranged with straps that pull the bottoms of the drawers over the insteps and heels of the feet, make as good a pair of tights when worn with trunks as any that can be rented from the costumer, and they are much more pleasant to wear than the often un-cleanly hired garments (Fig. 248).

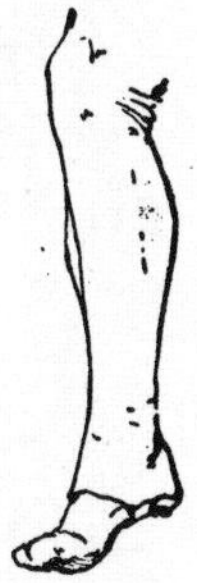

To Dress.

First put on your stockings ; then pull on the tights, allowing the straps to fit under the foot. Next put on the trunks, and pull the bottom of the legs of the latter garment up as high as possible, draw the strings and tie them tightly, this will make the trunks puff out and spread open the slashes. Next put on the doublet, and allow it to fall outside the trunks. Slippers or low shoes should be worn.

FIG. 248.— Leg with Tights.

A friend and myself once made a couple of suits like the one just described, using red knit underclothes for tights and white flannel pants slashed with red for trunks. Red-covered shoes and red feathers in our hats completed the costumes, which were exactly alike in every particular. So closely did we resemble each other when masked and dressed in these home-made garments, that our most intimate friends were una-ble to distinguish one from the other.

The Baby

is a mirth-provoking disguise when well personated. To transform yourself into a baby, remove your coat and vest, and, after procuring two long white skirts, fasten one at your waist, and let the waist-band of the other come just under your

FIG. 249.—The Baby.

arms, so that this skirt will fall over the first one adjusted. Let some one tuck up your shirt-sleeves to the shoulder, and run ribbons through them and out at the neck, tying the ends in bows at the shoulders. To do this, the shirt must be opened at the throat and the collar-band tucked under; this makes a low neck and short sleeves. A broad sash passed around under the arms and tied in a large bow-knot looks very baby-like (Fig. 249). The head should be covered with a hood. The latter can be made of a piece of white cloth, or a large handkerchief folded in the following manner :

How to Make a Handkerchief Hood.

Fig. 250 represents the handkerchief. Take the corners A and B and fold them under, as shown by Fig. 251. Allowing the handkerchief to rest flat upon a table, turn the corners made by the fold over as you would in making a paper hat; this will give you Fig. 252. Again proceed as you would in manufacturing a paper hat, and turn the bottom C D up over A B; roll this bottom piece up and over about three times (Fig. 253). Pick up the handkerchief by the ends C and D, and you will have Fig. 254, a pretty and complete baby-hood, which, when it is put on the head, and the ends C and D tied under the chin, will conceal the hair, and besides adding to the baby look, it will help to disguise the person wearing it.

Thus, I might go on until next year, telling how to make all manner of costumes ; but I have sufficient confidence in boys to believe that, as a rule, they only need a hint or two to start them in any project, and that their own ingenuity will carry them through. So far I have carried my descriptions of boy-

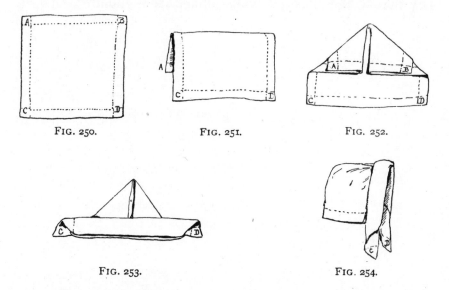

FIG. 250.   FIG. 251.   FIG. 252.

FIG. 253.   FIG. 254.

ish pastimes through the seasons, and I now halt at the recurrence of spring ; not, believe me, for lack of matter, for suggestion breeds suggestion, until there seems to be no end, and my greatest difficulty has been to avoid devoting too great a space to any one topic.

No boy need hope to achieve success as a manufacturer of any of the objects described in this book unless he carefully reads the description and masters the details. Remember that even in sports and plays no slipshod, careless, and partial effort can avoid failure. As a rule, the best and most earnest worker is the liveliest and heartiest companion.

It is not without regret that the author bids farewell ; and if the reader of this book derive half the enjoyment from the perusal that the author has from the writing, then the book is not a failure ; and if what little that has been said encourage and help any boys—be they few or many—to appreciate, love, and enter into all sensible sports, as every true American boy should, 'then has this book fulfilled its mission.

INDEX.

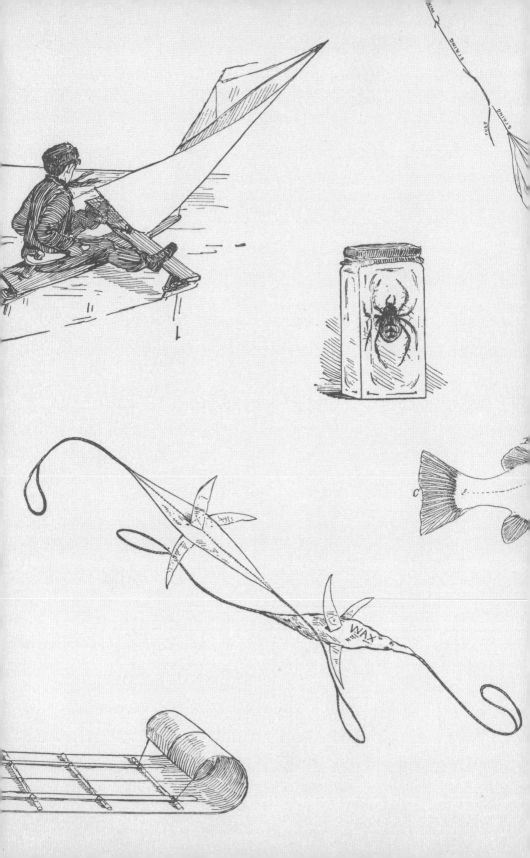